GIVING FORM TO AN ASIAN
AND LATINX AMERICA

Stanford Studies in
COMPARATIVE RACE AND ETHNICITY

GIVING FORM TO AN ASIAN
AND LATINX AMERICA

Long Le-Khac

STANFORD UNIVERSITY PRESS
Stanford, California

STANFORD UNIVERSITY PRESS
Stanford, California

Printed in the United States of America on acid-free, archival-quality paper

Library of Congress Cataloging-in-Publication Data
Names: Le-Khac, Long, author.
Title: Giving form to an Asian and Latinx America / Long Le-Khac.
Other titles: Stanford studies in comparative race and ethnicity.
Description: Stanford : Stanford University Press, 2020. | Series: Stanford
    studies in comparative race and ethnicity | Includes bibliographical
    references and index.
Identifiers: LCCN 2019031950 (print) | LCCN 2019031951 (ebook) |
    ISBN 9781503611467 (cloth) | ISBN 9781503612181 (paperback) |
    ISBN 9781503612198 (ebook)
Subjects: LCSH: American fiction—Asian American authors—History and
    criticism. | American fiction—Hispanic American authors—History
    and criticism. | American fiction—Minority authors—History and
    criticism. | Asian Americans in literature. | Hispanic Americans in
    literature. | Immigrants in literature.
Classification: LCC PS153.A84 L4 2020 (print) | LCC PS153.A84 (ebook) |
    DDC 813/.0095073—dc23
LC record available at https://lccn.loc.gov/2019031950
LC ebook record available at https://lccn.loc.gov/2019031951

Cover design: Amanda Weiss

Cover art: Shizu Saldamando, *Embrace Series, Grandstar Chinatown*
(detail), 2012, ball point pen on found bedsheet, approx 70 × 90 inches.
Courtesy of the artist.

Typeset by Westchester Publishing Services in 10.5/15 Adobe Garamond Pro

For my parents, brave migrants who lost a home but built a new one.

CONTENTS

ACKNOWLEDGMENTS

A recurring theme of this book is the necessity of collective solidarity in a nation and economic system that encourage us to think in individualist terms. The process of writing has affirmed this theme for me repeatedly. The greatest gift of this process has been the people, friendships, and communities it has brought into my life. This book is a collective project unimaginable without these alliances. It first formed under the guidance of exceptional mentors at Stanford University. Stephen Hong Sohn nurtured this project from its beginnings with a level of generosity and attention that remains my exemplar for the kind of advisor I aspire to be. Ramón Saldívar guided this project with a sure hand. And he continues to inspire me with his expansive work, kindness, and wisdom. David Palumbo-Liu offered crucial feedback, introduced me to many communities, and showed me what it means to be an ethical and committed intellectual. Alex Woloch's work and humane guidance have shaped my thinking about literature so deeply that his voice echoes alongside mine in many parts of this book. I'm grateful as well to John Bender, Gordon Chang, Ursula Heise, and Matthew Jockers, who also shaped my thinking. Special thanks go to Sianne Ngai for her energy and unflagging support and Gavin Jones, whose patience and wit never faltered. The writing would not have happened without Daniel Murray and Cristina Jimenez, the friends in my writing group, or without the great Borderlands Café, one of the last coffee shops where writers still write in San Francisco. And I wouldn't have gotten through graduate school without Aku Ammah-Tagoe, Tasha Eccles, Morgan Frank, Allen Frost, Ryan Heuser, Anita Law, Justin Tackett, and Claude Willan.

I wrote the bulk of this book during my time at Washington University in St. Louis. Many friends and colleagues made "Wash U" a wonderful place to start a career. I thank all the members of the English Department for their generous support. For opening up their homes, sharing memorable meals and sage advice, and offering a community that sustained me, I'm deeply grateful to Guinn Batten, Dillon Brown, Noah Cohan, Nathaniel Jones, Marshall Klimasewiski, Joe Loewenstein, Phil Maciak, Bill Maxwell, Melanie Micir, William Paul, Jessica Rosenfeld, Sara Ryu, Wolfram Schmidgen, Lynne Tatlock, Julia Walker, Rebecca Wanzo, and Rafia Zafar. My life at Wash U was also greatly enriched by Monique Bedasse, Linling Gao-Miles, Musa Gurnis, Lerone Martin, Jeffrey McCune, Edward McPherson, and Vince Sherry. I completed this book as I moved to Loyola University Chicago. Many thanks go to my colleagues in the English Department there for their warm welcome. I'm especially grateful to Suzanne Bost, David Chinitz, Ian Cornelius, Jack Kerkering, James Knapp, and Frederick Staidum Jr. for helping me acclimate to a new city and showing me the ropes at a new university.

This book benefited from the generous attention of many people. Special thanks go to Tina Chen, whose gifts for mentoring are unparalleled. Jean Allman, Miriam Bailin, Dillon Brown, Bill Maxwell, Steven Meyer, and Rebecca Wanzo were kind enough to read the entire manuscript, which is stronger for their suggestions. I first got to know Ralph Rodriguez, Rachel Greenwald Smith, and Min Song through a workshop on the manuscript, and I'm so glad I did, because they have become friends and scholarly role models. Several parts of this book are sharper because of the keen insight of Melanie Micir, Angela Naimou, Anca Parvulescu, and Rafia Zafar. Exchanging work with Elda María Román has been one of the great pleasures of the writing process. Another great pleasure was the chance to converse with and learn from a number of scholars I greatly admire: Marta Caminero-Santangelo, Marcial González, Peter Hitchcock, Hsuan Hsu, Daniel Kim, Lázaro Lima, Lisa Lowe, Ricardo Ortiz, Josephine Park, Crystal Parikh, and Cathy Schlund-Vials. The coolest perk of the writing process was talking with some of the authors I study. I thank Aimee Phan and Karen Tei Yamashita for their graciousness and insight and for being willing to listen to versions of "Here's what I think you're doing in this book."

This book was also made possible by generous institutional support. I thank the College of Arts and Sciences at Washington University in St. Louis for a leave that was crucial to drafting the manuscript. My semester at the Center for the Humanities at Wash U offered a haven for writing and introduced me to a wonderful intellectual community. Thanks go to Caroline Kita and Anika Walke for their camaraderie. Thanks also go to the center's director, Jean Allman, and the staff, especially Barb Liebmann and Kathy Daniel. A version of Chapter 1 was first published as "Bildungsroman Hermeneutics in the Post–Civil Rights Era," *American Literature* 90, no. 1 (2018): 141–70. I thank Duke University Press for permission to republish it here. A portion of Chapter 2 first appeared as "Narrating the Transnational: Refugee Routes, Communities of Shared Fate, and Transnarrative Form," *MELUS* 43, no. 2 (2018): 106–28. I thank Oxford University Press for permission to republish it. Chapter 3 contains materials from an interview with Salvador Plascencia. This interview, "Salvador Plascencia by Max Benavidez," was commissioned by and first published in *BOMB*, no. 98 (Winter 2007). © Bomb Magazine, New Art Publications, and its Contributors. All rights reserved. The BOMB Digital Archive can be viewed at www .bombmagazine.org. I thank Gordon Skene of the website Past Daily for pointing me to the remarkable photo of Santo Domingo featured in the Introduction. I also thank the photography staff at the Library of Congress for tracking down the original print. I'm deeply honored and grateful that Shizu Saldamando shared her piece *Embrace Series, Grandstar Chinatown* for the cover. Her extraordinary art brings to life an Asian and Latinx America in everyday acts of care and community connecting the lives of Asian Americans, Latinxs, and other marginalized groups in Los Angeles. I thank Ellen Yoshi Tani, my good friend and art world guide, and Rachel Cohen, the registrar at Charlie James Gallery, for making this possible. The Center for Comparative Studies in Race and Ethnicity at Stanford University bookended this project. Its intellectual community and vision were formative while I was a dissertation fellow and when I returned as a visiting scholar. I'm thrilled to publish as part of the center's book series. I'm grateful to the series editors, Hazel Rose Markus and Paula M. L. Moya. I owe a special thanks to Paula for believing in this book. I am thankful to my editor, Kate Wahl, for her sure guidance and to Leah Pennywark for her suggestions and patient answers.

I owe a great debt to the students I taught at Lee High School in Houston, Texas. Hailing from across Latin America, Asia, and the Asian and Latinx United States, their stories of migration, adaptation, and grit helped me see the connections that gave rise to this book. The deepest debt I owe is to my family. Matt knows what makes me laugh better than anyone else and remains the person I look up to. Nami (and Sammie too) helped me understand that home is not a fixed place but rather a bond that sustains across distances. My parents, Bi and Kim Chi, braved extraordinary circumstances to build their lives in the United States. Their stories have inspired and shaped me. What I owe to them cannot be expressed in English, the third or fourth language they learned on their journeys across the world. It can only be said, "con cám ơn Ba Me."

GIVING FORM TO AN ASIAN AND LATINX AMERICA

A TRANSFICTIONAL SOLIDARITY

ON OCTOBER 3, 1965, President Lyndon Johnson signed the Hart-Cellar Act into law, ushering in a new era of immigration that transformed the nation's social landscape. The act ended the discriminatory national origins quotas that for years had prioritized immigrants from northern and western Europe and restricted immigrants from much of the rest of the world. The story goes that by eliminating race and national origin as criteria for immigration, the law reshaped the nation's demographics and led to the explosive growth of two communities that have become the new faces of U.S. immigration: Latinxs and Asian Americans.

Asian American and Latinx communities were indeed remade by Hart-Cellar, but in different ways. By finally dismantling a system of anti-Asian restrictions that the U.S. government began constructing in the 1870s, the law opened the door to Asian immigration and the rapid growth of the Asian American population. With its preferences for skilled labor and family reunification, the law also transformed the class and ethnic character of Asian America. Latin American immigration also accelerated. Millions entered through family migration slots. A wave of highly educated Latinxs, particularly from South America, arrived, contributing to a broader stratification of the population along ethnic and class lines. But it would be a stretch to say that the law drove the tremendous growth of Latinx communities, because it placed numerical limits on Latin American immigration for the first time in U.S. history. By imposing restrictions on the robust flow of immigrants from Latin America, the law intensified undocumented immigration. The result was the consolidation and racial branding of "illegal immigration" as a specifically Latinx problem.[1]

From only 4 percent of the U.S. population in the 1960s, Asian Americans and Latinxs have grown to over 23 percent of the population today and are projected to reach almost 40 percent in the coming decades.[2] They have become the key figures of U.S. immigration, central players in the turbulent national drama sweeping Americans into an uncertain minority-majority future. But the existing story of 1965 and its legal reforms doesn't fully capture the forces feeding into this drama. Americans need a more nuanced story of the reforms. But more than that, we need other stories of 1965 and its aftermaths.

So here's a different story of 1965. This is a little known Cold War story that shifts our understanding of how this year transformed U.S. immigration and linked the fates of Asian Americans and Latinxs.[3] It's an obscure historical connection, because to see it requires looking across the histories of different migrations—of Dominicans and Vietnamese. One of the most powerful ways to perceive such connections is to turn to storytellers from these communities in an act of literary comparison. The imaginative work of writers who have been shaped by these histories and are shaping the historical materials they bequeath can reveal much if read together. It's this shaping, or more precisely, literary form, that can unveil the connection.

In trying to narrate the Cold War migrations that formed their communities, Dominican American author Junot Díaz and Vietnamese American author Aimee Phan develop a strikingly similar form in their first works. *Drown* (1996) and *We Should Never Meet* (2004) are short story cycles, interlinked yet discontinuous arrangements of short stories. Both works map national borders onto the narrative gaps separating stories. These national and narrative borders fragment the life stories of the migrants they depict. Meanwhile, the story cycles imply social relations and networks of effect across these gaps. Both works sequence their stories so that they cut between past and present, country of origin and the United States, intimating the historical links between these

settings. Díaz and Phan use this form to narrate the experiences of Dominican immigrants and Vietnamese refugees, contemporaneous but quite distinct
migrations. This shared form across different contexts invites us to consider
whether these works are grappling with convergent historical challenges. The
comparison places side by side two histories that we never think about together.
In juxtaposition, Díaz's and Phan's aesthetics are revealing. These story cycles
are fragmented, crisscrossed, and expansive because they are concerned with
how to narrate Cold War displacements that span national borders. They struggle to make perceivable life stories ruptured and communities dispersed by
violent histories that also span national borders. Their works take on a tangled
narrative form to insist on the deeply entangled histories of U.S. forces in the
Dominican Republic and Vietnam and of Dominican and Vietnamese migrants
in the United States.

Their aesthetic practices suggest a formal axis for tracing a global Cold War
migration history linking Asian and Latin American displacements generated
by U.S. interventions.[4] This axis links two scenes separated by half a world.
March 8, 1965: the 9th Marine Expeditionary Brigade lands at China Beach,
Đà Nẵng, the first U.S. combat troops deployed in the Vietnam War.[5] April 28,
1965: the 82nd Airborne Division lands in Santo Domingo, beginning the U.S.
invasion of the Dominican Republic. Less than two months apart, these dates
mark the moments when the Vietnamese and Dominican civil wars officially
became American wars, proxy pieces in the U.S. Cold War chess match. They
inaugurated wars whose violence and disruptive aftermaths displaced over a
million Southeast Asians and hundreds of thousands of Dominicans to the
United States.[6] These two seemingly separate arenas of U.S. militarism turn
out to be intimately related. The escalation of the Vietnam War in March 1965
informed the decision to invade the Dominican Republic just over a month
later. Records from the Johnson administration show that President Johnson
felt the need for a forceful intervention in the Dominican civil war to project
strength as the United States was diving headfirst into its Vietnam adventure. As
Johnson put it, "What can we do in Vietnam if we can't clean up the Dominican
Republic?"[7] He and his advisors saw the Dominican crisis as a crucial test of
the United States' anticommunist mettle. The connection between two U.S.
invasions 10,000 miles apart was not lost on Dominicans, as this remarkable
image from the streets of Santo Domingo in May 1965 reveals (see Figure 1).

Figure 1: Graffiti behind U.S. troops in Santo Domingo, the Dominican Republic, May 1965: "Yankees out of Vietnam."
SOURCE: Photograph by Douglas Jones. "The Grim Price of Power," *Look*, June 15, 1965, p. 43. Courtesy of the Library of Congress.

The graffiti, which translates as "Yankees out of Vietnam," demonstrates a Latin American–Asian solidarity with another country dealing simultaneously with U.S. imperialism.

This other story of 1965 opens a broader view of U.S. immigration history and the Asian and Latin American flows that altered its course. It compels Americans to consider what our country was doing in the world to generate migrations while it was debating immigration reforms to open itself to the world.[8] The broader story reveals that the United States was treating the borders of sovereign Third World nations as open to the bodies of U.S. military forces at the same moment it was exercising its sovereign powers to manage its borders, constructing a new immigration regime that would select and regulate bodies from the Third World.

Read together, the stories of Asian American and Latinx communities reveal unexamined connections that shift our sense of contemporary immigration history and concretize the relations between the groups most rapidly changing the

U.S. social landscape. *Giving Form to an Asian and Latinx America* argues that the transformations of these communities are not separate. These communities were formed in mutual relation by linked forces. They share an intertwined history that this book traces through a shared aesthetic paradigm, an interlinked yet discontinuous transfictional form that structures many contemporary Asian American and Latinx fictions. Phan's and Díaz's works are characteristic of a prevalent aesthetic that powerfully models social struggles linking Asian Americans and Latinxs. Within the shared history of these groups is the potential for solidarities that could confront the global military and capitalist forces buffeting so many of their members and intervene in the present and future of the United States and its relations to the world. This book explores the linked stories of the post-1965 period, from Cold War migrations to cross-ethnic organizing, that have made the United States of America a formation that we have not yet reckoned with: an Asian and Latinx America.[9] It considers literary works and their aesthetic practices as invaluable guides to an emergent formation that Americans do not yet perceive. This emergent formation can become a political force only if it's recognized across minority communities that currently see their fates as separate. Read together, literature by Asian Americans and Latinxs make this formation palpable. Their aesthetics give it a legible shape, frame it into shareable stories, make visible its tensions, and help us imagine its possibilities. They give form to an emerging Asian and Latinx America.

A POTENTIAL SOLIDARITY

It's easy to think of the stories of Asian Americans and Latinxs as separate. Our public discourse circulates opposed stereotypes: Asian Americans as model minorities, Latinxs as "illegal" immigrants. Feeding into this sense of separation are the fields of Asian American studies and Latinx studies, which have little interchange. There are also few widely recognized political alliances between these groups.[10] When mainstream media mentions their political interests together, the emphasis is usually on the conflicts between them. One story that caught the national attention in 2017 concerned the efforts by conservative Asian American groups to oppose affirmative action practices at Harvard University. The rhetoric surrounding the case pit Asian Americans against Latinxs and other minorities.[11] This book counters the image of separation to reveal the linked stories of contemporary Latinxs and Asian Americans.

There is a clear need for Asian American–Latinx alliances today. These groups are centrally involved in undermining the demographic basis for the white supremacy that has been a foundational premise of the United States. As the 2016 election and the Trump administration made clear, this demographic transition and the restructuring of power that it portends (but does not guarantee) will be a painful process marked by powerful opposition. Racialized as foreigners, Latinxs and Asian Americans are among the central targets of a nativist backlash of which the Trump administration is both a symptom and an instigator. In the wake of Trump's election, Latinxs were primary targets of hate incidents.[12] This is not surprising given the anti-Latinx nativism that Trump made central to his political rhetoric. Rates of hate crimes against Asian Americans also rose.[13] On closer inspection, this too is not surprising. An underappreciated theme of Trump-era nativist rhetoric is the linking of Asia and Latin America as a combined threat to the United States. Trump opened his first campaign speech by calling out the dangers that China, Japan, and Mexico pose to American success.[14] Given these shared threats, Latinxs and Asian Americans need to be able to perceive a connection pivotal to the nation's transition to a more racially egalitarian future. The backlash inevitable in that transition will only make shared resistance and solidarity more crucial.

Latinxs and Asian Americans are transforming the nation today, but this is not new. If it feels new, it's because U.S. historical narratives have tended to erase their long-standing presences.[15] These groups have had paradoxical roles within the United States. Nicholas De Genova observes that they have been central to the "social production of 'America' and 'American'-ness" by being framed as outsiders that are not part of the nation.[16] In these senses, the United States has long been an Asian and a Latinx America. But what has changed with the explosive growth of these groups in the past fifty years is that their presence can no longer be ignored.

As this growth drives the nation toward the minority-majority threshold, it is important to temper the political hopes invested in this demographic shift. Whatever potential it may have to decenter white supremacy depends on the formation of interminority coalitions that are far from inevitable. Central to the emerging minority-majority nation, Latinxs and Asian Americans exemplify its potential and its challenges. I argue that there is a potential solidarity here: that Asian Americans and Latinxs share crucial challenges and entangled fates.

At the same time, many differences and frictions exist. This solidarity cannot be taken for granted. We should not underestimate the racial order's power to divide and manage minority groups. As Claire Jean Kim argues, racial formation in the United States unfolds along multiple intersecting axes of difference that fuel interminority conflicts and obstruct recognition of shared challenges.[17] For an Asian American–Latinx coalition to emerge will require political imagination and on-the-ground work.

Giving Form to an Asian and Latinx America centers on this potential coalition and advances the cross-field dialogue needed to understand it. I draw on social science work that has opened the dialogue. Nicholas De Genova, Mae M. Ngai, and Eileen O'Brien have brought out some of the challenges linking Asian Americans and Latinxs. Both groups are navigating ambivalent places in a black-white racial order, and both are combating perceptions of foreignness.[18] I also build on the work of scholars who have taken Asian American–Latinx comparative work into literary studies. Crystal Parikh's pioneering research showed how Asian Americans and Latinxs are linked by alien racialization and charges of national betrayal.[19] More recently, Jayson Gonzalez Sae-Saue has traced the transpacific scope of Chicanx literature.[20] Jeehyun Lim has drawn out Asian American and Latinx literary engagements with the conundrums of bilingualism.[21] And Susan Thananopavarn shows how these literatures highlight histories of U.S. occupation, wartime racism, and Cold War ideologies.[22] This book builds on these issues and extends beyond them to make a broad claim: not just that Asian Americans and Latinxs share specific challenges but also that neither group, as they have formed in the last fifty years, can be fully understood unless we grasp how they have been shaped in mutual relation. I show literature addressing a sequence of historical situations that have transformed and linked these communities: the uneven openings of the post–civil rights era, the Vietnam War and Cold War in their global reverberations, the labor flows of neoliberal capitalism, and panethnic coalition building in an era of proliferating difference. These situations have been central topics of discussion in Asian American studies and Latinx studies. But the conversations have been separate, so they fail to recognize that these situations constitute racial projects that have relationally racialized Asian Americans and Latinxs.[23] Relational racial projects have often assigned these groups to different positions, encouraging the idea of separate struggles rather than linked fates. Against that idea, I show

how post–civil rights politics, migration policy, military strategy, neoliberal development, and panethnic institutionalization have acted on Asian Americans and Latinxs in tandem.

In extending the work on Asian Americans and Latinxs, I believe that the comparison of literatures presents a useful challenge. Linking minority literatures with issues that social science identifies risks reducing ethnic literatures to social and ethnographic content. This approach can perpetuate a historic lack of attention to the aesthetics of ethnic literatures and reinforce a tendency to judge minority works as socially interesting artifacts but not significant artworks.[24] More important, this approach can constrain our ability to perceive the imaginative range of Asian American and Latinx literatures. I sense this tendency to align minority literatures with their social content in Asian American–Latinx literary studies, where the analysis emphasizes content, themes, and tropes. Instead of taking social content as the starting point for comparative analysis, this book turns to the aesthetics emerging from the Asian and Latinx United States to glean the groups' shared history. It focuses on the aesthetic forms that are the surprisingly generative features of literature for comparative ethnic studies. As the case of Dominican and Vietnamese stories of the Cold War showed, comparison through form is powerful for perceiving solidarities across different social and racial positions, because related forms can suggest connections beyond overt parallels of social content and context. It's not just readers and literature scholars who should care about literary aesthetics. This book makes an aesthetic argument for bringing together two literatures, two fields of study, and two communities.

TRANSFICTIONAL FORM

The aesthetic at the center of this book is a transfictional form structuring many of the short story cycles and multiplot novels in contemporary Asian American and Latinx literatures. This form models the social struggles that link Asian Americans and Latinxs. Criticism has not adequately recognized it because its instances cut across the distinctions critics draw between short story cycles and novels. Building on the concept of transfictionality from transmedia narrative studies, I offer the first theorization of this form.[25] *Transfictional form* describes narrative works that create an effect of many distinct, semiautonomous stories, each focusing on different characters and events but taking place within the same imagined world. Readers construct a sense of this expansive storyworld by reading and thinking transfictionally, that is, by drawing relations across stories, and from one story to another.[26] But the stories do not merge into a single, causally interconnected narrative; the relations readers can draw are often not ones of direct causal relation and plot impact.[27] Many of the stories remain their own stories rather than subplots in a larger narrative spanning the work. The distinctness of each story is a key feature of transfictional form. While transfictional works are not linked by direct causal relations, they invite readers to perceive many other forms of connection, including character recurrences, social ties, and overlapping settings.[28] Questions of causal relation are by no means absent, but transfictional works consider more ambiguous causal relations—indirect, mediated, and tenuous networks of impact, communities of consequence that span distances and degrees of separation and defy clear mapping.[29] This range of ambiguous causal relations leaves unresolved the question of whether and to what extent one story affects another.

In a transfictional work the stories are distinct yet related. It's a difficult tension to sustain but a socially important one to recognize. This form offers a narrative shape for grasping the links among stories and people without eliding the differences and separations between them. By using this form, writers implicitly argue that the social world they shape into narrative is neither atomized nor unified. It cannot be grasped as completely separate stories, but at the same time, its many pieces and complexities cannot be contained within one story. One compelling example is Cristina Henríquez's *The Book of Unknown Americans*. The novel uses transfictional form to represent the experiences of migrants from across Latin America. This form challenges us to consider whether divergent Latinx migration experiences can be told in one story and, if not, whether there are still important ways that they are related.

A more familiar example is Maxine Hong Kingston's memoir *The Woman Warrior*, particularly the story "At the Western Palace." The story focuses on Maxine's aunt, Moon Orchid, who is bullied by her sister Brave Orchid into a disastrous confrontation with her cheating husband. Maxine, meanwhile, is not even a named character in the story. And Moon Orchid's story has no clear effects on Maxine's.[30] "At the Western Palace" focuses on several characters Maxine has never met and on settings that play no role in her story. Set off by page breaks and its own title (a common practice in transfictional works), the story stands relatively on its own. And yet, readers can draw resonant relations: the character ties between Maxine and her aunt, the echo between Brave Orchid's bullying of Moon Orchid and the famous scene in which Maxine bullies a female classmate. Whatever causal connections exist between the stories are ambiguous. To what extent does the story inform Maxine's actions in her own story? And to what extent does the story recognize the drama of her aunt's life in itself? A transfictional work doesn't clearly resolve such questions, though it's telling that in an interview with Elaine H. Kim, Kingston refers to multiple women's stories in the memoir rather than just her story.[31] Both Maxine and Moon Orchid struggle with forms of Chinese patriarchy and female agency, but their distinct stories show that their particular struggles cannot be conflated into one narrative.

It's also clarifying to consider examples that are not transfictional, such as story collections. The stories in a transfictional work take place in the same storyworld, so they differ from the stories in a collection, where each story implies its own world. Stories in a collection often focus on completely separate characters, events, and settings. Some collections take place in the same general location—for instance, the stories of Flannery O'Connor's *A Good Man Is Hard to Find* are all set in the American South—but share no other storyworld elements. Transfictional works are linked by closer and more numerous kinds of storyworld elements than story collections.

Transfictional form has a more complex relation to the short story cycle and the novel. Examples of the form extend across both genres. Story cycles and multiplot novels frequently span different protagonists, plots, and settings, and they ask readers to piece together a fictional world across many plots. They share these features with transfictional works. But transfictional form describes a distinct subset of story cycles and novels. It does not apply to works that open multiple plots but merge them into a larger, causally interconnected story. Think of Jennifer Egan's novel *A Visit from the Goon Squad* (2010). Encompassing the stories of dozens of characters involved in the music industry, it cuts across multiple periods and settings. Readers have to figure out how all these people are related and how their stories fit into a broader timeline. But in the end, the novel resolves into an interconnected story of two main characters, Sasha and Bennie, and the motley cast of characters whose stories affect their lives. Each plot has a clear entanglement with one or both of the narrative spines, which helps secure the novel's unity despite its freewheeling scope.

A transfictional work does not resolve its stories into the kind of cohesion that Egan's novel ultimately offers.[32] Some nontransfictional story cycles aim for a similar cohesion. Such story cycles circle back in their endings to gather many stories into a causally linked whole, usually by encompassing them in the story of a protagonist. The ending of Tomás Rivera's classic Chicano story cycle . . . *y no se lo tragó la tierra* (1971) shows the boy protagonist thinking back on all the stories in his community that were presented across the cycle. Flowing one into another, the stories integrate into one vision in his process of coming to consciousness. By cyclically integrating many stories into one, story cycles like this diverge from the transfictional possibilities of the genre.

The stories in a transfictional work are neither interconnected into a single narrative nor unconnected, as in a story collection. Exploring the possibilities for arranging narrative between these poles, transfictional works pull in conflicting directions. The resulting formal tensions distinguish the form. The potential unity of the work conflicts with the multiplicity of stories that jostle within it. The unity of the stories is an open question. For example, Karen Tei Yamashita's transfictional novel about the Asian American movement, *I Hotel*, encompasses dozens of stories of activism and questions whether they add up to a unified movement. Other tensions include narrative borders that separate stories and relations that cross those borders, the autonomy of stories and their interdependence, causal connection and disconnection. Transfictional form also highlights the conflict between a focus on an individual protagonist and attention to the stories of other characters in a community. This conflict keeps Sandra Cisneros's *The House on Mango Street* from encompassing the stories of diverse Latinas within Esperanza's story of formation. Transfictional works pull readers between the concerns of the story we're currently reading and parts of the storyworld on its periphery. One story hovers against many others, making clear that this story's circle of concerns is only a piece in a wider world. Think of the stories Junot Díaz sets in the New Jersey barrio in *Drown* and how they unfold against other stories across the Dominican diaspora. Such transfictional works challenge readers to attend simultaneously to divergent scales of narrative relations—the local ties within a story, indirect links between specific stories, and the global relations that span the whole work.

Unity and multiplicity, borders and border crossings, autonomy and interdependence, individual and collective, local and global—these are the sustained tensions animating transfictional form. When examined, they reveal that this form is more than a way to articulate a prominent aesthetic for Asian Americans and Latinxs—it is a way to structure, through literary form, some of their central social struggles. Borders and border crossings are a lived reality of the transnational migrations that characterize Asian American and Latinx communities.[33] Their stories bear witness to economic and military forces crossing the borders of Latin American and Asian nations while the migrant populations they displace confront militarized borders and legal barriers.[34] Asian Americans and Latinxs see themselves within and across local, national, and global scales of belonging.[35] They are also increasingly stratified communities where the managerial class and the undocumented, "model minorities" and the "underclass," coexist.[36] They are caught within uneven global labor flows and an unequal immigration regime. Economic prospects in these communities raise conflicts of individual mobility and collective blockages. Moreover, the very idea of community is fraught. Latinx and Asian American collective identities are consolidating at the same time that mass immigration and diversification undermine the premises of unity. The panethnic categories of Asian American and Latinx strain to encompass different ethnic groups, histories, and cultures.[37] Questions of unity and multiplicity, autonomy and interdependence are at the heart of Latinx and Asian American politics.

PERCEIVING AN INTERTWINED HISTORY

The shared struggles of Asian Americans and Latinxs remain obscure. To perceive this relationship requires comparative work that looks beyond direct crossings and similar positions to see a broader system of relational racialization and immigration management at work. Any comparison must acknowledge differences: the opposed images of "illegal immigrants" and "model minorities," the aggregate socioeconomic disparities, the fact that Latinx immigrants today bear the greater brunt of deportation and policing. But such differences do not mean these communities are unrelated. Their opposed positions are current snapshots that fail to capture their intertwining across the nation's history of regulating citizenship, race, and migration.[38] As Natalia Molina observes, the U.S. immigration system is structured by racial comparisons that influence which groups the nation welcomes and which it restricts.[39] As a result, "the lives of racialized groups are linked across time and space and thereby affect one another, even when they do not directly cross paths."[40] Latinx and Asian American migrations exemplify this point.

U.S. immigration policy and labor systems are relational racialization projects that have linked and interchanged Asian Americans and Latinxs around a needed immigrant / undesired immigrant contradiction. This binary paradigm entails distinct yet related positions that national interests can at different moments oppose, substitute, or converge. Two periods stand out as examples of this dynamic. The first is the turn of the twentieth century, when there was a decidedly different immigration landscape. The image of Latinxs as the quintessential "illegal immigrants" is so entrenched today that few recall that they were not the first illegal aliens in U.S. history. Asians were. As Mae M. Ngai shows, the U.S. government at that time patrolled the border with Mexico not for Mexican immigrants, but for Chinese immigrants who might be coming through Mexico to circumvent exclusion laws.[41] The first era of exclusion was aimed at Chinese and Asians more broadly.[42] In the same period, Mexican migration flowed across the border without numerical quotas or even inspections.[43] These different positions were part of a labor substitution. Asian exclusion created a labor vacuum in many industries that the United States filled with Mexican migration. An era of intensive recruitment of Mexican migrants began with efforts to replace Japanese immigrant labor when it was restricted in 1907. Demand and recruitment generated mass Mexican migrations into the 1920s.[44]

Mexican migrants were constructed as needed because of the simultaneous construction of Asians as undesirable. But key to U.S. immigration history is the instability of the two roles. Increasing Mexican immigration combined with the Great Depression turned the tide against Mexican immigrants. No longer needed for their labor and an easy target for economic scapegoating, Mexican immigrants became the next targets of nativist backlash.[45] The 1930s saw deportations that expelled nearly half a million people.[46] It was this period that framed Mexicans as the quintessential "illegal aliens," in a shift from earlier Asian figurations.[47] The ready slippage of Mexicans from needed immigrants to excluded threats alongside Asians shows that these groups were intertwined by their recruitment as racialized labor and also by the strategies of exclusion they faced. As Natalia Molina reveals, efforts to restrict Mexican migrants used arguments, legal cases, and patterns of violence that were first deployed against Asian immigrants. In some cases the same nativist groups that had lobbied for restrictions on Asians turned to work on Mexican exclusion.[48] A relational racialization view of the early twentieth-century immigration system reveals the exclusion of one migrant group, Asians, leading to the recruitment of another, Mexicans, as replacement labor until the nativist tide turned again to target Mexicans with strategies honed in excluding Asians. Even as they occupied different positions at particular moments, their fates remained intertwined. But as Mexican American activism of the time showed, the U.S. racial order incentivizes minority groups to claim whatever advantages they can instead of recognizing shared struggles with other minority groups. Because U.S. law classified Mexicans as white, some activist groups emphasized this racial privilege in fighting for full citizenship rights. "Mexicans were in a sense accepting the U.S. racial hierarchy," Molina explains. "They were not challenging the terms of the debates but rather saying that they were on the right side of the color line."[49] The differentiated immigration system is a powerful means of dividing and exploiting immigrant groups.

A second revealing period is the aftermath of the 1965 Hart-Cellar Act. The same legislation helped reconstruct Asians from threatening aliens to model minorities and reanimated the image of Mexican migrants as "illegal immigrants." Hart-Cellar opened borders to Asian and, to a lesser extent, African immigration while shifting restrictions to the Americas. The law's preferences for highly educated immigrants drew a wave of professional-class Asian migrants who arrived with advantages that explain much of the celebrated Asian American success story.[50] At the same time, the law intensified undocumented immigration from Mexico. Mexican immigration leading up to 1965 had been robust and needed, with hundreds of thousands of legal entrants each year resulting from the labor recruitments of the mid-century Bracero program. This consistent flow and the undiminished demand for it slammed into the new restrictions on legal migration from the Americas. The law effectively reclassified large swaths of Mexican migration as illegal.[51] Immigrants from across Latin America encountered the same restrictions, with the effect of expanding the racialized image of "illegal immigration" to Latinxs more broadly.[52] Hart-Cellar inaugurated a stratified immigration system with interlinked but differentiated effects on Asian Americans and Latinxs.

Asian American and Latinx migrations reveal the unstable distinction between needed and undesired immigrants. These figures result from colliding foreign policy, capitalist, and nativist interests whose contradictions play out on the lives of racialized immigrants. The needs of U.S. capital for cheap labor conflict with nativist desires to protect the nation from the racial difference that labor recruitment brings.[53] The needed immigrant is, crucially, not fully desired. For example, the employers who advocated for Mexican migration in the early twentieth century did not see Mexican immigrants as potential full members of U.S. society. Employers recruited what they saw as a lower race, which was "well suited for hard labor," and they framed Mexicans as "nonthreatening."[54] This nonthreatening aspect extends to contemporary model minority variations of the needed immigrant, in which public perceptions value Asian Americans as hardworking, politically quiescent others. Need, otherness, and repulsion coexist in varying balances. The contingent shifts in this balance affect and link Latinxs and Asian Americans.

There is an urgent but difficult case for forging a coalition across the intertwined positions of the immigration regime. The contingency of the positions makes clear that Asian American and Latinx communities should see their fates as linked even if they currently face different conditions. To be reprieved for now from the brunt of the system's racialized violence is no secure place if the logic of the "illegal alien" as a rights-less nonperson, the racially exclusionary idea of the nation, and the premise of exploitable foreignness endure. In an earlier period, some Mexican American activists failed to envision solidarities with those on the other side of this regime. Today many Asian Americans enjoy the more advantaged position. Asian Americans then must ask themselves, why, with an estimated 1.7 million undocumented Asian immigrants living in precarity, has the Asian American community not mobilized on a mass scale to join the immigrant rights movement spearheaded by Latinx activists?[55] Has the Asian American community been content to occupy the nonthreatening role, keeping its head down while the nation targets Latinxs as the threatening immigrants? Historical amnesia perhaps allows many to forget that Asian immigrants have also been the primary targets of exclusion. As Jeehyun Lim observes, the history of racial positioning in the United States shows that inclusion is not "once and for all achieved."[56] Many affluent Asian American immigrants today are clearly less threatened than earlier and present groups in the undesired position. But if nativism has consistently framed the histories of labor migration to the United States, what would it take for the nation to turn again against a needed group? Since 2010, new arrivals from Asia have surpassed new arrivals from Latin America.[57] If Asian Americans are hailed as model minorities today while they are 6 percent of the population, how might attitudes shift when their population more than doubles in the coming decades? The next turning of the tide may not be too far off.[58]

COMPARATIVE METHODS FOR A DIVIDED RACIAL ORDER

The stakes of perceiving interlinked histories across different positions are clear. So how might minority groups adjust their visions to see relationally across a divided racial order, stratified immigration system, and unequal world labor market? Comparative ethnic studies today is one part of addressing this question. Its scholarship can contribute to envisioning solidarities against the grain of the racial order. Putting forth unexpected comparisons and implicit links will be important for revealing the larger projects of relational racialization in which minority groups are embedded. This book holds that comparative ethnic literary studies helps reveal such links. It argues that looking to imaginative works can expand minority political imaginaries beyond the given and overt.

This book adds to a growing body of scholarship in comparative ethnic literary and cultural studies. Much of this work has focused on the relations between African Americans and other racial groups, which makes sense given the prominent position of African Americans in the U.S. racial order and minority politics. Scholars such as Daniel Y. Kim, Julia H. Lee, Fred Wei-han Ho, and Bill V. Mullen have advanced our understanding of Afro-Asian cultural and political connections.[59] Meanwhile, work by Emily Lutenski, Claudia Milian, and Elda María Román has illuminated the intersections of African American and Latinx cultures.[60] African American and Jewish American literary links have also been an important subject.[61] Less frequently, comparative studies have looked beyond the black pole of the black-white axis.[62]

Giving Form to an Asian and Latinx America makes an intervention in the comparative methods deployed in this field. While diverse in scope and argument, the works in comparative ethnic literary studies use recurring axes to connect the literatures of different racial groups: shared themes; histories of mutual influence; histories and portrayals of direct encounters; and reciprocal representations.[63] But comparisons between Asian Americans and Latinxs raise challenges for these methods, challenges that extend to other comparative cases as well. Comparative ethnic studies must consider the limitations of the established axes for groups that have been drawn into the nation and excluded in opposed ways, or groups without a vibrant history of alliance, or groups whose structural relationships within the racial order, immigration system, and global economy cannot be captured in histories of direct encounter.[64] How might these axes contend with cases in which neither party belongs to the black-white axis dominating U.S. racial thought? The influences of such groups on others may be less visible. In such comparisons, methods focused on direct encounter, reciprocal representations, and cross-influences will not capture the full breadth of the relationship. I argue for complementing these methods with comparison through historicized form. This approach can perceive relations that are not visible through overt links of social content, influence, and encounter, and it can reveal entanglements across opposed and seemingly separate social positions.[65] Comparison through form also has an advantage of highlighting the medium-specific contributions that literature can make to models of interminority coalition.

My approach stresses a fully social sense of artistic practice as an axis for comparative ethnic studies. Raymond Williams expressed this sense best. Williams saw writing as an embedded process of shaping materials within specific social conditions.[66] He approached aesthetic forms not as fixed features of a finished product but as living elements involved in multiple processes: working on materials, negotiating conventions, and constructing works that circulate in cultural systems of meaning. The comparisons at the center of this book draw out shared struggles in each of these processes. Asian American and Latinx writers wrestle with difficult historical materials marked by competing necessities. How, for example, does one represent migrant lives spanning national borders without covering over the ruptures that borders create in those lives? Attempts to do justice to these histories also conflict with a horizon of "available forms" that encode selective ways of seeing and interpreting.[67] For example, attempts to narrate migrations driven by U.S. militarism struggle against cherished plots of immigration that can only imagine migrations attracted by American freedom and opportunity. Writers are working through the limits on Asian American and Latinx histories, a struggle that manifests in their aesthetic strategies. Related formal strategies are clues, spurs to investigate the social challenges these writers may be jointly addressing: the linked contradictions in the histories they are depicting; the new kinds of political community they are imagining; the stories of nation, mobility, and empowerment they are rewriting.

Asian American and Latinx storytellers face many difficulties. As such, the works explored in this book do not tell stories of triumph. More often, they reveal continuing social and artistic struggles. In their forms, the contradictions of Asian American and Latinx histories and the constraints on their telling are still perceptible. These artistic attempts deserve attention precisely because they are qualified and partial. As Williams observes, incomplete aesthetic forms can offer the first signs of social changes in motion. New kinds of social relation and experience remain "at the very edge of semantic availability" until specific forms emerge that can grasp them. Developing forms are part of the social process that brings new possibilities into being, making "latencies actual" and "newly possible consciousness" available.[68] The transfictional forms across Asian American and Latinx literatures show writers struggling to envision types of social relation to address the challenges of their communities. Meanwhile, the social relation between these communities is itself one of the emergent possibilities that remains to be fully articulated.

TRANSFICTIONAL SOLIDARITY

Although widespread political alliances between Latinxs and Asian Americans have yet to form, this book shows that there are emerging artistic coalitions. Writers in distinct communities are converging on the same aesthetic strategies. I explore these strategies in the work of Latinx and Asian American writers in the post-1965 period, from emerging talents like Cristina Henríquez, Aimee Phan, Salvador Plascencia, and Rishi Reddi to established voices like Sandra Cisneros, Junot Díaz, Maxine Hong Kingston, and Karen Tei Yamashita. This range shows how transfictional aesthetics is energizing new voices and how a transfictional vocabulary offers fresh perspective on familiar texts. Panethnic coverage is beyond the scope of this book, but my investigation does span the literatures of many ethnic groups. While acknowledging some established centers of Latinx and Asian American literature, I also highlight the literature of more recently emerging ethnic groups. This book includes not only Chicanx but also Dominican and Panamanian American works, not just Chinese and Japanese American but also Vietnamese and Indian American literature. This is by no means an exhaustive survey of Asian American and Latinx transfictional works. The form is so generative in these literatures that there are fascinating examples that I am not able to include.[69] I am drawn to the works here for the ways their formal resonances enable us to perceive shared challenges during key periods in the formation of an Asian and Latinx America. I should also note that because one goal in this book is to develop methods of comparative ethnic study beyond overt connections of social content, I don't focus on the few intriguing works, such as Yamashita's *Tropic of Orange* or Cristina García's *The Lady Matador's Hotel*, that center on Asian American and Latinx characters interacting.[70]

I argue for a cross-medium collaboration in which scholars recognize the literature emerging from the Asian and Latinx United States as thought-provoking co-theorizers. Thinking alongside these works can open lines of comparison and structure Latinx and Asian American political thought in revivified ways. These works offer us a transfictional form for rethinking Asian American and Latinx solidarities. This theorizing power comes from the specific structure of the form, which I should specify further here.

Scholars in transmedia narrative studies use the term *transfictionality* to describe how a storyworld unfolds across many fictional texts and distinct packaged works—multiple films, books, comics, and so forth.[71] They are interested in how a storyworld spans multiple media,[72] but they recognize that transfictionality can also occur within a single medium.[73] Drawing on this work, the more specific idea of transfictional form holds that many of the world-building dynamics of transfictionality can occur within a single work. A narrative work with a transfictional form produces many of the elements that transmedia narrative scholars describe: adding more characters, giving minor characters their own stories, expanding the temporal scope, opening up new parts of the storyworld.[74] I propose that transfictional storytelling asks readers to think across not just many texts but, more fundamentally, many distinct fictions. Transmedia narrative studies implies intriguing questions about building one world across many stories. I address those questions and theorize the key formal tensions that result from this world building.

The tensions of transfictional form are best described by drawing on theorists in transnational and transgender studies. Scholars in these fields explain that the trans- prefix encodes senses of unsettled crossings. The prefix *trans* in *transnational* describes a tension between national borders and processes that move across them.[75] Similarly, the prefix *trans* in *transgender* expresses dynamic movements across gender boundaries while recognizing that these crossings do not dissolve gender boundaries.[76] These senses of borders and dynamic crossings are at work in transfictional form. Each story in a transfictional work sets the boundaries of its diegetic concerns, while transfictional relations link stories across these narrative borders.[77] Transfictional works can leave the gaps between stories unfilled, declining to resolve how the stories are related. When I asked Aimee Phan about the form of *We Should Never Meet*, she answered that it offered her the freedom to "leave a lot unsaid" and "not to answer every question."[78] Transfictional works can both invite links between stories and withhold information to frustrate readers' attempts to draw definite connections. By inviting links and also frustrating them, transfictional form embodies the trans tension between crossings and borders. The form challenges readers to think through principles of connection that relate without erasing the causal separations, diegetic borders, and gaps of knowledge between stories. These works invite us to consider the many kinds of relations that might link distinct groups and stories without conflating them, a thought process crucial to envisioning solidarities.

Much as the *trans* in *transgender* evokes an unresolved flux that does not settle on one side or the other of established gender divides,[79] transfictional form does not resolve conflicting aesthetic impulses. These sustained aesthetic tensions in Asian American and Latinx works give form to social contradictions that defy any easy resolutions that fictions might be tempted to imagine. Prematurely resolving such contradictions in a story can be a form of ideological fantasy.[80] Asian American and Latinx writers who use transfictional form take seriously social struggles that are ongoing, and they articulate them through sustained formal tensions.

With this form, transfictional works offer generative conceptual structures and modes of political imagination for grappling with Asian American and Latinx politics. This is especially welcome at a time when these coalitions are addressing a definitional crisis. Perhaps the most central conflict for Asian American and Latinx politics today is whether these groups should be thought of as groups at all. Rapid diversification has challenged the panethnic unity undergirding Asian American and Latinx coalitions. In the face of this impasse, the transfictional imagination can help reinvigorate the troubled concepts of Asian American and Latinx. Recently, scholars such as Sue-Im Lee, Colleen Lye, Marcial González, Jennifer Harford Vargas, and Ralph E. Rodriguez have explored the stakes of literary form for racial politics.[81] Meanwhile, Patrick Lawrence Hamilton, Kandice Chuh, and Min Hyoung Song stress the theorizing powers of minority literatures.[82] And Marta Caminero-Santangelo and Susan Koshy note the fictional nature of the concepts *Latinx* and *Asian American*.[83] I synthesize and advance these developments by arguing that transfictional literary fictions provide powerful forms for rethinking the political fictions *Latinx* and *Asian American*. While scholars debate doing away with these concepts, writers are elaborating a narrative paradigm that can give them generative form. Transfictional aesthetics can help structure political thought to draw affiliations without erasing the distinctions between groups, to engage the sustained conflicts within coalition without easy resolutions, and to envision distinct stories of struggle as part of a broader world of interconnected injustices. Drawing on the imaginative possibilities this paradigm opens, scholars and activists committed to Asian American and Latinx coalitions can rethink them as transfictional stories in the making, unfinished narratives of justice driven rather than disabled by their constitutive conflicts.

Transfictional aesthetics can go further to help us connect Asian American and Latinx political projects into an interminority coalition. A panethnic coalition, when rethought in transfictional terms as a story of struggle situated in a broader world of struggles, becomes coterminous with interminority coalition. An Asian and Latinx America, then, names a possible political formation, which would be a *transfictional solidarity* in two senses. First is the sense of relying on transfictional thought. The same operation of drawing out political affiliations without erasing distinctions that helps connect various ethnic groups into an Asian American or Latinx panethnic coalition does not end at the borders of a panethnic group. These affiliations carry beyond those borders as shared struggles extend to other minority groups. Second is the sense of a crossing between political fictions. Since the concepts of Asian American and Latinx are political constructions, an Asian and Latinx America would require a transfictional solidarity across political fictions, one that would keep their fictionality at the

forefront and acknowledge that aligning struggles across differences is a creative
process. There are urgent grounds for this transfictional solidarity. Fortunately,
transfictional literary works offer us ways to give it form.

THE STORY AHEAD

The first part of the story ahead weaves through a sequence of three historical
moments that shaped the Asian and Latinx United States into what it is today.
Each moment transformed, expanded, or diversified Asian American and Latinx
communities in different ways. This is a gradually expanding story that takes in
arriving groups and emerging differences. Intertwined with this plot of historical changes is a literary story of the situated powers of transfictional aesthetics.
Each chapter focuses on transfictional tensions that powerfully engage the
social contradictions raised by a particular moment in the formation of the
contemporary Asian and Latinx United States.

Chapter 1 examines the momentous changes wrought by civil rights move-
ments in the 1960s and the uncertain economic landscape in their aftermath.
Through Maxine Hong Kingston's *The Woman Warrior* (1976) and Sandra
Cisneros's *The House on Mango Street* (1984), alongside Gloria Naylor's *The
Women of Brewster Place* (1982), this chapter examines long established communities, Chinese Americans and Mexican Americans, as they confront the
uneven opportunities of the post–civil rights period, a period that transformed
African American communities as well. Cisneros, Kingston, and Naylor took on
a genre, the bildungsroman, or novel of development, that intersected with the
racial politics of economic mobility. Their attempts to rewrite the preeminent
genre of social incorporation and individual mobility unveil post–civil rights
divisions between minority individuals who rose with new opportunities and
the many who remained stymied by collective inequalities. These works use
transfictional form to decenter the bildungsroman's social vision and the politics
of individual development espoused during the backlash against civil rights
reforms. They stage conflicts between the protagonist's development and other
characters whose stories cannot progress, between the diachronic momentum
of individual mobility and an expansive attention to collective conditions.

Linked to established communities divided by domestic civil rights policy
were newer arrivals displaced by U.S. foreign policy and militarism in Asia
and Latin America (as Mary Dudziak and Cindy I-Fen Cheng have shown,

these two arenas of policy were linked).[84] Cold War displacements extending from the 1960s into the 1980s brought ethnic diversity and new histories of U.S. imperialism that transformed Asian American and Latinx communities. The second chapter follows a post–Cold War generation of Latinx and Asian American writers as they reflect on the migrations this global war generated. The fragmented form of their writings attests to struggles against American narratives that disconnected U.S. violence in the Third World from the Third World migrations entering the United States. The fictions of Junot Díaz and Aimee Phan deploy a transfictional tension of narrative borders and border crossings to capture the disrupted yet linked histories of the Dominican and Vietnamese diasporas. Reading their fictions together uncovers how Asia and Latin America were linked in a global military project and helps us see across the regional divides that structure histories of the Cold War.

The third chapter extends the vision of post-1965 migration to take in economically driven migrant flows. These flows arrived in the United States during a neoliberal age of stratified immigration that produces a discrepant range of immigrant fates—from undocumented labor to knowledge workers. The range of positions within Latinx and Asian American ethnic groups makes for uneven communities that defy attempts to represent them. Rishi Reddi's *Karma* (2007) and Salvador Plascencia's *The People of Paper* (2005) confront this challenge. These works transpose major and minor characters and unsettle narrative hierarchies that govern who does and does not serve as the center in stories of ethnic communities. These transpositions highlight the reduction of minority communities by racial stereotypes and neoliberal assessments of human capital. Scrambling perceptions of their communities, Reddi and Plascencia highlight, respectively, disadvantaged immigrants who belie the idea of Indian American success and upwardly mobile youths who complicate the idea of the Mexican American "underclass." Linking ethnic groups that seem to inhabit opposite ends of the immigration system, this chapter reveals their shared struggles to recognize the unequal life chances that neoliberal immigration has wrought. It unveils the linked projects of wealth and labor extraction in Asia and Latin America.

The post–civil rights period, displacements generated by the Cold War, and the neoliberal age of stratified immigration have expanded Asian American and Latinx communities in ways that culminate in a crisis of unity today.

They have spurred dramatic growth, fueling visions of potential power in U.S. politics. At the same time, they have generated deep cleavages that undermine the ideas of Asian Americans and Latinxs as unified, panethnic coalitions. The climax of this story will confront the current impasses of Asian American and Latinx coalitions. The unified minority identities driving earlier moments of identity politics can no longer be taken for granted, yet collective political organizing remains crucial. Developing ways forward from this impasse requires the full imaginative powers of Asian Americans and Latinxs. The final two chapters follow two ambitious fictions that attempt to encompass the range of panethnic differences: Cristina Henríquez's *The Book of Unknown Americans* (2014) and Karen Tei Yamashita's *I Hotel* (2010). These panethnic fictions use transfictional aesthetics to help reimagine the ideas of panethnic collectives. Chapter 4 brings together the debates on panethnic coalitions in Latinx and Asian American studies to reveal how their central impasses are aligned. It goes on to show how *The Book of Unknown Americans* uses transfictional form to express the antagonisms between panethnic unity and multiplicity. The novel tells parallel stories of migrants from across Latin America. Their life stories cross paths but do not merge into any narrative unity. Transfictional form, this chapter argues, recognizes the differences that prevent Latinx experiences from being told in any one story. At the same time, this form guides the comparative thought needed to envision new shapes of panethnic alliance that link Latinxs to each other and to broader formations. Chapter 5 follows *I Hotel* as it uses transfictional form to situate conflicts within the Asian American movement as part of social contradictions extending far beyond Asian America. Conflicts within panethnic coalitions, then, are generative, because they orient these coalitions to a systemic and utopian horizon of justice. Utopian horizons help us reconsider unity and closure, ideas critiqued by the politics of difference embraced in Asian American and Latinx studies. This chapter recasts panethnic unity not as a political premise but as a promise to struggle for, a horizon to aid in imagining the future that would make unity free of contradiction possible. Together these novels push Asian American and Latinx panethnic movements to look beyond their circumscribed borders and to see their internal struggles for unity as entangled with wide-ranging projects of justice that link them to each other.

A NOTE ON SCOPE

This book explores an emerging social formation and how transfictional form helps give that formation shape. My aim is not to offer a comprehensive survey of transfictional works across periods and contexts. That goal conflicts with my comparative methods. I'm not interested in comparison based on form alone. Similar forms can arise in multiple contexts (because a form can be put to a range of uses), but this is not enough for an illuminating comparison. In my view, the significance of form for comparative work is in how form may engage and allow us to see resonant historical materials and related social struggles across different contexts. That's what is striking about transfictional form in Asian American and Latinx literatures: how the same form addresses and reveals convergent challenges that come out of the distinct ways these groups are racialized and out of the particular histories of migration, stratification, imperialism, and political organizing they navigate. This conjunction defines my focus and the boundaries of the comparison.

Transfictional forms are present in other periods and traditions of American literature. The transfictional story cycle in particular has a longer history, especially in regionalist and modernist fiction around the turn of the twentieth century.[85] While it's not the focus, this longer history plays a role in this book, as contemporary writers reveal aesthetic possibilities latent in earlier examples. For instance, Aimee Phan's *We Should Never Meet* retrofits the locally focused regionalist story cycle and brings out its potential to map diasporic communities. Many of the works in this study stretch generic possibilities. In contrast to many earlier examples of transfictional form, which were unified by localized setting or a central character, these contemporary instances are more likely to dissolve the local setting to trace global movements and to let go of central characters. Far-ranging settings and character-systems also distinguish Asian American and Latinx transfictional works from many of their counterparts in Native American, African American, and Anglo American literatures.[86] Though this book focuses on the distinct challenges linking Asian Americans and Latinxs, it recognizes that racialization can be multiply relational. Some of the struggles that Latinx and Asian American transfictional works address also touch on other minority groups. In those cases, I expand the comparative scope to include transfictional examples from other traditions, as in Chapter 1, where I follow Asian American, Latina, and black women using the form to critique models of minority mobility.

Just as Asian American and Latinx literatures are not isolated from others, the concept of transfictional form developed here is not limited to these literatures. I hope that the concept will travel to help other scholars describe uses of this form in other contexts. Asian American and Latinx writers explore a range of transfictional possibilities that demonstrate the vast potential of the form, a potential which is not yet fully tapped. This is a rich archive with which to theorize the form's broader possibilities. As this form speaks to Latinxs and Asian Americans navigating the leading edges of transformations in the United States and the world, its narrative possibilities speak to and perhaps even prefigure broader changes to come.[87]

PART I

FORMS AND FORMATIONS

DECENTERING BILDUNGSROMAN HERMENEUTICS

Cisneros, Kingston, and Post–Civil Rights Mobility

A PROBLEM OF others haunts the most iconic female coming-of-age stories in Latina and Asian American literatures. Sandra Cisneros's *The House on Mango Street* (1984) includes forty-four named characters in a work that totals just 110 pages and forty-four vignettes. Of these vignettes that describe Esperanza Cordero's upbringing in a working-class Latinx neighborhood, eighteen are named after other characters in the community. Similarly, Maxine Hong Kingston's *The Woman Warrior* (1976) is a memoir "of a Girlhood among Ghosts." Kingston's story of negotiating identity unfolds amid the stories of many other women from her family, community, and cultural lineages. Why are these bildungsromane so full with the stories of others? This question leads to the political stakes of the bildungsroman in the aftermath of the civil rights period. This aftermath produced tensions between minority individuals who could take advantage of new opportunities and the many who remained in poverty, between individual rights secured and collective inequalities that continued to exclude minorities from social and economic incorporation. As the preeminent genre of social mobility and incorporation, the bildungsroman provided a compelling but fraught logic to mediate these tensions.

Our story of the contemporary Asian and Latinx United States begins here with long established ethnic groups—Mexican Americans and Chinese Americans—as they navigate the social transformations and political backlash unleashed by the civil rights period. The uneven landscape of economic mobility it produced contributed significantly to the class divides so clear in the Asian and Latinx United States today. These divides are central to the proliferating differences that have brought the ideas of unified Asian American and Latinx communities into crisis.

For writers from minority communities fractured by uneven opportunity, the post–civil rights landscape placed new risks on bildungsroman narratives. This chapter defines those risks. It examines the problem of bildungsroman hermeneutics in the post–civil rights era. Bildungsroman hermeneutics understands social relations as organized around the individual's development. This framework exerts a powerful hold that can be felt in the reading practices critics bring to minority life stories and, more consequentially, in the social policy visions that shape minority life chances. It pervades critical responses to *Mango Street* and *The Woman Warrior*, undermining the collective politics many critics sense in these works. Bildungsroman hermeneutics is troubling because its logic intersects with arguments developed in political reactions to civil rights reforms. By insisting that the achievement of racial equality be defined as opportunities for minorities to follow a path of individual development, a neoconservative backlash argued against the need for further reforms after individual rights were secured. To recognize the inequalities enduring after the civil rights movement, Americans need to circumvent a narrative template that has constrained our understandings of minority status.

Cisneros's and Kingston's works can help us do so. They crowd the traditional bildungsroman. Cisneros exposes the inequalities within its mobility narrative and refracts its individual focus toward a polycentric political consciousness that acknowledges the uneven circumstances stratifying Latinx life chances. Kingston also scrutinizes mobility from an ethnic community and employs a text full of others to examine the vexed politics of individualized models of female empowerment. To perceive these interventions though requires new ways of reading narrative and social relations that escape the pull of bildungsroman hermeneutics. The transfictional reading experience, with its tension between the individual protagonist and the stories of others, offers powerful possibilities for doing so.

Mango Street and *The Woman Warrior* decenter not only the form and social vision of the traditional bildungsroman but also the reproduction of that generic form in Latina and Asian American literatures. With its portrait of a working-class Latinx neighborhood and a girl's path to artistic maturity, *Mango Street* echoes the first Latina bildungsroman published by a major press, Nicholasa Mohr's *Nilda* (1973). But while Mohr's novel stays focused on Nilda's story and subordinates the stories of other Latinas, *Mango Street* opens its narrative structure to the lives of other Latinas as distinct stories.[1] Cisneros's transfictional development of the Latina bildungsroman reverberates in later works such as Denise Chávez's *The Last of the Menu Girls* (1986), with its discrete episodes and stories of others.[2] *The Woman Warrior* bears the influence of earlier Asian American female memoirs, such as Jade Snow Wong's *Fifth Chinese Daughter* (1950) and Monica Sone's *Nisei Daughter* (1953), which was modeled on Wong's successful book.[3] At the same time, it expands the protagonist-centered forms of these works to accommodate many female stories and narration that marginalizes the protagonist.

The contradiction of individual mobility and collective obstacles affected many minority communities in this period. It's not surprising, then, that other minority writers were also wrestling with the classic bildungsroman. While I focus on Cisneros's and Kingston's works, I will also touch on the African American woman's bildungsroman with Gloria Naylor's transfictional novel *The Women of Brewster Place* (1982). Naylor sets much of her novel in the aftermath of the civil rights movement and emphasizes the challenges that remained: "When all the smoke had cleared, you found yourself with a fistful of new federal laws and a country still full of obstacles for black people to fight their way over."[4] Drawing these writers together by observing their convergent aesthetic strategies, this chapter reveals a movement of women of color writers who worked to decenter the bildungsroman and address collective conditions. Within this movement, minority mobility had a particular charge for Latinxs and Asian Americans. Because these groups occupy the "racial middle" in a black-white racial order,[5] their handling of the politics of mobility has relational effects across the racial landscape. The success stories that come out of their communities can be arguments for blaming other minority groups, particularly African Americans, for their own fates.[6]

I begin with the question of others in the bildungsroman and then show the bildungsroman hermeneutics at work in post–civil rights debates on minority mobility. I then reveal this same hermeneutics driving critical approaches to the minority development narrative. In the final sections I turn to the transfictional aesthetics of *Mango Street*, *Brewster Place*, and *The Woman Warrior* to develop ways to decenter bildungsroman hermeneutics from our habits of social and narrative interpretation.

INDIVIDUAL AND COLLECTIVE, CANONICAL AND MINORITY BILDUNGSROMANE

Nina Baym, Susan Fraiman, and Bonnie TuSmith, among others, argue that the literature produced by women and minorities is communally oriented, in opposition to the autonomous individualism emphasized by dominant literary culture.[7] Many scholars consider the bildungsroman an important target for this resistance.[8] Minority writers transform "what were once efficacious vehicles for the representation of individually, atomistically oriented experiences into collective modes of articulation."[9] The crowding of characters into Cisneros's and Kingston's bildungsromane may be a formal consequence of this effort. My investigation builds on this work and on studies that propose the short story cycle as a framework for describing minority revisions of the bildungsroman.[10] I suggest that this scholarship should be advanced in two ways. First, scholars of the minority bildungsroman need a more nuanced view of the canonical bildungsroman's individualism. Second, many studies of minority revisions of the genre remain influenced by the traditional genre's hermeneutics, which undermines the collective politics critics champion in these revisions.

Critics are right to identify the traditional bildungsroman's resistance to communal politics. But classic examples and studies of the genre as well as the philosophy of *bildung* that informs it show that this resistance does not result from an atomistic individualism but from a social vision centered on the individual. The individual's relations with society have always been central to the genre. The bildungsroman is the genre of socialization.[11] Rather than developing apart from social demands, the protagonist of the *bildung* narrative finds fulfillment within the wider community. The end of Johann Wolfgang von

Goethe's *Wilhelm Meister's Apprenticeship* (1795–96), the prototype for the genre, leaves its protagonist well married, embraced by new friends, and inducted into a secret society that oversees the development of others. The philosophy of *bildung* holds that development occurs through rich relations with the social world. According to Wilhelm von Humboldt, one of the primary theorists of *bildung*, the individual reaches fulfillment by linking "the self to the world" in an "unrestrained interplay."[12] This literary and philosophical lineage suggests that the ideological elegance of the genre's individualism lies not in its alleged atomism but in its harmonious arrangement of self and society. As Alex Woloch notes, the genre's portrait of society forms a stable totality by subordinating other characters to the protagonist's plot.[13] What matters is not these others in themselves but the opportunities they provide for the protagonist's formation. This vision acknowledges the importance of social relations but remains incompatible with communal politics. For Humboldt, social relations are "instruments" for the individual's self-formation.[14] This premise informs his political philosophy, which argues that social policy should limit its attempts to mold the welfare of individuals and allow them to develop themselves from the opportunities around them.[15] As we will see, this individual-oriented policy perspective is why the bildungsroman intersects in such a fraught way with post–civil rights debates about collective inequalities. To sum up, the traditional bildungsroman does exhibit individualism, but its individualism does not take the form of the individual separated from society, as many critics argue. Rather, the genre's individualism stems from its contention that the meaning of social life lies in its organization around and for the individual. Others are there to serve the story of the self.

This more nuanced view of the canonical bildungsroman affects ideas of what it takes to revise the genre. One important precursor for my attempt to revise bildungsroman hermeneutics is Susan Fraiman's *Unbecoming Women*. Fraiman proposes ways to begin "decentering" the bildungsroman to attend to the stories of other characters, an idea I develop further. A "different way of reading for formation," Fraiman argues, would be to see it as dialogic, "a matter of social context." Yet Fraiman's push against the traditional genre rests on the familiar image of "isolate subjectivity," which obscures how formation in dialogue with others was always central to the genre.[16] The challenge of revising the bildungsroman for a communal ethos is not just shifting from autonomous to relational models of development. The challenge is remaking the relational model of development already in the genre to be more equitable and polycentric when that model offers such a powerful vision of social relations unified around the story of the self. This hermeneutics is difficult to unlearn because it's fundamental to the idea of a protagonist, and, as detailed next, to ideas of the social good.

BILDUNGSROMAN CONFLICTS IN THE POST–CIVIL RIGHTS ERA

The importance of the bildungsroman when it emerged at the turn of the nineteenth century was its power to resolve symbolically the contradictions of modern social mobility.[17] This mobility, of course, largely excluded women and minorities. But when Cisneros, Kingston, and Naylor were writing, these exclusions were opening in uneven ways. Joseph R. Slaughter observes that the bildungsroman becomes charged when the question of who is included in a nation reaches a crisis, because it has become the dominant genre "in which social outsiders narrate affirmative claims for inclusion."[18] The upheavals in the U.S. racial order during the 1960s and 1970s generated such a crisis. Protest movements opened some social freedoms and mobility to minorities by spurring civil rights legislation, immigration reforms, welfare programs, and affirmative action policies. These reforms improved the socioeconomic chances of minorities including Asian Americans and Latinxs.[19] But securing formal legal equality didn't mean liquidating long-standing economic inequalities. Most minorities remained poor.[20] The period's partial openings contributed to class divides within minority communities, as the few who could took advantage of new opportunities while the majority remained stymied.[21] Diverse waves of immigration further intensified the divisions within Asian American and Latinx communities. Many minority youths had to leave behind their communities to pursue greater mobility. For Chicanxs who had organized around working-class identities, upward mobility smacked of "betrayal."[22] Similarly, Asian American activists emphasized community-oriented, working-class politics.[23] These conditions intensified the conflicts of individual and collective negotiated in the bildungsroman. The political reaction to civil rights reforms made the genre even more fraught as its narrative logic intersected with the most contentious debates of the era's racial politics.

The post–civil rights period is part of a historical pattern that Philip A. Klinkner and Rogers M. Smith call an "unsteady march." Long periods of "stagnation and decline" have always followed bursts of progress toward racial equality in U.S. history.[24] Klinkner and Smith assert that the decline following civil rights achievements extends into the present. Many measures support their argument. Racial segregation rates and wealth disparities today are little different than they were during the civil rights period.[25] And the uneven condition of individual mobility amid mass challenges extended into the presidency of Barack Obama, the most spectacular case of a minority individual succeeding. Individual openings with collective blockages, de jure equality with de facto inequalities—these characteristics of the aftermath of civil rights endure today.

But if the post–civil rights period continues, I propose clarifying its internal shape by identifying a crucial subperiod of transition from the 1970s to the early 1990s. This transition saw a shift to a post–civil rights consensus that retreated from state interventions and further reforms. That consensus extends into the present, but I focus on the subperiod of debates before it consolidated. (I'll use the term *post–civil rights era* to refer to the period that extends into the present and *post–civil rights transition* to refer to this subperiod.) These debates formed the contentious context for the stories of mobility that Cisneros, Kingston, and Naylor were writing. Government interventions for racial equality were still being advanced, but a backlash was building. By the end of this transition, hopes that civil rights reforms might be expanded were dashed.

The transition began with the end of the civil rights movement, which ceded the stage for a new "racial reaction."[26] This reaction developed in the 1970s as public opposition to federal actions such as school busing became more widespread. The presidential administrations of the 1970s showed increasing ambivalence toward racial equality policies. Nixon's administration, for example, sought to roll back civil rights reforms yet also expanded affirmative action.[27] That "Nixon was not yet free to swing too sharply away from racially egalitarian policies" shows that the possibilities of securing and even extending civil rights reforms still hung in the balance.[28] By Ronald Reagan's administration, a critical shift had occurred. Reagan adopted the themes of the racial reaction, legitimating and normalizing it.[29] With this success, the president began reversing civil rights policies. The Reagan revolution spurred Democrats to distance themselves from "the political albatross of championing racial equality."[30] By 1992, with Bill

Clinton's election as a New Democrat, Democrats largely aligned themselves with Republicans, giving up on race-conscious policies and aggressive government intervention and adopting the rhetoric of individual responsibility so central to the backlash.[31] The post–civil rights consensus had arrived.

The transition was driven by a new rhetoric from the right. Conservative groups distanced themselves from overt racism and embraced the language of racial equality, debating its meaning and implementation so that it became a powerful line of attack against continuing struggles for actual equality.[32] The most sophisticated attacks came not from the conservative movement proper but from an emergent group of liberal intellectuals reacting against the New Left and radical racial politics. These neoconservatives, as they came to be known, influenced public debates in journals like *The Public Interest* and *Commentary*. Including figures such as Daniel Patrick Moynihan and Irving Kristol, the neoconservative movement laid the intellectual groundwork for Reagan's revolution and the roll back of civil rights reforms.[33]

Neoconservative arguments relied on a narrative template to which the traditional bildungsroman had greatly contributed: the story of individual mobility and development. This alignment is apparent in the book *Affirmative Discrimination* (1975) by Nathan Glazer, a distinguished sociologist of ethnicity. This was the first book-length attack on affirmative action, a text that became "required reading for American conservatives."[34] Glazer's argument rejects policies that consider the status of racial groups, because they abandon "the first principle of a liberal society, that the individual and the individual's interests and good and welfare are the test of a good society." Social policy should only focus on "the individual's capacity to work out an individual fate by means of education, work, and self-realization."[35] Glazer converges with the scheme the bildungsroman perfected, that social relations are meaningful insofar as they contribute to the individual's formation. Glazer's "test of a good society" echoes the centrality of the developed individual in Humboldt's political theory: "The State should test itself by his measure."[36] In both neoconservative and *bildung*-oriented political thought, this primary good prescribes "the limits of social policy" (the title of one of Glazer's books and a central theme of Humboldt's writings). As with the bildungsroman, neoconservatives did not advocate an atomized individualism; they believed that social institutions and policies matter.[37] But, as Glazer argues, "the proper objective of public policy" is ensuring conditions of "equal opportunity."[38] From there, individual merit should determine outcomes because the United States exhibits "easier mobility" than other developed nations.[39] For *bildung* theory, "the purpose of the state is to preserve (but not to administer)" the freedoms and conditions in which individual development can occur.[40] The bildungsroman's narrative of individual development implies a vision of limited social policy; conversely, the limited social policy neoconservatives advocate is justified by the central value of a narrative of individual development. In this way, the logic of the traditional bildungsroman reinforces neoconservative social policy.[41]

One consequence of this policy vision is that individual outcomes become the default scale for assessing racial equality, obscuring the more relevant scale of effects on racial groups. Glazer discounts the collective scale of analysis: "How the figures add up on the basis of whatever measures of group we use may be interesting, but should be no concern of public policy." By subordinating social structures to the story of the individual, this argument could avow support for racial equality, while eliding the very scale that would reveal the workings of racism. The neoconservative position contends that once the nation secures legal protections for individuals, the individual writes the rest of the story. This conclusion found support in the rhetoric of the civil rights period as a historic turning point. "No one," Glazer proclaims, "is now excluded from the broadest access to what the society makes possible."[42] This sense of achieved equality was a powerful argument against further interventions. Feeling that upheavals in the name of racial justice had gone far enough, neoconservatives rejected New Left activism.[43] The inclusion of the minority individual into the expanded rights of the state was a bulwark against more radical transformations. Individual inclusion as a diffusion of youthful revolutionary energy—this is the plot of the traditional bildungsroman, as Franco Moretti argues.[44] The genre affirms the existing nation-state, showing the opportunities for development available as alternatives to revolt.[45]

With opportunity for all seemingly achieved, minorities could blame only themselves if they failed "to work out an individual fate."[46] In this light, consider Georg Lukács's description of the bildungsroman: "In order to demonstrate the risk which everyone runs and which can be escaped by individual salvation but not by a-prioristic redemption, many characters have to perish because of their inability to adapt themselves."[47] The failures of others are necessary to highlight the achievement of success through individual effort and not categorical guarantee. Neoconservative thinking would find much to agree with in this scheme; they warned that the ideal of individual merit was being undermined by the doctrine of group equality and quotas.[48]

Juxtaposing the narrative form of the traditional bildungsroman and neoconservative arguments on race reveals the ideological work that can be done by focusing social relations around the individual. It's an elegant form for telling a minority mobility story that obscures structural inequities, makes state interventions appear unnecessary, channels collective struggles into the pursuit of individual opportunity, and contends that individual rights are enough.

The post–civil rights transition posed particular risks for minority writers telling stories of social mobility.[49] These writers had to negotiate an incomplete opening of the racial order, class polarization, further reforms to be championed, and achieved reforms to be defended against a backlash whose arguments aligned with the narrative logic of the bildungsroman. Cisneros, Kingston, and Naylor were finishing their bildungsromane from the mid-1970s to the early 1980s, when the retreat from racial equality efforts was accelerating but was not yet dominant. The U.S. public, "weary of racial conflict," was eager to hear minorities testify that the nation should move beyond race.[50] In 1978, African American sociologist William J. Wilson published *The Declining Significance of Race* and received national attention. And in 1981, Mexican American writer Richard Rodriguez's *Hunger of Memory* arrived to critical acclaim and controversy for its account of upward mobility and its attacks on affirmative action. In this context, a minority story of mobility could be taken as emblematic of the opportunities supposedly available to all. Crystal Parikh observes that the narratives of minority neoconservatives like Rodriguez both marginalize and are haunted by others in their ethnic communities who do not fit their plots of inclusion and meritocratic opportunity.[51] The risk of erasing the conditions of others under an emblematic plot is built into the classic bildungsroman. Lukács observes that the *bildung* protagonist is a universal figure whose outcome is "potentially accessible to all."[52] The bildungsroman in this period could elide the contradiction between the post–civil rights narrative of individual opportunity and the systemic inequalities that continued to constrain racial groups. These questions become more complex for the feminist ethnic bildungsroman, which exposes racism in U.S. society and sexism in ethnic communities. Could one express a desire to escape from sexist domination in one's community without being taken as endorsing assimilation to liberal individualist values, the values that conservatives were invoking to dismiss the struggles of minority communities? Cisneros and Kingston navigate these risks in remarkable ways, trying to hold within one narrative structure the new openings for a few and the blockages that persist for the many. But their attempts confront a pervasive bildungsroman hermeneutics that interprets narrative relations as organized around the individual. Beginning with Cisneros, I turn now to examine this hermeneutics.

BILDUNGSROMAN HERMENEUTICS

Critics have subjected *The House on Mango Street* to widely divergent readings. They have critiqued its individualism, celebrated its individualism, lauded its collective values, and seen it as a synthesis of these values.[53] *Mango Street* has generated such varying interpretations because its coupling of individual and collective values addresses unresolved tensions of Latina social mobility. In doing so, the book revises the classic bildungsroman and demands different reading practices. Nevertheless, the hermeneutics of the traditional bildungsroman remains difficult to resist. As Paula M. L. Moya notes, genre conventions of the novel and the classic bildungsroman have dominated critical approaches to *Mango Street*, despite recognition that the book is generically hybrid.[54] Even critics who argue—rightly, I believe—that *Mango Street* revises the genre to express a collective politics often fall back in their reading practices on the traditional bildungsroman's individual-centered rubric, which is antithetical to those politics.

Ellen McCracken's work offers an example. McCracken argues that *Mango Street* counters individualistic literature with a modified bildungsroman that "roots the individual self in the broader socio-political reality of the Chicano community."[55] The problem arises when she considers other characters, particularly the women of Mango Street. Despite arguing against the individual-centered tradition, in practice she reads these characters in relation to the presumed center of Esperanza. McCracken rehearses a theme that recurs repeatedly in criticism of minority bildungsromane: These other women are "role models."[56] In the traditional bildungsroman the lives of others are meaningful insofar as they contribute to the protagonist's formation, whether as warnings or models.[57] McCracken reproduces this interpretation. The character of Sally, whose stories make up a substantial portion of *Mango Street*, becomes a "role model for Esperanza . . . symboliz[ing] the process of sexual initiation for her younger friend."[58] The horizon of meaning for Sally's stories is not her own development but Esperanza's. McCracken's attempt to describe the communal orientation of Cisneros's text slips back into the reading habits of the classical bildungsroman via the logic of the role model. To be clear, I agree that Sally and other female characters help and inspire Esperanza. The issue is when bildungsroman hermeneutics subsumes the stories of other women to a functional role in Esperanza's development, thus overlooking the ways that *Mango Street* recognizes their particular concerns in themselves. Such readings are pervasive in *Mango Street* criticism.[59]

Often the result of this interpretive practice is that the other female characters become negative foils highlighting Esperanza as the exceptional individual who challenges the constrictions of race and gender in her community. Margot Kelley argues that Cisneros uses a story cycle form to reorient the bildungsroman toward collective values. But this claim is difficult to reconcile with her reading of Esperanza's relation to the other characters: "To clarify the difficult task Esperanza undertakes in trying to evade the strictures of these systems, [Cisneros] presents images of women who do not challenge the systems (like Rafaela) and images of women who unsuccessfully challenge them (like Sally). Finally, Esperanza . . . maintains that she will exit this world."[60] Rafaela's and Sally's experiences become foils setting off Esperanza's determination to prevail. They symbolize the "risk" Lukács perceived in the world of the bildungsroman, where many will perish. Other critics echo this view.[61]

The exceptionalist reading of Esperanza undermines the collective politics argued for by these critics and raises problems for understanding post–civil rights minority mobility. Consider how readily this reading practice lends itself to individualist politics. Ellen C. Mayock takes up the theme of counterexamples to celebrate *Mango Street* as a story of individual triumph. Esperanza's escape from her community's sexism depends on a "willingness to reject certain characteristics of negative female role models." Mayock's reading demonstrates how bildungsroman hermeneutics can shift attention away from conditions of poverty and patriarchy toward individual character, the scale emphasized by neoconservative accounts of minority status. Moreover, this interpretive practice can obscure a sense of collective struggle. "This rebellion," Mayock asserts, "is not an effort of a 'sisterhood,' but rather an individualistic approach. . . . Esperanza refuses to join the ranks of Mexican-American women who serve men."[62] This reading ignores the many ways Latinas support each other, which *Mango Street* amply portrays. The exceptionalist escape trope also plays into the pitfall that troubles the feminist ethnic bildungsroman: the temptation to suggest escape from one's ethnic community into U.S. individualism as the "way out" when conservative voices were using this ideology to dismiss the struggles of minority communities.

Bildungsroman hermeneutics continues to organize ways of reading *Mango Street* even as critics seek to understand how Cisneros revises the genre for the communal struggles of Latinxs. The disjuncture attests to the powerful hold of this way of making meaning.

TRANSFICTIONAL FORM AND THE STORIES OF OTHERS

The slippages in *Mango Street* criticism testify to the ambitions and difficult legibility of Cisneros's revisions of the traditional bildungsroman. The challenge for criticism is to develop approaches that maintain fidelity to the collective aim many sense in the novel. An approach that recognizes the transfictional form of *Mango Street* can do so. Many of the stories in *Mango Street* remain semiautonomous rather than subplots to a larger story. Its form does not strive for the unity that in the classic bildungsroman is predicated on the centrality of the protagonist. The result is a multicentered storyworld. *Mango Street* decenters bildungsroman hermeneutics by sustaining formal tensions between the unity of the whole work and the multiplicity of stories within it, each story's autonomy and its interrelations with others, and an individual focus on a protagonist and a transindividual attention to stories beyond this focus. I'm inspired by Paula Moya's call to change reading habits shaped by the novel form so that we can look beyond Esperanza's character and attend to the many characters and relationships in the book.[63] While Moya makes an important turn to the poetic aspects of Cisneros's work to read beyond Esperanza's story, I explore how *Mango Street* invites other ways of reading within the genre of narrative. Narrative's world-building powers, it shows us, can be oriented toward multiple centers rather than around a protagonist.

Cisneros notes of *Mango Street*, "It can be read as single stories or as a novel."[64] The stories can stand on their own and yet they are related, so reading them together reveals a richer storyworld. This quality is also apparent in other women of color narratives that attempt to decenter the bildungsroman. *The Women of Brewster Place* is subtitled "a novel in seven stories." The stories focus on different women while revealing instances of communal ties among them. Kingston conceived *The Woman Warrior* as a collection of women's stories and she narrates the lives of her mother and aunt in separate stories.[65] Together, these texts invite readers to recognize the semiautonomy of the stories of others in the community.

Consider how *Mango Street* emphasizes other characters' stories in themselves. In a story like "Meme Ortiz," Esperanza's individual voice is absent. She narrates through the "we" of the neighborhood kids. In describing Meme's name, dog, and house, Esperanza constructs a character portrait. She is hardly a protagonist here; rather, she is an observer. "Louie, His Cousin & His Other Cousin" recounts what Esperanza calls an "important" event in Mango Street history, the day Louie's cousin stole a Cadillac.[66] As important as it is, the children of Mango Street experience it collectively and Esperanza's "I" appears just once. These stories don't affect Esperanza's plot, and she plays only minor roles in them. In stories like these, Cisneros says she was trying "simply to chronicle" figures in her community.[67] Not bound by tight plot relations, transfictional works can include stories not for the role they play in the protagonist's arc but to recognize other stories in the community.

In chronicling other lives, Cisneros pays attention to stories that cannot be fully linked to Esperanza's history. A poignant example is "Geraldo No Last Name," which describes a Mexican migrant laborer whom Esperanza's friend Marin meets one night. He is killed in an accident and only Marin is there to explain his identity to the authorities. Esperanza recounts, "Marin can't explain why it mattered, the hours and hours, for somebody she didn't even know. . . . He wasn't anything to her. . . . Just another *brazer* who didn't speak English." It's clear however that it does matter. Even though he has no relationship to Esperanza, he matters enough that Esperanza tries to imagine his life: "They never saw the kitchenettes. They never knew about the two-room flats and sleeping rooms he rented, the weekly money orders sent home." But the story makes clear that she does not have access to Geraldo's life. His story comes secondhand from Marin who knew little about him. The "far away" people central to his life lie beyond Esperanza's world (66). If traditional *bildung* is a process in which one "creates a single circle" and "a closed system" around oneself out of the infinitude of the world,[68] what's intriguing is how this moment highlights the limitations of Esperanza's circle. The story's transfictional autonomy from Esperanza's plot shows how much world there is beyond the circle of her life. Geraldo's story raises issues of migrant labor and citizenship status (the term *brazer* alludes to the Bracero program, which imported temporary Mexican workers) that Esperanza does not face but that are crucial to many Mexican Americans. Stories that do not directly touch Esperanza's and cannot be encompassed in hers still have their place in *Mango Street*. The book is about more than one Chicana growing up; it is also about others in the Latinx diaspora living unrecognized lives of struggle. Transfictional aesthetics evokes a sense of beyond, directing attention to parts of the storyworld beyond one story's concerns. In *Mango Street* this form breaks open the closed system around the self to reveal the inadequacy of individual-centered social visions for understanding the distinct circumstances in a minority community.

The stories we've surveyed so far are significant in that they do not advance Esperanza's bildungsroman.[69] Perhaps this is why they have received so little attention in the criticism. Standing relatively on their own, downplaying Esperanza's role, unable to be read as formative encounters with role models, these stories fall outside the purview of bildungsroman hermeneutics. This hermeneutics has obscured a crucial element of *Mango Street*'s aesthetics: a spatial movement circling outward into the community that pulls against the diachronic movement of Esperanza's story. As a transfictional dynamic, this pull can be felt in the relations between stories. Notice how spatial contiguity rather than temporal sequence links many of the stories. After Meme Ortiz's story, "Louie, His Cousin & His Other Cousin" begins: "Downstairs from Meme's is a basement apartment that Meme's mother fixed up and rented to a Puerto Rican family. Louie's family" (23). And after "Edna's Ruthie," "The Earl of Tennessee" begins: "Earl lives next door in Edna's basement" (70). Spatial aesthetics pervades Cisneros's fiction. In her story collection, *Woman Hollering Creek*, it likewise creates a dilatory narrative form that delays plot movement.[70] In *Mango Street*, this spatial imagination links narrative units into a panorama of the community rather than the progression of an individual life. These expansions to other parts of the community delay Esperanza's story. *Mango Street* enacts in its form the trade-off between following the individual

development narrative as neoconservative analysis advocated and attending to
the life circumstances across a community.

THE EXCEPTIONAL ONE AND THE "ONES WHO CANNOT OUT"

More than mere foils for Esperanza's development, these other stories complicate
the minority mobility narrative by broadening its vision beyond the individual
and registering the unequal conditions that frame Latinx life chances. Because
many of the stories are causally separate, each story can prompt readers to consider the particular circumstances that inform its outcomes. This transfictional
autonomy lends itself to differentiation, a significant move in a moment when
conservative rhetoric took individual mobility stories as emblematizing the
fate of whole communities. Cisneros uses this autonomy to note the relative
advantages that enable Esperanza's development. The interpretive framework of
foils, however, has obscured these advantages. For all the attention paid to Esperanza's desire for a "real house" (5), critics rarely mention that her family owns
their house on Mango Street. This implies that the Corderos enjoy a moderate
level of wealth that isn't widespread in a poor neighborhood. Esperanza also
attends private schools. Her access to good education is pivotal for her dreams
of becoming a writer. Cisneros's experiences are relevant here. In "Notes to a
Young(er) Writer," she recognizes the contingent opportunities that allowed
her to develop, wondering what would have happened if she hadn't taken her
first creative writing class or hadn't gone to college. Cisneros also notes that
she was fortunate that her mother relieved her from the gendered demands of
household labor. "I'm here," she admits, "because my mother let me stay in
my room reading and studying, perhaps because she didn't want me to inherit
her sadness and her rolling pin."[71]

Esperanza never appears doing the domestic labor that is so often the lot
of the young women around her. The image of inheriting a rolling pin echoes
a line in the story "Alicia Who Sees Mice," setting up a revealing comparison.
In contrast to Esperanza and Cisneros, Alicia *has* inherited "her mama's rolling
pin" and has to get up early to cook food for her family before taking "two
trains and a bus" to her college classes and studying "all night" (31–32). An
ambitious young woman like Esperanza, Alicia struggles with a far heavier load
of domestic work. The narration consistently attends to the constraints other

women face. Esperanza tells the story of Rosa Vargas, a poor single mother trying to raise a large family. Esperanza insists, "It's not her fault you know, except she is their mother and only one against so many." The story mentions the father who abandoned them "without even leaving a dollar for bologna." The kids' wild behaviors are likewise not their fault: "how can they help it with only one mother who is tired all the time from buttoning and bottling and babying" (29). In this story and others, Cisneros commits to understanding broader conditions rather than assigning individual blame.

This commitment connects *Mango Street* to Gloria Naylor's *The Women of Brewster Place*. Rosa Vargas's story resembles Naylor's story "Cora Lee," which portrays the struggles of an African American mother raising seven children. Both stories detail the resources stretched thin in caring for so many. Cora wonders, "How could she do all that—be a hundred places at one time?" (110). A turning point in Cora's story is an encounter with Kiswana Browne, a young woman in the same building who is organizing a tenants' association to stand up to their negligent landlord. While giving each woman's story its own space, the novel registers how these lives intersect in the tenants' association. As in *Mango Street*, this independent yet interdependent structure recognizes different circumstances while drawing out the collective struggles of a community. Kiswana's story reveals the difference in her background. She hails from an affluent family and comes to Brewster Place to be in "day-to-day contact with the problems of [her] people" (84). Prominent among these problems is the threat of patriarchal violence, which links stories from "Mattie Michael" to "Lucelia Louise Turner" to "The Two."

Cisneros also exposes patriarchal violence as a pervasive condition framing the life chances of young women. Sally, a character often taken as a counterexample for Esperanza, is perhaps most vulnerable. A beautiful girl with a domineering father, Sally endures a restrictive home and frequent abuse. When she ends up marrying young and living under similar but attenuated threats from her husband, the story cycle helps us see this outcome of continued entrapment in relation to what Sally has endured. As Esperanza surmises, Sally has probably done it "to escape" her father (101). This background must inflect any comparison between Sally's and Esperanza's life paths. The framework of the negative role model can't recognize their different backgrounds. It made a pivotal difference in her development that Esperanza did not come from a home defined by patriarchal violence. She has a loving relationship with her father and a mother who supports her ambitions.

Cisneros and Naylor use the relative autonomy of other stories to unfold the particulars of each woman's circumstances.[72] Juxtaposing distinct stories within the same social world, their works challenge readers to understand the multiple scales, from individual to familial to socioeconomic and infrastructural, that govern different minority outcomes, in a distinct break from neoconservatism's insistence on the individual scale. But their works also differ in an important way. *Brewster Place* has no central protagonist, and it does not feature a character leaving her ethnic community. Early in the novel, Naylor recognizes the upwardly mobile as anomalous: "the few who would leave forever were to be the exception rather than the rule" (4). But after this, Naylor's attention stays with the women who cannot leave Brewster Place. As a result, the rift between the exceptional individual and "the ones who cannot out," as Esperanza memorably names them, is less pronounced in *Brewster Place* than in *Mango Street* (110).

The minority individual achieving mobility was a central protagonist in the narratives of racial equality advanced during the post–civil rights transition. More directly than Naylor, Cisneros confronts this fraught figure. In a moment in which the language of individual opportunity became a discourse of equality masking sustained inequalities, Cisneros's narration of Latina mobility eschews this language to recognize the differentiated conditions Latinas navigate. These unequal circumstances complicate the unity of this community portrait. In the traditional bildungsroman, unity is premised on the lives of others finding their meaning in the story of the protagonist. *Mango Street*'s transfictional form, however, resists the merging of many stories into one. The distinct stories of others emphasize their particular challenges and the comparative advantages the protagonist enjoys. These stories cannot find their resolution in Esperanza's plot. In this way, Cisneros begins to dismantle the bildungsroman hermeneutics that tethers the stories of others to the protagonist.

BEYOND BILDUNGSROMAN HERMENEUTICS

As we recognize the transindividual aspects of *Mango Street*, we must acknowledge Esperanza's plot, which is clearly prominent in the story cycle. Given the patriarchal constraints in the community of Mango Street, a young woman's individual empowerment is an important story to tell.[73] The challenge is how to read this story without recentering it as the horizon for the other stories, which would suppress the measure of autonomy we have seen in them. The critical debate over *Mango Street* has registered the complex relations of individual and collective orientations in Esperanza's development. But ultimately even readings that argue that Esperanza achieves a collectivist consciousness cannot meet the challenge. This is because the premises of the debate remain within the outlines of bildungsroman hermeneutics.

The ending of Esperanza's story looms large in arguments that *Mango Street* reorients the individualism of the traditional bildungsroman. Leslie Gutiérrez-Jones, for example, insists that Esperanza leaves "behind her selfish desire to escape, alone, from the barrio" and resolves to return to help her community.[74] The oft-quoted sentences that close *Mango Street*—"I have gone away to come back. For the ones I left behind. For the ones who cannot out" (110)—support this conclusion. Such arguments take an important step toward recognizing how Cisneros revises the bildungsroman. Esperanza's plot reverses the direction of the genre's individual-collective relation: Instead of the meaning of the community concentrating in the formation of the individual, the meaning of individual formation here is to gather strength to work for the community. This reading squares with Bruce Robbins's contention that many upward mobility stories actually resolve the conflict between self-interested mobility and the common good.[75] Such narratives show that one can rise by working for the community. In these terms, Esperanza's plot reconciles the poles of the individualist versus collectivist debate.

That Esperanza commits to her community is important, but interpretations that end here cannot move beyond bildungsroman hermeneutics. Susan Fraiman's diagnosis of the critical tradition addressing the canonical bildungsroman helps explain why. This tradition has fetishized the protagonist, conflating the texts and the genre "with the destiny of this one figure, whose movements are tracked, detectivelike, to the exclusion of other movements."[76] Fraiman's critique sheds light on the bildungsroman hermeneutics underlying the critical debate over *Mango Street*. Regardless of what side they're on, critics have largely conflated the question of whether *Mango Street* is an individualist or collectivist text with the question of whether Esperanza develops an individualist or collectivist consciousness.[77] Once again, the protagonist is the horizon of meaning for the whole work.

Moving beyond bildungsroman hermeneutics requires expanding the protagonist-centered vision. *Mango Street*'s transfictional aesthetics asks readers to develop a broader interpretive practice that understands Esperanza's development story in its unequal relations with the development stories of others. These relations capture the uneven post–civil rights landscape of openings for a few amid blockages for the many. As she experienced social mobility in her own life, Cisneros was sensitive to this inequality. It's palpable in her recollection of the affluent students around her at Loyola University Chicago: "How nice to think of nothing other than getting a job and making as much money as possible. . . . They didn't feel guilty and sad when they looked out the window of their sportscar and passed the poor tenement apartments of Uptown."[78] Cisneros's awareness of this inequality helps explain why she stays relatively close to the classic bildungsroman form instead of breaking from it more definitively as Naylor does. Without a central protagonist showing an individual path out of the neighborhood's struggles, *Brewster Place* argues that the only path is a collective one: "Black people were all in the same boat . . . and if they didn't row together, they would sink together" (142). With its decentralized structure, *Brewster Place* dramatizes this argument, but it's less focused on rendering the uneven openings of the post–civil rights era than *Mango Street* is. More centralized than *Brewster Place* and yet also more crowded with other characters, *Mango Street* zeroes in on the contradictions of individual mobility and collective conditions. These contradictions cannot be resolved by the trajectory many critics celebrate, that Esperanza will return to help lift up her community. I argue that it's not Esperanza's individual rise as she works toward the collective good that makes *Mango Street* productive of a Latinx political consciousness. Cisneros's more important provocation is to expose how the achievement of the individual agency to work for the collective good is dependent on the inequality of the others one seeks to help.

The conditions allowing the flourishing of an individual who can help her community and the conditions constricting those she would help are entangled. This is most evident in *Mango Street*'s exploration of privacy. Esperanza's desire for solitude has always troubled readings of *Mango Street* as communally committed. She dreams of a private space: "A house all my own. . . . a house quiet as snow, a space for myself to go" (108). Recounting how she grew up in a crowded home, Cisneros reflects on the necessity of privacy: "the whole idea of not having a bedroom with a door or not even having a separate bedroom makes the whole idea of yourself, your sexuality, and your awareness different." Privacy is a material condition that allows the space for development in one's self, sexuality, and perception—and in one's art as well. Writing, Cisneros feels, is "a very solitary act."[79] In a convincing attempt to reconcile Esperanza's desire for privacy with her commitment to the community, Geoffrey Sanborn proposes that the value of private enjoyment Esperanza espouses is not apolitical. Rather, privacy may become "the precondition of new collective formations."[80] Cisneros, he contends, infuses a sense of contingency into the private self, which then recognizes alliances with others who also negotiate such contingency. Sanborn has hit on something key.

But I inflect the idea of privacy's contingency differently to show how it links the conditions of self and others through disparity, not affinity. *Mango Street* is sensitive to the contingent conditions that affect the life chances of other women. And Cisneros is aware of the contingent opportunities that allowed her to become a writer. Reflecting on one of her idols, Emily Dickinson, Cisneros connects the chances of others to the writer's path:

> What I didn't realize about Emily Dickinson was that she had a few essentials going for her: 1) an education, 2) a room of her own in a house of her own that she shared with her sister Lavinia, and 3) money inherited along with the house after her father died. She even had a maid, an Irish housekeeper who did, I suspect, most of the household chores. . . . I wonder if Emily Dickinson's Irish housekeeper wrote poetry or if she ever had the secret desire to study and be anything besides a housekeeper.[81]

This analysis places the private space needed for individual development and artistic creation in relation to the unacknowledged others whose labor makes this space possible. And in an imaginative leap that, like the form of *Mango Street*, refuses to subordinate another's life to the development of the artist, Cisneros wonders about the housekeeper's own ambitions. Her attention to the housekeeper recalls the many stories of women who nurture Esperanza's artistry while lacking the conditions to pursue their own. A space of her own may be crucial to Esperanza's development of the resources of self and art she needs to address the inequalities her community faces, but it is also inseparable from those inequalities.

Esperanza's achievement of a private space helps develop a Latinx politi-cal consciousness by emphasizing the contingency of her achievement. This emphasis is possible because *Mango Street* is not simply Esperanza's story, but a panorama of the uneven stories of Mango Street's women. The broader scale enables a clear vision of the inequality of access to privacy and development. Another name for this productive contingency is the transfictional tension between the protagonist's story and the stories of others that cannot progress in the same way. These stories are related to Esperanza's—as fellow Latinxs, segregated minorities, and women of color, as friends and neighbors—but they are not resolvable within her story. Patricia Hill Collins reminds us that "individual empowerment is key," but "only collective action can effectively generate the lasting institutional transformation required for social justice."[82] *Mango Street* sustains its transfictional tensions of individual and collective, autonomy and relation, diachronic development and expansive attention to insist that the story of individual mobility and commitment cannot resolve the more fundamental inequalities shaping a minority community.

This perspective reevaluates the ending of *Mango Street*: "I have gone away to come back. For the ones I left behind. For the ones who cannot out" (110). Esperanza does come to a communal commitment. But what these lines em-phasize more than the outcome of her story is the unequal conditions of others. That Esperanza yearns to bridge the rift between her and her community attests to the reality of that rift, which encodes the openings for a few and blockages for the many in the post–civil rights era. The reconciliation of individual and collective values within Esperanza's story points to a deeper irreconcilability on the social scale. This clash of scales is pivotal to the book's call for a collec-tive politics. To heed this call, we must follow *Mango Street* as it wrestles with the individual mobility story and pulls interpretation beyond bildungsroman hermeneutics.

RACIAL COMPARISON IN *THE WOMAN WARRIOR*

In the last story of *Mango Street* Esperanza refers to her community as a "ghost" that haunts her (110). This evocative image links *Mango Street* to another work about leaving ethnic community, which was published just a year before Cisne-ros began writing hers: Maxine Hong Kingston's *The Woman Warrior: Memoirs of a Girlhood among Ghosts*.[83] Like *Mango Street*, *The Woman Warrior* follows the development of a second-generation immigrant woman from a working-class, minority community. Maxine also struggles with constraints on female identity in her community and U.S. society. As Esperanza does, she craves escape, but she must reckon with her ties to a community that remains blocked by racial and economic barriers. And in critiquing patriarchy in her community, Kingston navigates a bind like Cisneros's: how to lodge this critique without absolving American society of its role in gender and racial violence.[84] Like Esperanza's *bildung* plot, Maxine's narrative is crowded by the stories of others, "ghosts" from the past and present of her community that pull at her story.

Cisneros complicates the classical bildungsroman's comparative logic of role models, highlighting inequalities of race, gender, class, and life chances. In Kingston's hands, the focus on racial and gender difference is even sharper, because her protagonist becomes obsessed with standards of normality and navigates a more complex mix of standards. Women appear as powerful subjects and subordinate figures within her ethnic culture. (In contrast, Esperanza finds few models of unfettered female agency within her community.) *The Woman Warrior*, then, brings out another concern in the bildungsroman's comparative logic. For individuals racialized as foreign, this logic intertwines with assimilation's demands for comparison. As Anne Anlin Cheng notes, the imperative to assimilate installs an endless anxiety of how one compares to society's racial norms and also to others whose racial difference might reflect back on one's failures to measure up. In Cheng's reading of Kingston, this comparative anxiety initiates an escape narrative, but the possibility of escape comes up against the irreducibility of racial difference, which "cannot be metabolized by the drive of the ethnic *Bildung*."[85]

Intersecting norms suffuse Maxine's mobility story with comparative obsessions. Having internalized racist and sexist views of Chinese female voices, she tries to define herself against their "chingchong ugly" sounds.[86] But when she tries to make her voice "American-feminine" by adopting a whisper (172), this tactic founders against American standards of confident speech. Maxine's struggle with voice culminates in a speech near the end of the memoir in which she declares her intention to go to college and become an American success, leaving behind the constrictions of Chinese gender norms. But even in this speech her language remains bound to standards of beauty, speech, and intelligence; she calls herself "ugly and clumsy," "stupid" and sickly (201). Specters of abnormality haunt her desired development toward normality and success. The memoir presents a panorama of deformity including several "crazy girls and women" and a mentally disabled Chinese boy (186). She lives in fear of her similarity to such outcasts. *The Woman Warrior* exposes the web of comparisons that hobbles the ethnic *bildung* plot. Kingston attempts to write herself out of the matrix of normality and deviance. The relations between Maxine and the others surrounding her narrative are the sites of this attempt.

As critics read these relations, bildungsroman hermeneutics creeps in. Maxine's penchant for fantasy complicates the sense of the other characters. The memoir leaves their imagined status an open question. Maxine's negative role models may be psychic projections. This possibility is apparent in the famous scene in which Maxine tortures another Chinese American girl. Many critics read the scene as Maxine's projection of racial self-hatred onto another. What's interesting is how readily these readings accept the elision of the other girl as merely a screen for Maxine's psychic struggles. Sau-Ling C. Wong reads the girl as a "racial shadow"; Sidonie Smith sees her as "a mirror image of Kingston herself"; and King-Kok Cheung, David Leiwei Li, and Elaine H. Kim all interpret her as an "alter-ego."[87] In these views, the other girl has little significance in her own right. She is a part of Maxine's mind, a figure of the racial difference from which Maxine seeks to distance herself. Some evidence in the scene supports that reading, but the chapter also suggests that the quiet girl is an actual person. We see other children interacting with her and we learn of her later life with her family. What I'm interested in is not a quibble over the reality of this girl (a difficult thing to decide in Kingston's text), but how these readings frame her meaning. They practice a variation of bildungsroman hermeneutics. If the bildungsroman hermeneutics of comparison can subordinate the meaning of others to the protagonist's formation, that comparison can extend so that others are, in effect, parts of the self. This slippage is not surprising given that the bildungsroman played an important role in developing the psychological interiority of the protagonist as a norm for novels.[88] The racial double, like minor characters in the bildungsroman, becomes functional in the protagonist's development. As Sau-Ling Wong argues, encounters with the racial double lead to the "growth of the first self."[89] To read the girl as Maxine's double is to accept the terms of this intensified bildungsroman hermeneutics, a structure of continual comparison to the self that's inseparable from the comparative compulsion installed by the racist logic of assimilation. To read this way is also to accept Maxine's own reading of the girl, with all its violence.

Maxine's violence compromises her narrating perspective and provokes us to read against her portrayal of the other girl. King-Kok Cheung observes that Kingston's portrait of her younger self is an unreliable narrator, whose perspective the text complicates.[90] To read against Maxine's perspective, bildungsroman hermeneutics, and racial comparison requires paying attention to the case of the other girl. The text cues readers to do so. Toward the end of the torture scene, Maxine reflects, "It seemed as if I had spent my life in that basement, doing the worst thing I had yet done to another person" (181). This reflection frames the scene as an intersubjective encounter. Alongside the psychic violence that Maxine experiences, it insists on the intersubjective violence this other girl experiences. Maxine's bildungsroman reveals that the primary violence resulting from developing as a racial and gender minority is not the skewing of individual formation but of collective political formation. This violence is most palpable in the relations one has with coethnic others. Much as *Mango Street* looked beyond the development of the protagonist's consciousness as the horizon of its political vision, *The Woman Warrior*'s vision of racial and gender violence is fully perceptible only by looking beyond the vicissitudes of the protagonist's psyche. The memoir guides readers to this interpretive practice through its transfictional form. As we'll see, it includes other female stories that resist being subordinated as projections or examples for the protagonist's story even as Maxine's perspective, obsessed by comparison, seeks to position them as such. The narrative is riven by these conflicting impulses. Placing an individual-centered vision against other distinct stories, the memoir reckons with the politically divisive consequences of racial and gender comparison.

"THE WORDS AT OUR BACKS": TOWARD A COLLECTIVE NARRATIVE OF STRUGGLE

The Woman Warrior has been widely celebrated as a story of constructing Asian American feminist subjectivity and voice.[91] But much as *Mango Street* celebrates individual empowerment while revealing its shortcomings for the broader concerns of Latinas, *The Woman Warrior* traces a forceful paradigm of agency while exposing its limits for other women. In the torture scene and others, Maxine distances herself from women who fail the standards of voice and agency that she craves. Exposing this process of comparison, the memoir shows how the script of achieving individual power and voice, which seems crucial to contesting patriarchy, can reproduce standards of normality and deviance, speech and silence, power and weakness that structure both Chinese patriarchy and the U.S. racial order. This model of resistance may silence other women, and often the most vulnerable. "These unnamable beings," David Leiwei Li observes, "are powerful presences that permeate the work."[92] A reading sensitive to the transfictional autonomy of narratives beyond the dominant stories of Maxine and her mother, Brave Orchid, can recognize their presences.

Counter to the established reading of Maxine's achievement of voice, I propose that her coming-of-age as a storyteller is not the torrent of speech to her mother at the end of the memoir but rather her uneven stumbling toward a different, decentered model of narration. I suggest attention to Maxine's development of an other-oriented narration that pulls away from her own *bildung* plot. We should examine the moments when the narrative of female heroism is destabilized by the stories of other women that don't fit its norms of agency and speech. Rather than showing the individual failures of these women, these moments open narrative space for the specific conditions they face. I argued earlier that the stories of others are crucial to *Mango Street*'s nuanced engagement with the social conditions of Latinas. The transfictional elements of *The Woman Warrior* are equally illuminating.

There is a case for reading this memoir in transfictional terms. It bears close relations to Kingston's next book, *China Men* (1980), with its more overtly divergent, multiprotagonist, multinarrative structure.[93] Some critics note tensions in *The Woman Warrior* that are recognizably transfictional. "For all her assertion of individualism," King-Kok Cheung observes, "the narrator has introduced a community of women into her 'autobiography.'" Cheung undercuts this insight by arguing that the inclusion of this community acknowledges "the familial and cultural influence on her formation," once again resolving the conflict between the stories of others and the story of the protagonist by reading the significance of others in relation to the individual.[94] Recognizing the transfictional qualities of *The Woman Warrior* means attending to how it sustains this conflict.

Like *Mango Street* and *Brewster Place*, *The Woman Warrior* makes space for the specific conditions of many women's lives. But its treatment is more fraught because of a narrator who invests in racial comparison. Maxine's perspective recoils from many of these women as abnormal deviants that warn of her potential fate. But looking closer at their stories reveals moments when the text recognizes the distinct conditions and social worlds that shaped their outcomes. The crazy woman next door is a victim of traumatic displacement. She is "bought" by her immigrant husband, taken from her home in China, and settled in America (186). Another woman was abandoned as a toddler when her parents left for the United States. By the time they made enough money to send for her twenty years later, she had gone "crazy" (187). These extraordinary circumstances strain the impulse to interpret these stories as comparable warnings for Maxine's story. Much as Geraldo's story exceeded the bounds of Esperanza's limited social world, these women's stories reveal gendered experiences in the Chinese diaspora beyond the circle of Maxine's story: the transnational displacement of brides, economic constraints that compel emigration and child abandonment. Challenging us to read across stories related to Maxine's and yet distinct from it, *The Woman Warrior* sketches a variegated portrait of women's struggles in the Chinese diaspora.

These stories of deviants are not true examples of transfictional autonomy. Even as they pull attention away from Maxine's story, they causally affect it as she obsesses about them. This linkage leaves them open to bildungsroman hermeneutics. The conflict between autonomy from the protagonist's story and subordination to it indexes Maxine's struggle to attend to others without pulling them into her psychic drama of comparison. The memoir formally dramatizes the difficulty of undoing bildungsroman hermeneutics.

The quasi-transfictional quality of these stories point to the possibility of a more fully other-oriented narration. That possibility comes to fruition in "At the Western Palace," which is, not coincidentally, the story that most pointedly registers the violence of the heroine plot on other women. As Sidonie Smith observes, the story shows Maxine's mother, Brave Orchid, imposing a heroic script on her sister, Moon Orchid.[95] Brave Orchid moves her sister to the United States and goads her to confront her husband, who has abandoned her. Forced into a model of female agency, Moon Orchid breaks under the pressure, ending up another in the line of "crazy women." What's significant is that Maxine largely disappears from the story. Unlike the story of her aunt in "No Name Woman" or of her mother in "Shaman," Maxine's commentary falls away in this chapter. The narration is focalized through Brave Orchid, Moon

Orchid, and Moon Orchid's daughter. Maxine in the story is merely one of Brave Orchid's Americanized children. Even the projective desire for "ancestral help" that drives her narration of "No Name Woman" diminishes here (8). Readers learn later that Maxine wishes her aunt had gotten in at least "one nasty word" against her husband (163). Given this desire, it wouldn't be surprising if "At the Western Palace" were a fantasy of female resistance in which Moon Orchid claims justice. But that's not what happens. Instead, Maxine retreats as a present narrator to tell a story that is not about herself, does not directly affect her story, and questions the model of female heroism. This story lays out a paradigm of other-oriented narration and unheroic plot that conflicts with the investment in individual expression and agency in Maxine's bildungsroman.

Unheroic stories and moments are significant because they are not easily contained within the woman warrior storyline. With semiautonomous stories, Kingston's memoir considers women's experiences that diverge from Maxine's path and the template of female agency in which she invests. These divergent stories reveal the limitations of individual heroism as a scalable model of empowerment. As Brave Orchid confesses how years of toiling as an immigrant laborer in the United States have worn her down, Maxine turns her attention away: "I do not believe in old age. I do not believe in getting tired" (104). "You have no idea how much I have fallen coming to America," she tells Maxine (77), and indeed Maxine doesn't really know, because Brave Orchid's stories have trained her to look away from female weakness. Brave Orchid's incompletely told story of struggle reveals how the woman warrior plot of individual agency can foreclose the recognition of the broader social conditions in which immigrant women struggle. In a confounding way, this model of individual empowerment, which emerges to contest racial and sexual inequalities, actually aligns with the scale of individual development that conservatives were using so effectively to obscure the collective nature of such inequalities. Maxine's perspective turns away from the other sides of her mother's story and the larger struggles they imply, but hints of these other sides nevertheless emerge. The memoir offers glimpses of Brave Orchid's downward mobility. It hints at her suffering as a refugee of the Japanese invasion of China and alludes to racialized labor—long days in the laundry, stints picking vegetables—and how urban development undermines this labor. Clashing with the heroism Maxine desires, these dissonant notes speak to the grinding collective conditions many immigrant women endure.

Stories that exceed the purview of the protagonist's development pull the traditional bildungsroman toward a collective vision that spans the challenges of Chinese and Chinese American women by constructing commonalities across distinct stories of struggle. Maxine does register systemic injustices. She notes the economic forces that marginalize immigrant workers and "deny [her] family food and work" (49). She observes racist backlashes to the civil rights movement. She struggles to understand the Chinese Revolution and how it victimized her family. Her anger is clear. But in thrall to the woman warrior legend, her vision of resistance is flawed: "To avenge my family, I'd have to storm across China to take back our farm from the Communists; I'd have to rage across the United States to take back the laundry in New York and the one in California. Nobody in history has conquered and united both North America and Asia" (49). The impossibility stems from her adherence to an ideal of individual vengeance. The development Maxine must undergo is to shift from a singular model of resistance to a collective struggle. If read against the grain of Maxine's perspective, the memoir offers hints of this development. "White Tigers" ends with an oft-quoted passage:

> The swordswoman and I are not so dissimilar. May my people understand the resemblance soon so that I can return to them. What we have in common are the words at our backs. . . . The reporting is the vengeance—not the beheading, not the gutting, but the words. And I have so many words—"chink" words and "gook" words too—that they do not fit on my skin. (53)

The usual interpretation is that Maxine is identifying with the woman warrior in her singular quest against sexual and class injustice. But the "we" in the third sentence could also forge a commonality with "my people," Chinese and Chinese Americans who collectively bear the injustices of "'chink' words" and "'gook' words" on their backs. Read this way, the passage expresses a group's common inscription into the crimes of a racial order. Maxine's lonely effort then becomes part of a collective vengeance. The divergence of these readings expresses the broader tension I've been tracing: The female avenger with the strength to take on collective grievances is a powerful way to imagine selfhood for a struggling minority woman, but this model can also divide that very sense of collectivity.

This division returns us to where we began: in the bathroom with Maxine and the quiet girl. What is most disturbing about the way Maxine treats the other girl as an abject part of herself are its divisive political consequences. The demands of racial comparison that lead Maxine to shore up her sense of agency and normality against another Chinese American girl preclude seeing her as a coethnic woman struggling with similar binds of racism and sexism. As Sau-Ling Wong notes, Maxine's attempts to differentiate herself cannot resolve the collective nature of racialization.[96] Individual escape from a denigrated Chinese America only reinforces the standards that propel this imperative to escape. Only by reading against Maxine's narration and recognizing this girl as her fellow subject is it possible to analyze the divisive consequences of racial comparison. Moments of transfictional distinctness throughout the memoir guide readers toward this recognition by inviting us to attend to the others alongside the woman warriors. If our ways of seeing remain constrained by the individual-centered scope and comparisons of bildungsroman hermeneutics, we risk eliding the collective realities of racial and sexual violence and the vision that makes coalitional resistance possible.

The political battles and uneven openings of the post–civil rights transition placed pressures on minority writers to contest the traditional bildungsroman and its compelling hermeneutics. The genre offered a narrative template that converged with neoconservative arguments proclaiming individual equality and limiting radical interventions. A further hurdle was the difficulty of critiquing American inequalities while also indicting the gender inequalities in their own communities. Along with other women of color writers like Gloria Naylor, Cisneros and Kingston confronted the bildungsroman's social vision. Their works challenged the default scale for interpreting the social worlds presumed by our policies and imagined in our novels. *Mango Street* embeds the minority development story in a broader vision of other lives and collective conditions. This vision informs its refusal to subordinate other stories, its attention to uneven circumstances, its tensions of diachronic progression and spatial expansion, individual and communal focus. Cisneros embraces this aesthetic to write her freedom from the patriarchal strains in her ethnic culture without reinforcing the individualist values used against her community. Kingston also traces individual mobility and the struggle with patriarchy. She reveals the difficulties of articulating feminist resistance without producing alternative norms of agency that remarginalize many women. She shows how these norms participate in the violence that comparative assimilation inflicts on minorities and how they vitiate the possibilities of collective struggle. To pull against the lure of the lone heroine, *The Woman Warrior* confronts the individual voice with the distinct stories of others.

The transfictional tensions in these works render the social contradictions that cannot be resolved within an individual's story. In meeting the interpretive challenges posed by this aesthetic, we are disabused of that familiar paradigm for giving form to the plots of narrative and social change. We are left with the harder work of forming collective visions and transformations. That is a plot we should know. It's the story of the continuing struggle for equality in the post–civil rights era.

CHAPTER 2

NARRATING COLD WAR DISPLACEMENT

Junot Díaz and Aimee Phan Trace the Migrations of U.S. Empire

IF THE NOVEL is the preeminent form for narrating the nation,[1] what form can narrate the transnational?[2] Few subjects pose this question more urgently than the life histories of refugees. Their displacements from one nation to another, their status outside the protections afforded by nation-states, and the ties they maintain across borders make clear a transnational tension: borders with the power to cleave lives versus the relations that span those borders. I pursue the opening question by examining a narrative of Asian American refugees, whose migrations cannot be grasped without recognizing their links to the routes of U.S. Cold War violence in Asia. Aimee Phan's 2004 short story cycle *We Should Never Meet* develops a transfictional form that makes perceptible the linked trajectories conditioning transnational displacements. Mapping the fallout from the Vietnam War and the evacuation of children from South Vietnam, it traces the relations among the vectors of U.S. power, the mass displacements they produced, and the uncertain positions the displaced inhabit in the United States.

This challenge for narration, however, is not limited to refugee histories. I place Phan's work alongside another story cycle, Junot Díaz's *Drown* (1996), which depicts Dominican migration to the United States during the same period of the Cold War. Both works develop a similar form. Both map national borders onto the narrative gaps separating stories while drawing elements across those gaps. Both cut between past and present, country of origin and country of settlement. But they use this form to narrate the experiences of Dominican immigrants and Vietnamese refugees, distinct migrations. This shared form invites comparison. The joint form, I argue, reveals alignments across the histories of Vietnamese and Dominican displacement. It helps us map a broader history of Cold War migrations, connecting the usually separate stories of diasporas shaped by U.S. interventions in different regions. This comparison complicates the distinctions between immigrants and refugees. It reveals that the history of Dominican immigration also calls for mapping the vectors of U.S. Cold War militarism. And it points to the unremarked impacts of the Vietnam War on the U.S. invasion of the Dominican Republic. Díaz and Phan share a representational challenge: to narrate the transnational routes of U.S. Cold War violence and the lives it displaced.

Phan and Díaz hail from Asian American and Latinx communities entangled in the histories of U.S. militarism. As scholars such as Jodi Kim, Ricardo L. Ortiz, and Susan Thananopavarn have emphasized, the presence of these communities in the United States is testimony to the migrations propelled by warfare in the most proximate arenas of U.S. Cold War interests: Latin America and the Asia-Pacific.[3] Respectively considered the United States' "backyard" and "lake" in the nation's military imagination, these regions suffered a disproportionately heavy share of the "hot wars," invasions, and interventions that belied the idea of a Cold War. The diasporas these conflicts generated reshaped Asian American and Latinx communities. While Chapter 1 focused on established ethnic groups and racialized domestic policies, this chapter expands the story to consider the nation's racialized foreign policies that brought many new ethnic groups to its shores. While the civil rights period and its aftermath opened new stratifications within Asian American and Latinx communities, they unfolded against (and were driven by) Cold War conflicts the United States was conducting. These conflicts exacerbated the divisions within the Asian and Latinx United States by displacing millions of desperate people into the nation. The displaced brought with them distinct cultures and experiences of U.S. imperialism. The injustices they endured create imperatives for Asian American and Latinx politics to reckon with U.S. violence against communities of color not just within U.S. borders but across the world.

With their first works, Junot Díaz and Aimee Phan were writing in an immediate post–Cold War period in which the United States emerged victorious. They are part of a generation of Latinx and Asian American writers wrestling with triumphant national narratives of the Cold War that repress the violence that formed their communities.[4] The Vietnamese child refugees Phan depicts are the subjects of dual narratives. A "rescue" narrative of America as a refuge for Vietnamese fleeing communism elides the memory of American militarism.[5] And a narrative of Americans saving abandoned Third World children suppresses family ties and the geopolitical power that conditions transnational adoptions.[6] Displaced by U.S. interventions but coded as immigrants, Dominicans are subject to linear models of immigration that split apart home and host countries.[7] Such models again cover over the historical entanglements between the United States and Third World nations. Díaz's and Phan's fictions rewrite these narratives with a transfictional form. In their hands, the transfictional story cycle's capacity to invite and frustrate links among its stories captures the coexistence of interconnection and dispersion in these diasporas. Spanning the histories of the United States and Third World nations, their story cycles remap Dominican and Vietnamese migrations as inseparable from the global webs of U.S. power.

To envision justice within networks generated by mass displacements requires grappling with a tension between borders and flows. Many scholars are exploring the possibilities of relations beyond the powers of the nation, but we must keep the extent of those powers squarely in view, particularly as they act on disadvantaged migrants. Views of transnationalism can be too sanguine if they do not sustain attention to the material borders that migrants confront and the role of nations in generating and blocking migrations.[8] As Dalia Kandiyoti observes, "the age of global flows is also the era of fences and walls." Militarized borders, exclusionary immigration policies, and the segregation of diasporic populations coexist with movements of people across borders, creating a "tension between enclosure and translocality." This tension places formal pressures on diasporic narratives, which must register both mobility and enclosure.[9]

Transfictional texts like *Drown* and *We Should Never Meet* can powerfully express these tensions between borders and flows. In a transfictional work, relations of storyworld elements like character and setting flow across the stories. At the same time, the stories remain semiautonomous and bounded. Transfictional works ask readers to attend to the gaps between different stories as much as to the stories themselves. While describing the distinct experience of reading this form, the *trans* prefix also expresses the form's productivity for narrating the transnational. This capacity stems from a series of tensions: divergent scales of narrative relations; narrative borders and connections that cross those borders; gaps between stories that invite connections while simultaneously frustrating them.

More so than examples focused on local community, like *The House on Mango Street*, transfictional texts with transnational ambitions emphasize distant and mediated social and causal relations. These texts provoke a question: To what extent does a story set in one place affect a story set elsewhere? As we will see with *We Should Never Meet*, these indirect relations are well suited to trace transnational networks of effect that exceed direct contacts and sustained social ties. The social connections linking characters in different stories tend to be mediated. They span degrees of separation and different social circles. Phan's story cycle suggests relations among widely dispersed groups of Vietnamese and Americans, while Díaz's reveals links across the scattered parts of the Dominican diaspora. These story cycles can disperse their stories across wide ranges of characters and settings. While other multiplot forms can span similar ranges, Aimee Phan explains that the story cycle is amenable to looser connections between stories, which allows a distinct freedom to "start a new setting . . . or a new character just like that."[10]

In *Drown* and *We Should Never Meet* the narrative borders separating stories express the violence of national borders. Meanwhile, relations of setting, character, and ambiguous causality cross these borders. This separate yet linked structure captures the "undecidable" nature of the transnational, which is "neither in nor out of the nation-state."[11] Just as transnational relations unsettle national coherence and boundedness,[12] transfictional relations destabilize the sense of any narrative being complete in itself. Crossing from one story to others, they intimate that the delimited circle of events, people, and places

concerned in one story is implicated in indirect yet consequential relations
with other stories in parts of the world beyond this circle. Transfictional form
can model the force of national borders and vast distances in its fragmentation
of narrative continuity while recognizing that migrant stories are not defined
entirely by separations. Out of the experiences of the most disadvantaged migrants can come "emergent forms of social relation."[13] Imagining new forms of
political community is crucial to address the injustices endured by the migrants
Díaz and Phan depict. *Drown* and *We Should Never Meet* spur this imaginative work. They confront readers in their form with the fragmenting effects of
displacement, and challenge us to develop new principles of connection across
narrative and national borders.

DROWN AND THE TRANSNATIONAL CHRONOTOPE
OF IMMIGRATION

Drown makes clear that Dominican migration to the United States is opaque
if we view this nation's history as separate from that of the United States. This
is a crucial intervention because, as Nina Glick Schiller observes, "The study of
U.S. immigration is typically confined within the borders of the United States
and told as a national tale of redemption."[14] This limit impedes engagement
with the role that U.S. hegemony plays in driving migrations. And it reinforces
ideas of America as a beacon of immigrant opportunity.[15] Migration scholars
argue for revising models that posit a teleological movement to countries of
settlement, which cannot describe migrants whose social lives and histories
span nations.[16] *Drown*, as we'll see, breaks open the containment of migrations
within U.S. borders and registers how U.S. economic and military power drove
Dominicans abroad. But the U.S.-oriented model of immigration is difficult
to dislodge, because it's a compelling narrative central to the idea of the nation
of immigrants. This narrative, Ylce Irizarry observes, emphasizes an endpoint of
arrival and integration that may speak to the experiences of early European immigrant groups but overlooks the distinct challenges of contemporary racialized
immigrants.[17] Patricia Chu analyzes this narrative as a "myth" that focuses narrative interest in the United States, where the immigrant overcomes challenges and
acts in a setting of wider possibilities. Following the paths of American *bildung*
requires a "containment" of the past.[18] American immigration myths rely on
a linear, bifurcated chronotope that maps the past and enclosed possibilities

onto countries of origin and the future and open opportunities onto the United States.[19] This split contains experiences that span emigration and immigration, returns and continuing ties, and histories of U.S. imperial violence within a U.S. national and narrative horizon as primarily immigration stories.

Drown spans this split chronotope, expanding a national narrative into a transnational one. To see how, we need to attend to the way Díaz arranges stories of the Dominican Republic and the United States. The sequencing of the stories in *Drown* is a good example of why a transfictional framework matters. When viewed as a story collection as critics tend to do, *Drown* is read as effectively a bag of stories, whose order and arrangement are insignificant.[20] But because it offers no genre tags, neither "a novel" nor "stories," *Drown* invites scrutiny of the generic frames readers bring to it. *Drown* includes ten stories set either in the Latinx communities in northern New Jersey or in the Dominican Republic. Four of the stories, "Ysrael," "Fiesta, 1980," "Aguantando," and "Negocios," present pieces of the migration saga of Yunior and his family. Four other stories feature unnamed protagonists who might be Yunior. Finally, two stories focus on other characters, a young man in the same neighborhood in "Aurora" and a disfigured teenager named Ysrael who appears in the first story and returns as the protagonist of "No Face." *Drown* is not simply a story collection; a family migration story forms a narrative spine through the work and the same characters and neighborhoods recur across multiple stories. At the same time, *Drown* features semiautonomous stories like "Aurora" and "No Face" that unfold in the same world but are not intertwined with Yunior's family. *Drown* is a transfictional story cycle. When read in this way, its links, sequencing, and separations become salient. It matters that the narrative of Yunior and his family unfolds in a sequence of fragments whose gaps encode the rifts created by U.S. imperialism and disadvantaged migration.

The tale of Yunior's family unfolds in the first, second, fourth, and final stories. The stories jump back and forth in time and cut between the Dominican Republic and the United States. These movements, I argue, are not haphazard. The stories form a crosscutting sequence that disrupts linear models of immigration. *Drown*'s arrangement embodies a pattern in Dominican American migration fictions. Clear-eyed as they are about U.S. intervention and its violent impacts on the Dominican diaspora, these fictions regularly refuse linear narrations of integration into the United States. Consider the work of Julia Alvarez.

Her 1991 novel *How the García Girls Lost Their Accents* moves in reverse chronology, turning away from stories of assimilation to dig into the political history that propelled this family into exile. The novel gradually reveals a CIA plan to overthrow the dictatorship of Rafael Trujillo, a plan in which the family was embroiled and which forced them to flee the island. Alvarez's 2000 novel *In the Name of Salomé* has a mother's plot moving forward in time while her daughter's plot moves backward in time. These trajectories piece together a family history scattered by the 1916–1924 U.S. occupation and Trujillo's U.S.-backed regime. *Drown*'s migrant temporality is equally unorthodox and introduces transfictional gaps that the forms of Alvarez's novels hint at.

Drown does not begin with arrival in the United States or with life in the homeland leading to immigration. Instead, the first story, "Ysrael," depicts ongoing life in the Dominican Republic, focusing on the children left behind by an immigrant, Ramón, who leaves in the hopes of reuniting his family in the United States.[21] His two boys, Rafa and Yunior, often think about the promise of life in the United States and their father who has been away for five years. This is a family stretched across borders. Their stories concretize the transnational ties of migrants and present a scheme that models of immigration do not accommodate: the co-presence of the home country, which cannot be relegated to the immigrant's past but continues as part of his transnational present.

The promise of the United States in "Ysrael" points to an ending: a family reunion that would redeem their painful separation. With a shift to three years later when the family has been in New Jersey for several years, the second story, "Fiesta, 1980," seems primed to show this endpoint. But this promise deflates on the first page, which alludes to an affair that splits the family apart as much as the staggered migration did. (As we'll see, the demands of the staggered migration are a factor in Ramón's infidelity.) The sequencing and revelations of the first two stories mark a break from the immigration plot. Twenty pages in, a failed ending hangs over this family migration story before we even know most of the story. *Drown* uses abrupt shifts in setting to disrupt the trajectory of narrative promise in the United States.

In "Aguantando," the family narrative cuts back to the Dominican Republic and the family waiting for Ramón's return. The story fills in some of the gap between the first and second stories, showing how the family endured the separation. With this shift back, the sequence of stories sets aside a future- and U.S.-directed narrative for a circling process of reconstructive work, in which readers piece together a family history fragmented by disadvantaged migration. The final story, "Negocios," is Yunior's reconstruction of his father's years away from the family. It resembles the immigration myth of leaving home and building a life in the United States, except that its endpoint has already been undermined by the earlier stories. The ending of "Negocios" shows Ramón leaving New York to get his family after five years of struggles. But readers already know that this ending has been superseded, rendered moot by the family's future disintegration. Perhaps this is why none of the stories narrates the family reunion even though many of the stories anticipate this moment. Díaz pushes the moment offstage, its resolution a false endpoint on transnational migrant lives that cannot be so cleanly shaped.

The linear, coherent form of American immigration myths cannot accommodate the missing years and material barriers that define staggered and disadvantaged migrations. While *Drown* invites readers to reconstruct this family's narrative, in the end it frustrates our attempts to do so. Each of the four stories presents a different segment of the family's timeline but chunks of the timeline remain missing between the stories. An example of this occurs when Ramón returns to the Dominican Republic, plans to visit his family, but never does. His sons wait for this return in "Aguantando." In "Negocios," Yunior tries to figure out what happened but his limited perspective encounters an aporia: "Maybe Papi stopped there and couldn't go on, maybe he went as far as the house . . . . In the end, he never visited us . . . . if a strange man approached me during my play and stared down at me and my brother, perhaps asking our names, I don't remember it now."[22] The aborted visit is the point where "Aguantando" and "Negocios" come closest to touching, but Díaz withholds the information that would reveal what happened and resolve the ambiguous proximity of the two stories. As Christopher González notes, Yunior attempts to reconstruct his father's years away but a major portion of Ramón's interiority and intentions "remains out of Yunior's, and subsequently the reader's, grasp."[23] Sustaining such gaps at the seams between stories and offering no final moment of reunification, the family story remains in pieces.[24] Díaz argues through narrative form that the process of staggered, disadvantaged, and legally blocked migration irreversibly cleaves the wholeness of a family. These cleavages cannot be resolved on the symbolic level; they compel attention to the material conditions of transmigrations.

"A PART OF HIM WAS DETAINED ELSEWHERE"

The pull between intimate relation and yawning separation is at the core of these moving family migration stories. We can sense it in the narrative gaps between the represented parts of the family's saga. We might also note the way that each story is set in one national space or the other, with only the last story spanning the two. This containment recognizes the bifurcated immigrant chronotope and the material barriers that obstruct migration. At the same time, *Drown* draws attention across the national and narrative split. The other national setting is a destabilizing source of continuing ties and responsibilities. *Drown*'s jagged sequencing enhances this effect, drawing attention repeatedly to the other side of the chronotope. Each story is simultaneously contained within a setting and troubled by an elsewhere.

Separation and relation, the delimited circle of the world in one story and the parts of the world beyond this circle—these are transfictional tensions. But approaching the stories of Yunior's family in transfictional terms raises a complication. Can we describe the relations between the stories of one family as transfictional when a defining quality of the form is semi-autonomy? The family saga after all has long been an effective way for writers to causally link many plots into a whole. The presence of semiautonomous stories like "Aurora" alongside the pieces of the family narrative invites us to consider whether this autonomy seeps into the family narrative at all. Being open to this possibility helps to recognize the formal tensions that make this family saga so distinctive. These tensions capture the separation and intimacy that define this Dominican family.

The stories set in the Dominican Republic emphasize this Janus-faced feeling of separation. Left behind while their father works abroad, Yunior and Rafa experience life on the island as separate from the United States but defined in relation to it. Their longing for their father becomes entangled with their desire for the transformative potential of the United States. This horizon orients their narratives. While "Aguantando" portrays the painful disappointments when their father's promises of return do not materialize, the idea of his return continues to capture their imaginations. It's the deferred endpoint that makes the story one of waiting and enduring, as the title "Aguantando" suggests. The story ends with the boys imagining their father's return. In Rafa's vision, "he'd come in the night, like Jesus . . . . Too real to be believed. He'll be taller . . . . Northamerican food makes people that way. He'd surprise Mami on her way back from work, pick her up in a German car . . . . They'd drive down to the Malecón and he'd take her to see a movie, because that's how they met and that's how he'd want to start it again" (87). The fantastical quality of this vision is not just a result of a child's imagination. It speaks to the emotional stakes of his projection onto the American side of the immigrant chronotope. The miraculous changes the boys desire are the kind of transformations it would take to justify the fracturing of their family. Rafa's fantasy couples Papi's American transformation with the identical reconstruction of the family's bonds; Papi and Mami would replicate their original meeting. There is wishfulness in this idea that Papi will be utterly changed by the United States but retain the same family ties, that in making their family rich and American, they will remain the same family. Rafa's vision is an imagined reconciliation of conflicting promises: the transformative potential of the American dream and the sustaining of family bonds across all the miles, years, and changes. The daydream exposes the difficult, even fantastical premises of extending the individual American immigrant myth to a whole family, especially in cases of disadvantaged, staggered migration. *Drown* expresses the conflict between the transformative American path and the endurance of family bonds as a transfictional tension between the gaps that separate its stories and the bonds that link them.

"Negocios" is the most interesting case of bending toward the other side of the immigrant chronotope among the U.S.-set stories. But before turning to that story, I want to recognize the brief story that precedes it, "No Face," which shows how an autonomous story creates a transfictional reading experience that bleeds into the family narrative. "No Face" follows Ysrael, the disfigured boy that Rafa and Yunior accost in the first story. Ysrael returns here as the protagonist of his own story. As he waits for a promised trip to Canada for reconstructive surgery, he crafts a superhero persona that allows him to survive the abuse and deprivation he suffers as a disfigured youth in the Dominican Republic. Like Kingston's "At the Western Palace," "No Face" stands apart. Yunior and his family do not figure in it at all and the narration is depersonalized third-person. By this point in *Drown*, readers have followed Yunior's family to the

United States and "No Face" comes after four straight stories set there. It's then that *Drown* opens this autonomous story to recognize the uneven mobility among Dominicans and the continuing lives on the island. The autonomy of "No Face," the way it isn't tightly tied to Yunior's story or any of the U.S.-set stories, allows it to re-immerse readers in the Dominican Republic after many of the stories have effected a seemingly definitive shift to the United States. To interpret the Dominican community requires sustaining attention across many distinct settings and lives, a practice that *Drown*'s transfictional form elicits.

Leading in to the final story of Yunior's family, "No Face" plants ideas of transfictional autonomy and sustained attention to those still in the Dominican Republic. These are crucial concerns in "Negocios." Among the family stories, "Negocios" is the one that comes closest to autonomy because Ramón attempts to follow the American immigration myth and leave behind his past. But much as "No Face" interrupts a string of U.S.-centered stories, the Dominican side of Ramón's life pulls on his story in the United States. He arrives with only a few necessities, confident that "two hands and a heart as strong as a rock" will be enough here (168). But steep barriers block Ramón's integration into the nation: capital, education, and language barriers, racial marginalization, and the need to generate surplus income for his family. He finds himself in a world of unending labor that strains his family ties. He is often too tired from work to write home and makes too little to send money regularly. The other major barrier is citizenship. Ramón arrives an undocumented immigrant as a result of Cold War calculations that did not offer refugee status to Dominicans leaving a devastated country and oppressive regime. I'll return to this point later on. Díaz reveals the contortions and doublings of family ties the citizenship barrier produces. The path to the citizenship Ramón needs to bring over his family is well worn: "Find a citizen, get married, wait, and then divorce her" (178). The legal barriers create a paradoxical situation in which doubling the family, in the form of a second wife, is what it takes to reunite a family. He finds a citizen-wife in a Dominican American woman named Nilda. Because of immigration exclusions, Ramón's path into the nation takes the form of infidelity, confirming the conflict of family unity and American mobility felt in "Aguantando." The economic and legal barriers between nations split Ramón's life and both families. At the same time, in thrall to the future-oriented ideology of American immigration, Ramón embraces the split. He tries to contain his past, settling into a comfortable life with his new wife. The story shows material barriers to incorporation and the ideology of American immigration converging to split the immigrant's life from his country of origin.

"With the hum of his new life," Yunior remarks, "Papi should have found it easy to bury the memory of us" (191). Ramón, however, finds the claims of a transnational community difficult to ignore. Accusatory letters from his first wife, criticisms from fellow immigrants, and a diasporic social network prevent him from distancing his ties. Nilda eventually finds out about his other family through "a chain of friends that reached back across the Caribe" (187). The network maintains a claim on any immigrant who tries to embrace the logic of American immigration by splitting his life in a past-there / future-here scheme. The story of his abandoned family troubles his new life. After Nilda gives birth to a son, he calls him "Yunior" by mistake several times. Nilda senses the split, "that a part of him was detained elsewhere" (192).

This complication of the immigrant chronotope's split is crucial but we should dwell on just how close Ramón's story comes to splitting itself off. "Negocios" approaches narrative autonomy from the other family stories. It involves settings like Miami and Virginia that the rest of his family never encounter and characters like Nilda whom they do not know. Yunior narrates the story but there are events that lie beyond his knowledge, which recalls the way Geraldo's story lies beyond the purview of Esperanza's experience in *The House on Mango Street*. The causal connection to the other family stories remains clearer; these five years of absence determined the family's wait in the Dominican Republic. But there are mediated connections here that approach the relations we'll see in *We Should Never Meet*, which narrates disparate lives entangled by warfare. At the end of "Negocios," Yunior meets Nilda years after Ramón has left both of their lives. Yunior evokes warfare as one of the metaphors to describe the connection they share: "two strangers reliving an event—a whirlwind, a comet, a war—we'd both seen but from different faraway angles" (207). They are intimately and consequentially related and yet distant strangers. Díaz writes this family saga so that transfictional autonomy erupts within a genre that traditionally takes a tightly interwoven form. This formal contortion testifies to the pressures Dominican diasporic families negotiate: structural barriers that force staggered migrations, ideologies that split lives at the national border. These are family experiences that cannot readily be shaped into progressive, cohesive stories.

If U.S. understandings of immigration continue to follow such narrative terms, they will occlude the struggles of families like this.

With its form, *Drown* places pressure on American immigration myths and their mapping of past and future. Its narrative gaps register the splitting force of borders and citizenship barriers. Meanwhile, the relations among its stories rewrite immigration myths so that part of the story is always "detained elsewhere" beyond the national setting. Its transnational chronotope holds home and host nations in co-present relation. Where we saw a there-then to here-now scheme in immigration models, *Drown*'s emphasis on the ongoing stories of those left behind introduces a there-now term that troubles the splitting of space-time. This there-then, here-now, there-now scheme advances an idea that is difficult to accommodate within American exceptionalism: that the United States is not the positive term against which the country of origin is defined in binaries of here/there, now/then. It's a setting among other settings. *Drown* places the progression toward national incorporation against a spatial axis of transnational ties. In *Mango Street* we saw a tension between the temporal progress of individual mobility and a spatial attention to others in the community. While the transfictional relations in *Mango Street* insist on how much world there is beyond the protagonist's development story, in *Drown*'s diasporic variation they show the vital transnational contexts cut off by migration stories focused on the individual striving in the United States. This expansive vision emphasizes the situation of Latinx immigrants in transnational communities and, as discussed next, in histories of imperial war.

IMPERIAL HISTORIES IN AMERICAN IMMIGRATION

Detaining immigration with stories elsewhere does more than disrupt myths of American promise and recognize diasporic responsibilities. It registers the broader histories of U.S. imperialism driving immigration. Narratives of American promise obscure these histories. "Immigrants from the Caribbean," Ylce Irizarry rightly observes, "have not simply come to the United States to begin a new life." Their movements must be understood within the "neocolonial web of the United States" that stretches across the region.[25] There is a fourth chronotopic term that *Drown* alludes to: the here-then and its relationship to the there-then. In other words, the past relationship between the United States and the Dominican Republic, a relationship marked by a 150-year history of imperialism, economic and political control, multiple invasions, and as Díaz puts it in *The Brief Wondrous Life of Oscar Wao*, "one of the longest, most damaging U.S.-backed dictatorships in the Western Hemisphere," that of Rafael Trujillo.[26] The United States' 1965 invasion and backing of another oppressive regime, that of Joaquín Balaguer, gave rise to the devastating economic and political conditions that spurred the migrations of people like Ramón. At several moments, this history breaks into the narrative. In "Aguantando," Yunior mentions the 1965 invasion, which responded to the civil war that erupted following Trujillo's CIA-backed assassination.[27] At the time, Yunior's mother was pregnant. She suffered a miscarriage because of injuries from a rocket attack. U.S. military violence leaves gaps in this family.

An allusive scene in "Drown" places this history in a global framework of U.S. militarism. The unnamed narrator (who could be Yunior) encounters a U.S. military recruiter targeting youths in his impoverished New Jersey neighborhood. The recruiter asks if he would like a "real career, more than you'll get around here" (100). The man claims that the military can take him around the world. The global reach of U.S. military power enables mobility. The narrator avoids the recruiter from then on: "These days my guts feel loose and cold and I want to be away from here. He won't have to show me his Desert Eagle or flash the photos of the skinny Filipino girls sucking dick. He'll only have to smile and name the places and I'll listen" (100–101). The recruiter acknowledges the lack of opportunity in this community, which increases the vulnerability of its youths to the call of the military. The irony of the recruiter's proposal is that behind the lack of opportunity is the unacknowledged history of U.S. militarism in the Dominican Republic. The scene alludes to a circuit in which U.S. military intervention abroad displaces populations into underdeveloped enclaves like this, where the nation draws on this racialized lower-class population as a military labor force to send overseas to continue the cycle in other parts of the world under U.S. imperial power, such as the Philippines. If the global mobility offered by U.S. military power stands in stark contrast to the narrator's utterly enclosed life chances, it is the mobility of U.S. power that shaped this enclosure in the first place.

These allusions to imperial histories, however, reside on the margins of *Drown*'s stories. The geopolitical and military histories that made migration to the United States "something folks planned on" are present but not fully elaborated (73). To encompass them would require expanding beyond the familial scale that Díaz explores to such moving effect. Through family ties, *Drown* expresses the splitting of selves and families generated by histories of imperialism and displacement. But this scale is less able to map the geopolitical scope of those histories. To push further in mapping America's imperial past in the lives of its immigrants calls for narrative relations that move across scales and beyond the diasporic family. Aimee Phan's *We Should Never Meet* does this by developing a similar form to *Drown* but with its transfictional links organized along relations of mediated consequence.

INTERWEAVING THE SPLIT NARRATIVES
OF OPERATION BABYLIFT

We Should Never Meet confronts the histories of displacement generated by the Vietnam War and an evacuation known as Operation Babylift. Highlighting transfictional form's expansive possibilities, it jumps from wartime Vietnam to wartime America to Ho Chi Minh City and Orange County's Little Saigon years later. This form encompasses separate people, places, and times, allowing attention to the ruptures and reverberating impacts generated by the war and Babylift. Years of warfare in Vietnam resulted in mass orphaning and a class of con lai, the mixed-race children of American GIs and Vietnamese women. Near the war's end, children overwhelmed South Vietnam's orphanages, and their fates as the North Vietnamese took control were the subject of mass fears.[28] In April 1975, as South Vietnam fell, Operation Babylift, a joint effort of the U.S. government and private orphanages, evacuated over two thousand children and placed them with adoptive families in the United States. Debate raged over whether the evacuees were actually eligible for adoption and why Americans were permanently removing them from Vietnam.[29] The chaotic effort severed children from identifying documents that tied them to their pasts.[30] "On every level," Dana Sachs assesses, "from the original decisions about which children would be airlifted to the protocols for finalizing adoptions, Operation Babylift suffered from acute disorder and a nearly complete lack of oversight."[31] Placements were haphazard and though many adopting families provided supportive homes, in some cases the experiences were traumatic.[32] Many who came via the Babylift struggle with their national, racial, and personal identities. Many do not know their family, parents, birth dates, or names. These are lives ruptured by the devastation of one nation and displacement to another. The trajectories created by Operation Babylift are dizzying, and not just for the orphans. Each touched the lives of many others: birth and adoptive parents, orphanage workers, doctors, adoption agency staff.

These are the trajectories Aimee Phan tracks across the eight interlinked stories of *We Should Never Meet*.[33] The vast networks of involvement pulled in members of Phan's family. Her mother was a social worker who helped with the operation, and her aunt and uncle came to the United States on the flights.[34] This family involvement may explain why her attention to the impacts of the Babylift is so wide-ranging. Phan explains that she sought to supplement the pervasive attention to the military dimensions of the war: "The book deals with not only [the] consequences in the orphans' lives, but many other civilians' lives that were affected by the war and the Babylift."[35] Her story cycle traces these impacts across an expansive spatiotemporal scope that emphasizes the enduring effects of the war and their transnational reverberations.[36]

Marguerite Nguyen and Catherine Fung argue that Southeast Asian American writings intervene through their aesthetic strategies in the discourses framing refugees.[37] This is certainly true of *We Should Never Meet*. Its range and crosscutting structure are strategies for untangling the web of narratives enclosing the Vietnamese refugee and adoptee in the American imagination. As reminders of a morally troubling war, Vietnamese refugees remain a key site of ideological work. Yến Lê Espiritu observes that a narrative of Americans rescuing Vietnamese refugees from communism emerged to recuperate the moral justification for U.S. warfare in Vietnam and beyond.[38] This story allowed Americans "to remake themselves from military aggressors into magnanimous rescuers," thus suppressing the central role of U.S. warfare in creating the refugee crisis.[39] With Operation Babylift, the plight of Vietnamese orphans became a highly publicized cause, a way to "salvage something from the horror of the war."[40] The disproportionate interest placed in these 2,500 child refugees (a fraction of the millions of displaced Vietnamese) attests to their ideological importance in the process of replacing the history of U.S. militarism with the deeds of U.S. humanitarianism. These ideological investments split the narrative of Vietnamese displacement, disconnecting the history of U.S. forces entering Vietnam from the history of Vietnamese refugees entering the United States. The latter story becomes one of helpless Vietnamese offered salvation in America; the former, that of American soldiers losing their innocence in the hell of Vietnam.[41]

Reinforcing this split was the framing of Cold War Asian adoptees. These narratives posed the adoption of Asian children as evidence of American benevolence rather than a legacy of Cold War military interventions.[42] Laura Briggs observes that transnational adoption policies were themselves interventionist. She traces an ideology of adoption whose central theme was "American paternalist responsibility" for rescuing Third World children from communism, poverty, and "Asian 'barbarism.'"[43] These narratives helped decide child refugee policies emphasizing adoptions and permanent separation from birth families and nations in contrast to pre–World War II policies of supporting children until they could be returned to their parents.[44] These practices created pressure to suppress racial identities, birth families, and histories in Asia so as to fit adoptees into American families.[45] This split scheme contained the roles U.S. interventions played in creating the conditions from which Asian children needed to be "rescued." The elision helped foster a view that further American intervention in the form of permanent removal was what such children needed. In the framing of Operation Babylift, the narratives of Americans saving Vietnamese refugees from communism and Americans saving children from Asian backwardness intersect to overdetermine a separation of what the United States does to people "over there" from what the United States does for people "over here."

Phan's representation spans this split. The stories interweave U.S. actions in Vietnam with the paths of refugee children in the United States. Interweaving national settings is a prominent impulse across Vietnamese American narrative because the life stories of many Vietnamese Americans were dispersed by war. Important examples include Le Ly Hayslip's *When Heaven and Earth Changed Places* (1989), Nguyen Qui Duc's *Where the Ashes Are* (1994), Lan Cao's *Monkey Bridge* (1997), lê thi diem thúy's *the gangster we are all looking for* (2003), and Linh Dinh's *Love Like Hate* (2010). What makes Babylift refugees stand out here are the gaps in their knowledge of their lives and families. The presence of these gaps is why such subjects are important (and why they lend themselves to transfictional form); they push Vietnamese American narrative beyond its usual genres of personal memoir and family sagas.[46] The stories of many Babylift children are illegible within these scales. They cannot reconstruct a continuous personal narrative or family history. In taking on this subject,

Phan expands the scope of Vietnamese American narrative to grapple with ethical and political relations that cannot be grasped within the purview of an individual life or family ties. Her story cycle makes evident the entanglements of refugee routes with agents on multiple scales, from individual aid workers to the U.S. military. The political community of the U.S. nation-state, with its investments in containing large swaths of the histories affecting Vietnamese refugees, cannot encompass these webs. Phan's story cycle outlines a different, transnational shape of community to map these diffuse networks of effects and the claims of justice they generate.

We Should Never Meet draws on a story cycle form that has roots in regionalist fiction and traditionally depicts local community.[47] Phan adapts the genre's subnational spatial rubrics to tell stories of transnational displacement. This surprising adaptation suggests the largely unrecognized potential of the story cycle to narrate global routes. Recent studies of American literary regionalism have uncovered the genre's attention to global networks.[48] I argue that regionalism did more than register transnational relations as it portrayed local communities. It developed a form that offers surprisingly rich possibilities for narrating diasporic communities. Many critics note the story cycle's capacity for representing place and local community.[49] A shared location often unifies the stories,[50] and the structure of individual stories forming a greater whole functions as an analog of community. But little attention has been paid to the form's potential for narrating collectives beyond the local even though story cycles spanning transnational settings emerged at least as early as Ernest Hemingway's *In Our Time* (1925). One exception is Susan Koshy's essay "Minority Cosmopolitanism," which reads Jhumpa Lahiri's *Interpreter of Maladies* (1999) as a story cycle that develops a cosmopolitan ethics.[51]

Koshy opens a line of inquiry that I pursue further. Criticism needs a more capacious theory of the story cycle's possibilities, which extends beyond examples depicting local community to explain the genre's powers for narrating transnational community. The concept of transfictional form expands story cycle theory in this way. It allows for analysis of the gaps and relations between distinct narratives, the aesthetic means by which story cycles grasp social relations across national borders. I see the story cycle's capacity for tracing global connection as an extension of, rather than a break with, the regionalist tradition. Acknowledging that early regionalist story cycles recognized global ties, I follow the counterintuitive idea that the genre's capacity to map local community may be a strength in mapping transnational relations. This capacity can bring ideas of community into perceptions of distant ties that seem to exceed the contours of recognizable community. In the face of displacements propelled by global networks of effects, transfictional story cycles meet the need for aesthetic forms that can make transnational relations of interdependence feel as palpable as the ties binding local communities.

We Should Never Meet retrofits the regionalist story cycle for global networks. It disintegrates the rooted location and central character that unified many regionalist story cycles (by doing away with a central character, it also stretches the form further than *Drown* does in its transnational adaptation of the story cycle). Its dispersed settings and character system stretch the idea of community to encompass refugee routes. The regionalist focus on mapping community remains, but the sense of community expands, no longer a rooted group. The discontinuous collective traced by Phan's stories is a transnational network of the Vietnam War's chaotic conditions, difficult choices, and far-ranging impacts.

NETWORKS OF UNRESOLVED RESPONSIBILITY

The opening story, "Miss Lien," takes place during the war. It centers on a teenage girl from the Mekong Delta sent by her parents to the city of Cần Thơ to make desperately needed money. The family's crop has been destroyed as fighting sweeps the countryside. After she endures months in the city, her parents insist she stay longer because "the money was too valuable."[52] In circumstances left implicit (the story hints at a rape by an American GI), Lien becomes pregnant. She realizes she cannot tell her parents: "They would only blame her. They would never believe that they were partly responsible" (22). The phrase "partly responsible" expresses the ambiguous relation this story cycle charts within and between its stories: neither direct connection nor disconnection between the actions of one party and their mediated effects on others. Feeling unable to care for the child, Lien leaves the infant on the steps of a Catholic orphanage. In a moment that will prove resonant, the nun who answers the door looks around for the mother and pauses to give her a last chance before taking the child inside. Feeling her responsibility lifted, Lien thinks, "This child was safe. This child would not have to suffer" (23). The story ends there.

But as the next story unfolds, transfictional relations emerge that trouble this closure with ties of partial responsibility that may bind Lien's story to others.

The next story, "We Should Never Meet," is set nearly twenty years later in Little Saigon, Orange County, California. Kim, a Vietnamese American teenager, is a high school dropout with few prospects and no family to support her. As the story reveals that Kim is a mixed-race Babylift orphan who suffered abuse in various foster homes, possible connections begin to form across vast distances, timespans, and what seemed a definitive story break. Is Kim the same child left at the orphanage in Vietnam years before? The story continues to suggest resonances but does not resolve the question. When a Vietnamese shopkeeper lets Kim off for stealing, Kim is drawn to her, seeing this woman as a substitute for the mother she never knew. The woman gives Kim a jade bracelet, which echoes a bracelet Lien's grandmother gives to her. Interpreting the gift in familial terms, Kim asks the woman for money, which, in another echo, she needs to address an unexpected pregnancy. But the shopkeeper rejects her. With that, "the woman became a stranger again. Her features were not so similar to Kim's, her face, body language not so loving." Kim walks out, "half-hoping the woman would call out to her" (50), but she doesn't. For readers, the moment implies a path back to the orphanage in Vietnam when a mother had a chance to call out and take back her child. Kim lashes out at what she feels is a second abandonment by sending her boyfriend's gang to rob the store. Staying behind, she realizes the gang often attacks the merchants they rob. The story ends with Kim trying to reach them, "still convinced she could undo what was happening" (54). In a reverberation of the end of "Miss Lien," Kim also commits an irreversible act. But this ending revises the previous one, in that Kim realizes that she has not fully reckoned with the impacts of her decision.

As this opening pair reveals, the stories of *We Should Never Meet* form vertiginous narrative structures that suggest networks of effects and responsibilities linking separate times, places, people, and stories. These transfictional links are rarely explicit and often resist definitive answers. Readers construct them across pronounced spatiotemporal and narrative gaps. The crosscutting arrangement of stories exacerbates these gaps while outlining the extent of the potential links. The first, third, fifth, and seventh stories are set in wartime Vietnam. They trace the path children take from their beleaguered mothers ("Miss Lien") to a rural orphanage ("The Delta") to a Saigon adoption center

("Gates of Saigon") to their evacuation ("Bound"). This sequence alternates with another set largely in Orange County's Little Saigon in the 1990s. This latter series follows the troubled paths of the teenage orphans as they grow up ("We Should Never Meet," "Visitors," "Emancipation," and "Motherland"). Like *Drown*, this story cycle cuts back and forth between narrative series, evoking them as different pieces in the fragmented life histories of the Babylift children. These movements ask readers to link present conditions to past events while also considering how the chains of events that altered the children's lives may concatenate, producing further chains of effect, such as the impact Kim has on the shopkeeper.

The transfictional relations in this story cycle are ones of distant effect stretching across time and space. The third story, "The Delta," centers on a Catholic nun at a convent in the Mekong Delta overrun by orphans. The story suggests (but again does not confirm) that Phuong may be the same nun who took in Lien's child. The relief that mothers feel in delivering their children to an orphanage obscures the displacement of responsibility onto others. The story observes how this burden affects Phuong and those around her, generating a further tier in the network of effects. To devote herself to the orphans, Phuong breaks off a long-standing engagement. "Her decision," the story notes, "traveled a devastating path" (82), splitting neighboring families, and dividing a village. Phan traces such devastating paths of effect across her stories. By the end of the story, Phuong transports some of the orphans to an adoption center in Saigon. An employee named Hoa takes them in, another transfer of responsibility. Hoa reappears as the protagonist of "Gates of Saigon," in which the staff scrambles to secure passage out of the country for the children before Saigon falls. The story portrays the chaotic conditions in which they make evacuation decisions and forge records with incomplete data, choices with permanent consequences for the children. Meanwhile, the fate of Hoa and her family remains unclear. The North Vietnamese government condemned the evacuation of orphans. Involvement with the operation places employees like Hoa at risk. As their decisions affect the orphans' lives, these caretakers bear the effects of that responsibility on their own lives.

Phan traces these effects beyond the Vietnamese affected. The story "Bound" concerns Bridget, an American pediatrician whose long volunteer stint at the Saigon adoption center devastates her family. The stories also register the effects on the orphans themselves and those they affect in the United States. "Visitors" focuses on Kim's boyfriend, Vinh. Vinh joins a gang of Vietnamese orphans who feel that "their new country and government-issued families" had "denied" them everything. They rob houses and stores "to break even," believing "they had no other choice" (52). "Visitors" ends with Vinh robbing and assaulting an elderly Vietnamese man who had befriended him. The implied connections among the stories invite readers to situate this story's outcome within the chain of events that disrupted the lives of the orphans.[53] This form evokes how actions of agents in one place create distanced effects that shape the situations within which other agents act and affect others still further away.

The "community" that *We Should Never Meet* elaborates is a transnational network of partial responsibility and mediated effect. It is a community centered on child refugees and encompassing the many people shaping and shaped by the contingent paths they take. The links binding them are characteristic of trans-fictional character and causal relations; they are tangential and indirect touches between people in separate social worlds. These links differ from traditional community ties because they do not involve sustained or even direct contacts. They are unexpected, impermanent connections. A chance viewing of a news special on Vietnamese orphans draws Bridget to the adoption center in Saigon; the children pass from one pair of hands to the next according to circumstance; the Vietnamese man attacked by Vinh's gang meets Vinh when he gets lost in Little Saigon. Other connections are indirect. Without ever having met them, Phuong, Hoa, and others bear the impact of decisions made by mothers like Lien. Likewise, the life of the shopkeeper is indelibly changed by the figure of Kim's biological mother. Phan focuses on these forms of glancing and indirect connection. The title *We Should Never Meet* expresses a sense of collectivity that exceeds direct contact, a "we" whose members are linked in ethically significant ways even if they should never meet.

COMMUNITIES OF FATE ACROSS SCALES AND NATIONS

The links Phan depicts are not bound as a community is. One could argue that what this story cycle portrays is not a community in any recognizable sense. But the fact that *We Should Never Meet* draws on regionalism's form for rendering community encourages readers to examine the stakes of that term for refugee routes. I argue that the urgency with which this story cycle leads us to draw links beyond the contours of recognizable community is the urgency of envisioning new forms of community that can encompass the ethical and political relations generated by global disruptions like the evacuation of South Vietnam. Without some form of collectivity to understand these connections, we might not recognize them at all. If regionalist works made clear the "tangible social relations" of local community,[54] can more distant relations of consequence be made similarly palpable? With the capacity of transfictional form to render a dispersed character system exceeding direct contacts, this story cycle calls on us to imagine an expanded form of community whose stakes are intensified by refugee displacements. Buffeted by diffuse forces, the Babylift children raise the question of how to claim justice in networks of effect that seem impossible to map.

Envisioning collectivity matters in the case of the Babylift because the questions of responsibility it generates cannot be resolved on an individual scale. Trying to make sense of the Babylift's outcomes on her life, Kim ends up blaming herself. She wonders why her adoptive family rejected her when she was only three years old and concludes that "she must have done something wrong" (48). Kim's self-blame indicates that the scale of individual responsibility presents serious problems for refugee children and adoptees. The rhetoric of transnational adoption tends to tell the story of adoption in individual and private terms.[55] Meanwhile "damage-centered" perspectives on refugees locate the presumed "problem" of refugees within the "bodies and minds" of refugees themselves.[56] The individual scale in these discourses can pathologize adoptees and refugees, rooting whatever problems of formation they may have within the realms of the private and familial instead of within the histories of imperialism and militarism that produced mass displacements. As David L. Eng argues, we need to restore a collective historical scale of understanding to these experiences of displacement.[57]

Addressing this need, Phan's stories recognize the importance of individual actions while insisting that the scales of agency involved in the Babylift are diffuse. In "Motherland," one orphan, Mai, concedes that she cannot expect her parents or anyone else swept up in the war to have done right "when everything here was wrong" (243). The stories consistently view individual actions within broader contexts. For instance, Lien's decision to abandon her child, which seems to precipitate effects across the stories, is itself shaped by a web of forces and decisions stemming from her parents, the troops that ravage their crops, and the U.S. military intervention that places Vietnamese women in a sexual economy with American GIs. Tracing one chain of effect back to Lien's parents, "Miss Lien" reveals the difficulty of their decision to send her to the city. They feel they have "no other choice" (15), a phrase many of the stories repeat as they depict individuals caught in circumstances they cannot control. The personal costs of Phuong's and Bridget's commitments to the orphans stem from the overwhelming burdens they attempt to shoulder. More abandoned babies show up each day; mothers scream at Bridget to take their children. The scale of human need the war produces is simply impossible to meet or adjudicate on the level of individual responsibility.

Phan deploys transfictional form's divergent scales of narrative relations—from the direct relations within a story to the more distant relations across the stories—to map the trans-scale causes and effects of the evacuation of South Vietnam. The relations of partial responsibility linking the stories extend beyond any one scale or narrative. Kim's story implicates the social worker who placed her in foster homes where she was abused. This is an immediate factor affecting Kim's life, but one passage points to factors lying beyond the story's scope: "Kim was classified as an orphan when she arrived in the States as part of Operation Babylift. But that didn't mean her parents were dead, only that they'd given her up. No identification on her but her name" (36). The passage alludes to settings, agents, and events represented only in other stories. The reference to giving up children reinforces the potential link to "Miss Lien," which depicts the impacts of birth parents and militaries on child abandonments. Kim's missing identification invites a connection to "Gates of Saigon" in which an adoption agency forges documents to evacuate the children under its care. The relations within and between stories implicate many agents, from individual caretakers to the institutional scale of adoption agencies and social work offices to the geopolitical scale of Cold War military conflicts. The cycle weaves non-kinship relations, institutions, and public histories into the stories of the adoptees' seemingly private suffering. And it challenges readers to synthesize these pieces into a community of consequence whose links resist the tendency to see different scales as unconnected, which Hsuan L. Hsu argues "atomize[s] political struggles" and conceals the relations among agents.[58]

We Should Never Meet pushes us to imagine the discontiguous networks generated by warfare and refugee displacement as a community bound by distant yet ethically consequential ties. It contributes an aesthetic form expressing mediated yet powerful connection to current political theory that is grappling with similar questions. Political theorist Melissa S. Williams describes a term that dovetails with the model of social relations Phan's story cycle develops: "communities of shared fate." The concept holds that in a globalized world the actions of agents in one place affect distant others in unexpected ways. As Phan's story cycle shows, we do not necessarily know the extent of our actions' reverberating consequences. The word "fate" expresses a sense of conditions surpassing intention: "ethically significant relationships . . . are not all of conscious choosing. There are forces not of our own making that bind us to one another, like it or not." These networks binding us to others raise questions of political accountability. The concept is a foundation for envisioning political agency and justice within the kinds of discontiguous relations Phan maps. Williams argues that this sense of community can transform networks of actions and unintended impacts into sites where people practice intentional politics toward a collective good. Through the different modes of fiction and academic theory, Phan and Williams expand the boundaries of community beyond traditional measures of shared culture and place. In this model, what binds a community "is not necessarily a shared identity, a shared sense of membership, . . . it is a system of social interdependence, often characterized by inequalities of power in which individual-level actions generate effects beyond the parties immediately concerned."[59] Not premised on identity or contiguity, this is a model of relationship that recognizes difference and separation as irreducible elements of the transnational political communities we need to envision. Relation across separation, the interpretive challenge that transfictional form poses, is at the heart of the urgent and difficult work that communities of shared fate call us to.

Phan and Williams present an alternative mapping of community: actions, consequences, agents, and affected parties, not necessarily contained or even recognizable within traditional community boundaries. Communities of fate cut across borders and "jump scales," to borrow Neil Smith's formulation.[60] Though Williams develops the concept to meet the demands of transnational ties, communities of fate are not exclusive to the transnational; they connect agents on national, subnational, and other scales. Communities of fate and local communities, then, are not mutually exclusive, and the adaptation of the regionalist story cycle to refugee narratives may not be so strange. Several of

Phan's stories focus on the ethnic enclave of Little Saigon, but the local focus in each of these stories hovers against the transnational horizon of the Vietnam War's community of fate, which produced this enclave. This horizon becomes apparent through links to the other stories that range from wartime to the present, Vietnam to the United States. As Susan Koshy notes, the story cycle can place "individual lives and stories against an ever-shifting cosmopolitan horizon of meaning."[61] Coupling local and global scales of community, Phan's work develops a tension that was latent in the regionalist story cycle. Scholars of regionalism have shown that its local focus encodes an awareness of globalization. Not just depictions of provincial places, regionalist texts revealed local sites to be porous to the world, penetrated by the foreignness the genre is assumed to preclude.[62] We can connect the tension of local and global in regionalist fictions to the parallel tension of local and translocal that Dalia Kandiyoti perceives in diasporic fictions.[63] This connection helps makes sense of Phan's adaptation. In expanding the story cycle's scope, *We Should Never Meet* doesn't break with regionalism; it foregrounds the connections to broader communities already in the genre's background.

The connection to regionalism highlights a third scale of community: the imagined community of the nation. Regionalism, Stephanie Foote observes, emerged as a literary strategy for managing difference in a period of anxiety about immigration. It expressed an ideal that regional and cultural difference could be incorporated into a unified nation.[64] But to do so, the genre often had to suppress the contradictions among local, national, and transnational communities. For diasporic communities that are racialized as foreign, the regional is an important scale, because its unsettled place within the nation can reveal these suppressed contradictions, highlighting the problems of "abjection and *dis*-unity" in the nation.[65]

Few minority subjects are caught more fully within the conflicts of local, national, and transnational communities than the displaced orphans Phan depicts. In "Visitors," Vinh expresses his alienation from the United States: "It's like I'm visiting, and I've overstayed my welcome" (97). Uprooted from his country, failed by the state, and bounced among foster homes, Vinh transforms his feelings of rejection into a defiant stance against assimilation. He condemns "selling out to the Americans" and pities the orphans who integrate into American families and society successfully. The less fortunate orphans may have suffered in their foster homes, but at least "they knew where they stood with the Americans" (103).

The U.S. national horizon of identification does not square with the orphans' place in the Vietnam War's violently dislocated community of fate. As Vinh bluntly says of Americans, "They destroyed our country, then they left. To ease their guilty conscience, they took some of us in" (96). Refugees are expected to disappear "from plain sight when incorporated into the national body," Timothy K. August observes, a process that helps the nation leave behind the violent histories abroad that produced the refugee condition. But the histories refugees bear are not so easily contained; "lingering contradictions" continue to play out in refugee lives.[66] If regionalism had difficulties suppressing contradictions while fitting marginal subjects into the nation, the contradictions Vinh identifies are even more difficult to reconcile. For what must be suppressed is the reality of a community of fate utterly shaped by the actions of the United States. Phan's story cycle works against that suppression by mapping the displaced Vietnamese not just as a community that does not fit in the United States but within a transnational sense of community that encompasses the war's web of actions, effects, and responsibilities. This mapping does not allow Americans to disconnect the racial difference entering the nation from U.S. actions in Southeast Asia. To borrow Lisa Lowe's formulation, the mixed-race orphans of Operation Babylift are a "material legacy of the repressed history of U.S. imperialism in Asia."[67] Bridget explains, "These Amerasians are children of the U.S. military; they're products of this war" (194). Offspring of an American war, their liminal racial and national identities are markers of history. When acknowledged, these refugees dredge up unresolved feelings about one of America's most difficult wars, and they unsettle paradigms of national identity that suppress histories of U.S. imperialism. Phan portrays the world of the Babylift orphans with a transfictional form that links the past and present of the United States and Vietnam, spans the split narratives of the adoptee or refugee saved by the United States, and expands the purview of Vietnamese American narrative to trace relations of consequence exceeding the individual or family scale. *We Should Never Meet* advances its expansive scope and sense of community to historicize the problem of placing this group of displaced subjects within America as inextricable from the problem of the actions and responsibilities the nation would rather forget.[68] It raises two related questions:

Have Americans developed a sense of citizenship commensurate to the unbound communities of fate in which our actions have involved us? And is our sense of national community commensurate with the claims of those already here whose fates have been shaped by our involvements elsewhere?

NARRATING COMMUNITIES OF FATE INTO BEING

Communities of fate, Melissa Williams insists, are not just there to be seen.[69] The relations that constitute them are often distant and difficult to perceive. Before we can act on them, we need to be able to envision these networks of effect as communities whose members bear political responsibilities to each other. For literary scholars, Williams makes an intriguing proposal: What we need are "storytellers" who bring communities of fate to life. "Through their words and their actions, they attempt to persuade other parties to these relationships that the connections between them are real and that their actions have real consequences for others."[70] Williams makes a strong case for why the kind of work done in *We Should Never Meet* matters. If transnational communities of fate must be narrated into being, Phan's cycle offers a transfictional form for doing so.

We Should Never Meet invites readers to participate in constructing the narrative relations that bring communities of fate to life. But in doing so we confront the challenge of recognizing border crossings without ignoring the force of borders. The formal means by which this text invites participation, the gaps between stories, recognizes this challenge. Encoding vast rifts in time and space, these gaps call us to draw connections between stories while simultaneously obstructing that impulse. Consider how Phan avoids specifying the gender of the abandoned child in the first story. The narrator uses the gender-neutral "it" (18, 21, 22).[71] This choice makes any identification between this child and the teenage Kim in the second story even more difficult to establish despite the resonances between the stories. Kim is not the only character whose story invites links to "Miss Lien." The final story, "Motherland," follows Huan, another mixed-race Babylift orphan, as he returns to Vietnam to reconstruct his past. This return holds out the promise of the story cycle circling back to resolve its unanswered questions and tie its stories together into a clearly connected whole. Tantalizing details emerge. Huan traces his path back to the Saigon adoption center where Hoa and Bridget worked and to the convent in the Mekong

Delta where Sister Phuong still lives. There, he finds an intake record, "the first evidence of his existence" (237–38). His weight, six pounds, and age, a few days old, resemble the details of Lien's child, but even in this detail Phan introduces ambiguities. The weight of Lien's child is only estimated in the first story, around "six, seven pounds" (17). The trail ends at the convent because there is no record of Huan's birth parents. Even this, the most investigated of the life stories, cannot be resolved. The gaps in these lives and in the story cycle's form remain.

Invited but never quite realized connections span the story cycle. This distinctively transfictional move is a formal recognition of the interconnected yet fragmented world of the orphan refugees. It withholds from readers the comfort of believing that life stories disjointed by warfare can be smoothly reconstructed. It would be far easier, when confronted with the complexities of transnational responsibilities and mass displacements, to have smooth stories to clarify political life. The resistant form of this story cycle does not allow readers to indulge this desire. Instead, it confronts us with the difficult task of imagining political communities that address rather than smooth over the ruptures in refugee life stories. The refusal of definitive narrative links on the scale of the individual life argues that we cannot limit mappings of consequential affiliations to any one scale. To link Kim and others to Lien's child, readers must think through the broader scales of adoption agencies, refugee policies, and militaries. We can only complete the links by following relations of individual responsibility as they are mediated through institutional, national, and geopolitical scales of connection. Williams admits that telling stories to fill in the "indeterminacy of political space" in a globalized era presents huge difficulties.[72] But in the face of networks of consequence that state institutions cannot adjudicate and nation-based models cannot grasp, writers and scholars are refusing to accept that such difficulties permit us to abdicate the responsibilities that bind us together. Transnational responsibilities call for a form that can give them shape. With *We Should Never Meet*, we see a transfictional literature developing to narrate elusive communities of fate into being.

A BROADER COLD WAR HISTORY
Together Díaz and Phan develop a transfictional form whose tension of narrative borders and border crossings captures a Cold War contradiction: the splitting force of U.S. borders on the lives of "foreigners" who are here because of the

ease with which U.S. forces crossed the borders of their nations. The convergent aesthetics they develop offer a formal axis for tracing what Jesse Hoffnung-Garskof calls a "Cold War migration history."[73] This history connects the usually separated stories of migrations from countries sharing the experience of U.S. invasion and proxy wars. As I touched on in the introduction, the comparison of Díaz's and Phan's works leads to the little known links between Asian and Latin American displacements generated simultaneously by a U.S. military strategy spanning the globe. The United States' official entry into the Vietnam War in 1965 determined the contemporaneous invasion of the Dominican Republic. The need to project military strength in the context of the drastic escalation in Vietnam committed the Johnson administration to a forceful intervention in the Dominican civil war.[74] Johnson suspected that the civil war was a Soviet-backed retaliation for the U.S. entry into Vietnam and treated the Dominican crisis as a crucial test of the United States' anticommunist strength.[75]

Though linked, these migrations were categorized differently, with Vietnamese entering the United States as refugees and Dominicans entering as immigrants. This comparison, then, also reveals links across the immigrant/refugee distinction. The Dominican case shows how politically constructed this distinction was. As Hoffnung-Garskof reveals, U.S. imperialism and invasion played a key role in the political crisis and oppressive government of Joaquín Balaguer that Dominicans sought to escape in the 1960s and 1970s.[76] But the United States accommodated fleeing Dominicans under immigrant and even tourist visas.[77] Ramón in *Drown* arrives on a tourist visa and overstays it, an occurrence that the State Department fully anticipated. U.S. refugee policy was focused on those fleeing communist regimes, such as the Vietnamese, so the category's Cold War functions precluded recognizing those, like Dominicans, who were escaping countries suffering under U.S. interventions and U.S.-backed regimes.[78] The Cold War refugee/immigrant split is a variant of the needed/undesired binary that links Asian American and Latinx migrations. In addition to filling labor needs, the management of migrants helped fulfill foreign policy needs. The figure of the refugee fleeing communism bolstered the international image of the United States as a haven from tyranny while the asylum claims of those fleeing U.S.-backed regimes were unwelcome reminders of U.S. disruptions of sovereign nations. Coding Dominicans as immigrants accomplished the impressive feat of reinforcing narratives of U.S. opportunity even in the midst of U.S. invasion. With Marines fighting on the streets of Santo Domingo, hundreds seeking to flee the country mobbed the U.S. embassy. The embassy interpreted the mob in an amazing way: "USA STILL 'LAND OF PROMISE' HERE."[79] The political functions of the immigrant and refugee categories, then, are more intertwined than the distinction suggests. This pertains as well to the Vietnamese on the other side of the distinction. Refugee status did not prevent media representations from conscripting Vietnamese into immigrant-inflected stories of success that shifted attention from U.S. violence to U.S. opportunity.[80] The comparison reframes the immigrant and the refugee as intertwined categories through which the United States narrates migrations to justify its interventions, contain its histories of imperialism, and reinforce its self-image.

The historical links we perceive through Díaz's and Phan's aesthetics raise questions about how we have regionally divided our Cold War histories. The military connection between the Dominican Republic and Vietnam and the Latin American–Asian solidarity felt by Dominicans in this moment fall through the cracks of Cold War historiography. Many studies of the Cold War in Latin America do not emphasize connections to Asia, nor do they deeply explore the impacts of the Vietnam War on this region.[81] Meanwhile, the rich body of scholarship on anti-imperialist solidarities in this period have focused on Afro-Asian connections.[82] This focus stems partly from the symbolic visibility of the 1955 Afro-Asian conference at Bandung, a crucial moment for Third World solidarity among the newly decolonized nations of Africa and Asia. Historians have rightly emphasized the explosive intersection of post–World War II decolonization struggles and the Cold War, but this focus points our attention to Asia and Africa and away from Latin America. Much of Latin America had long been independent of European colonialism and during the Cold War was struggling with the neocolonial power of the United States.[83]

The focus on Afro-Asian solidarities and decolonizing nations has obscured the transnational solidarities Latin Americans envisioned.[84] As I noted in the introduction, many Dominicans saw very clearly their connection to Vietnamese who were simultaneously enduring U.S. invasion. This Latin American–Asian solidarity is not legible through the framework of Bandung. It's better understood through another key conference, which Bandung has overshadowed. The 1966 Tricontinental Conference in Cuba hosted delegates from eighty-two nations, including the Dominican Republic and North Vietnam, to form the

Organización de Solidaridad de los Pueblos de África, Asia y América Latina (OSPAAAL). The Tricontinental Conference, Robert J. C. Young argues, "brought together the anticolonial struggles of Africa and Asia with the radical movements of Latin America," initiating a global anti-imperialist solidarity.[85] While it's important to recognize the differences between decolonizing struggles in Asia and Africa and struggles with neocolonialism in Latin America during the Cold War, these distinct spheres were linked by simultaneous U.S. efforts to contain communism. In Asia and Africa, the United States often supported European colonial powers as a bulwark against decolonizing movements that might side with the communist bloc. Meanwhile, Latin Americans saw U.S. anticommunist interventions in their nations as a form of neocolonialism. As a result, peoples across three continents began to see a shared enemy in U.S imperialism.[86] Distinct stages of anticolonial struggle came together in the Tricontinental's platform. The Vietnam War was crucial to this vision since it showed the continuity between an anticolonial struggle against the old European imperial order represented by France and a struggle with a new imperial order led by the United States.[87] OSPAAAL supported liberation struggles against all types of military and economic imperialism, in Vietnam, the Dominican Republic, South Africa, and beyond.[88] Relational work connecting Asia and Latin America is crucial to expanding our understanding of Cold War anti-imperial solidarities.[89] To grasp the full scope of U.S. imperialism during the Cold War, its militarism across the Global South, and the transnational solidarities that connected U.S. imperialism to the older colonial powers, we cannot isolate the Cold War in Latin America from Asia and Africa. With Latin America integrated into histories of the period, we may bring more visibility to the Tricontinental as a crucial antithesis to the U.S. Cold War imperial order. Rather than starting comparative analysis through recognized historical links, I've argued that attending to shared aesthetic strategies across distinct arenas of the Cold War can help us cross regional divides in our historical narratives to see solidarities obscured by those divides.

Writing from an Asian and Latinx America formed by the Cold War, Díaz and Phan span the national limits on our political and historical imaginations. To contest the historical amnesia enabled by immigration myths and refugee narratives and to understand the Asian and Latin American communities displaced to the United States by the Cold War requires a different story of migration that spans global routes and vectors of U.S. power. With a transfictional aesthetics giving form to transnational power, displacement, and community, they attempt to change our understandings of America in the world and the world in America. Their efforts hold out hope for an enlarged sense of political community that rejects the easy line between here and there in our responsibilities, that instead sees our fates as Americans as intertwined with those our nation affects overseas and those over here because we have been, far too often, over there.

CHAPTER 3

UNSETTLING STRATA AND TYPE

Divided Communities of Neoliberal Immigration in Karma *and* The People of Paper

"LAKSHMI CHUNDI, first-generation Indian immigrant, forty-seven-year-old homemaker, wife of a gainfully employed computer-software engineer working at a reputable computer-manufacturing corporation, mother of two grown sons, is melancholy."[1] This jarring sentence opens the story "Lakshmi and the Librarian" from Rishi Reddi's 2007 story cycle *Karma*. The sentence's sudden shift in register expresses the rifts between demographic data and personhood, economic position and interiority. Lakshmi's emotional life jars with a view that parses her identity by ethnicity, immigrant category, age, occupation, and gender and understands her in relation to her husband, whose salient attributes are his gainful employment in a hi-tech industrial sector and his corporate affiliation. Alongside Reddi's story, consider Salvador Plascencia's 2005 novel *The People of Paper*. The novel centers on a Mexican American writer in an elite creative writing program whose novel about Mexican American farmworkers and gang members is funded by a corporate foundation. The foundation's lawyers comb through the novel "page by page, with a mechanical counter in hand, . . . quantifying the breadth of sorrow" before the contract is drafted and "the money allotted."[2]

In Reddi's and Plascencia's works, we encounter some racial types familiar in Asian American and Latinx literatures: the first-generation Asian immigrant, the Mexican farmworker, the Mexican gang member. These figures connect Reddi's and Plascencia's works to a long-standing struggle to write against racial types. On the first page of their introduction to the pioneering 1974 anthology of Asian American literature, the editors of *Aiiieeeee!* address the specter of the "laundryman, prostitute, smuggler, coolie."[3] Américo Paredes's groundbreaking 1958 study *"With His Pistol in His Hand"* advanced an analysis of the "Anglo-Texan legend," a stereotyped discourse about Mexicans that justified the crimes against Mexican Americans.[4] *Karma* and *The People of Paper* continue this tradition of struggle, but their range of characters and themes of economic datafication index a significant shift in the social landscape. In the twenty-first century, new figures are complicating attempts to represent Asian American and Latinx communities.[5] Writers must wrestle not only with the Asian laundryman but also with the hi-tech Asian worker and transnational Asian capitalist; not only with the Latinx gang member and the Latinx farmworker but also the multicultural token of corporate America, the NAFTA refugee, and the Mexican billionaire. A neoliberal era of economic restructuring and stratified immigration has normalized the parsing of immigrant lives into demographic types and categories of human capital while producing stark inequalities of class and citizenship in Asian American and Latinx communities. The differentiated economic types of neoliberal analysis overlay the long-standing reduction of immigrant lives by racial stereotypes. Stereotyping's tendency to homogenize ethnic groups clashes with the rapid stratification of these groups today. This clash is arguably more intense for Asian Americans and Latinxs than for other U.S. minority groups because immigration driven by neoliberal policies has formed such a large proportion of these populations.

In Chapter 2, I described Cold War displacements that vastly expanded the range of national origin, ethnicity, and class among Asian Americans and Latinxs. This chapter turns to the other major migrations that re-formed the Asian and Latinx United States: economic migrations. While communities displaced by the Cold War were arriving in the United States, the nation was constructing a new immigration system in line with a restructuring global economy. These parallel developments were not separate. Cold War imperatives to disseminate an image of U.S. racial equality and to ensure U.S. economic and technological superiority propelled reforms to abolish the discriminatory national origins system and draw in valuable immigrants.[6] The 1965 Hart-Cellar Act turned away from explicit racial preferences and codified the beginnings of a new immigration system based explicitly on economic utility to the nation. This emerging immigration criterion was developed more fully in the following decades as a neoliberal orthodoxy came to dominate economic thought, fashion immigration policies, and restructure world labor markets. The intertwining of immigration policy with the interests of the global economy has generated migrant categories ranging from millionaire investor visas to undocumented laborers. The stratification of migrant categories has cleaved not only the pan-ethnic categories Asian American and Latinx but also the many ethnic groups within those categories. Vastly different economic, legal, and material conditions pertain within the same ethnic communities.

How does one write against homogenizing stereotypes to represent Latinx and Asian American communities when these communities are so rapidly strati-fying that they seem to outrun any attempts at community representation? This chapter brings together two works that wrestle with this question in formally inventive ways. Chicano author Salvador Plascencia's *The People of Paper* and Indian American author Rishi Reddi's *Karma* are centrally concerned with the stereotypes framing ethnic communities and the stratifications dividing them. They employ related transfictional techniques of characterization that destabilize the distributions of discursive space and scramble the topographies of center and periphery organizing perceptions of an ethnic community. Convergent formal strategies in works sharing parallel concerns with stratification enable a revealing comparison between Indian and Mexican economic migrations, which are paradigmatic of Asian and Latin American labor flows under neoliberalism. *Karma* and *The People of Paper* focus on the most starkly opposed immigrant groups in American public perceptions. Indian Americans are stereotyped as paragons of professional immigrant success, while Mexican Americans are seen as the face of the illegal immigrant "underclass." Reddi and Plascencia's shared form for addressing stratification allows us to cut across the opposition of the two groups to bring out their linked challenges as communities caught within an interrelated neoliberal immigration system. The comparison opens a cross-regional and cross-class view of neoliberal labor migration. Studies that focus in isolation on Asian or Latin American migration to the United States cannot comprehend the linked roles of these mass labor flows in a restructured U.S. economy and a flexible global capitalism that thrives on stratified migration.

Read together, *Karma* and *The People of Paper* help us grasp shared challenges of stratification and human capital across the range of global labor migrations as well as the aesthetic problems these challenges generate for writers of ethnic community. Reddi's and Plascencia's works converge on the distribution of narrative discourse as a key area of intervention in depicting divided communities and navigating stereotype. This focus points to questions that ethnic studies has not explored in its long-standing engagement with stereotype: What are the formal mechanisms of stereotype? Might these mechanisms be as important as the content of stereotypes? Recognizing the representational "moves" of stereotyping changes our view of the techniques ethnic writers themselves use to deliver minority communities to the public. As this chapter describes, *Karma* confronts us with the insoluble difficulties of knowing and representing complex ethnic communities. *The People of Paper* questions ethnic literature's much-lauded impulse to give voice to marginalized communities. It shows how this impulse resonates with the formal mechanisms of stereotype, and it reveals the fraught politics of writing ethnic communities when stratification divides ethnic writers from the communities they write.

THE CHANGING WORTH OF IMMIGRANTS

The internal stratification of Asian American and Latinx communities results in large part from a contemporary immigration system differentiated according to neoliberal criteria of human worth. In the late twentieth and early twenty-first centuries, Aihwa Ong observes, "neoliberal criteria have come to dominate our norms of citizenship" and our assessments of prospective citizens.[7] The ideal immigrant is now the "value-added" elite subject who contributes to the nation's competitiveness in the globalized economy.[8] As Jeehyun Lim puts it, this is "an environment where an economic understanding of the value of racialized lives dominates."[9] Through targeted preferences and restrictions, the neoliberal immigration system invests in some immigrants while divesting from others "depending on their potential for GDP enhancement."[10]

The demand for Asian capital and elite workers played a central role in this transformation of immigration policy. As Madeline Y. Hsu has shown, U.S. corporations seeking Asian knowledge workers explicitly informed the legislation encoding human capital preferences.[11] In 1990, this lobbying effort resulted in the H1-B visa program, which offers work permits and pathways to residency for immigrants filling specialty occupations. Asian immigrants have dominated the H1-B program.[12] As many Asian economies became global powers in the late twentieth century, the United States sought to draw Asian capitalists as well. Congress created an investor visa that gives green cards to immigrants who bring $1 million in investments. The category brought to a culmination the neoliberal logic of the U.S. immigration system: human being and capital are conflated and citizenship has a quantifiable price. Immigration policies, Aihwa Ong concludes, have become strategies for the nation-state to accumulate capital and compete in the global economy.[13]

As the elite Asian immigrant became an ideal, a wave of undocumented Latin American immigrants also entered the United States. They too are framed by human capital metrics. Targeted recruitment reconstructed Asians from excluded aliens into model immigrants while Latinxs replaced Asians in the public imagination "as the chief immigration threat, . . . incorrigible lawbreakers illicitly crossing into America . . . to become drains on public resources."[14] The understanding of racial difference "in terms of differential economic contribution" has consolidated two key economized racial stereotypes of the neoliberal era of immigration: the Latinx "underclass" and the Asian "model minority."[15] Mexican Americans and Indian Americans are central to these stereotypes. The Indian American population is the Asian American ethnic group most completely constructed by neoliberal preferences. Numbering just 12,000 in 1960, this community has swelled by millions, most of whom came with college degrees under employer sponsorship and H1-B visas.[16] Not surprisingly, they are the U.S. ethnic group with the highest median income. Meanwhile, Mexicans numerically dominate migration from Latin America and are perceived as the ethnic face of the Latinx "underclass."

Representing Indian American and Mexican American communities today raises the challenge of writing against race-class stereotypes that inform immigration policy and obscure the stratification within these communities. The image of the Indian American model immigrant hides the growing mass of undocumented and struggling Indian immigrants, who number in the hundreds of thousands. The issue extends to other ethnic groups, as Asian migrants have become the fastest growing segment of undocumented immigrants.[17] This vulnerable population is invisible to many Americans. Similarly, the illegal underclass type conceals the significant portions of highly skilled migrants from Latin America who have entered the United States through legal channels.[18] Raúl Delgado-Wise calls for greater attention to the nearly quarter million Mexican immigrants who came from highly educated backgrounds.[19]

To grasp the material conditions of Latinx and Asian American communities in the twenty-first century entails grappling with the uneven legal and economic topographies in each of these communities. Latinx and Asian American immigrants index the ways that global capitalism and state immigration policies generate stark inequalities within economic migration. Flexibly organized companies thrive by dispersing production across differentiated tiers of workers around the world, taking advantage of the labor and legal landscapes in different sites. Meanwhile nation-states manage immigration to attract human capital and restrict supposed burdens in order to maximize their positions in the global economy. This complex matrix of state and capital regimes, Ong argues, assigns migrants "disparate forms of legal and labor conditions," "unequal life chances," and "different political fates" according to "their specific location in geographies of production and of administration."[20] These stratifications do not align neatly with existing lines of ethnic and racial difference; they overlay and intersect with those lines so that divisions of life chances proliferate within and between ethnic communities. Contemporary projects of economic justice for Latinx and Asian American migrants must survey this stratified terrain.

TRANSPOSITIONS OF INDIAN AMERICAN COMMUNITY

Rishi Reddi's *Karma* exposes the inequalities within an Indian American community in the greater Boston area. Each of its seven stories focuses on a different individual in the community. The story cycle's juxtaposition of distinct lives and stories registers the differences of class, gender, immigration category, and generation that cleave the community. These inequalities are central themes of *Karma* and also shape its formal choices of narrative attention and characterization.

In interviews, Reddi shows a keen awareness of the class and gender divisions within her community. And she is sensitive to the stakes of her own representation as she focuses on a little-known segment, the Telugu-speaking population. "Very few non-Indians that I knew in the United States had ever heard of the language," she observes.[21] Her portrayal acknowledges the community's divisions and alludes to the neoliberal immigration systems that inform them. In light of this, her choices of narrative attention are striking. Rather than focusing her stories on the male professionals who are highly valued by the U.S. labor market, she is drawn to less visible and less valued figures. The story "Bangles" considers an elderly woman who emigrates to live with her son, a wealthy doctor, only to realize her utter dependency in this new country. And the story "Karma" focuses on Shankar Balareddy, who is searching for work after failing as a taxi driver and convenience store clerk. The story foregrounds a precarious working class incompatible with the image of the model immigrant community.

We might be wary of such an inversion of attention from the powerful to the disadvantaged, which could solidify an alternate but equally one-sided image of Indian Americans. But what's fascinating is how this story cycle's transfictional form keeps the community portrait from settling into any fixed image or perspective. Reddi draws character links across distinct stories, inviting readers to compare divergent views of the community from different social positions. She juxtaposes distinct distributions of narrative attention in the various stories to destabilize hierarchies of major and minor characters, and in turn our sense of the community's social topography. Sustained formal tensions of major and minor, center and periphery keep this portrait of a community as unsettled and dynamic as the community itself. As Rajini Srikanth observes, South Asian American writing disrupts the "grammar of expectancy" readers bring to depictions of South Asian American communities by confronting them "with a complex landscape of indeterminate unpredictability."[22] Reddi's story cycle exemplifies this tradition. It richly develops a formal grammar of *un*-expectancy that shakes up our views.

Driving *Karma*'s dynamic instability is a transfictional technique, the *minor-major transposition*. The independent yet linked structure of the transfictional story cycle allows for a minor character in one story to reappear as a major character in a separate story and vice versa. This move can disturb the conventions of narrative organization. A large swath of narrative theory sees unequal distributions of attention as the normative arrangements of narrative elements. With character, we distinguish between major and minor, "round" and "flat," and this unequal arrangement almost always persists.[23] Stories arrange events hierarchically between plots and subplots, "nuclei" and "catalysers," "kernels" and "satellites."[24] They differentially weight settings as well as periods of time.[25]

Narrative "resources" like attention and focalization tend to concentrate in certain centers more than others, and this hierarchical distribution feels more stable, even more "natural" than a decentralized one.[26]

An example of the transposition occurs with the character of Lakshmi Chundi. Lakshmi is the protagonist and primary focalizer in "Lakshmi and the Librarian," whereas in "The Validity of Love" she is a minor character, appearing for barely half a page. Lakshmi's transposition raises formal questions of character position as the stories unfold a character who occupies a vulnerable legal and social position. "Lakshmi and the Librarian" introduces her as a first-generation immigrant woman married to a successful computer engineer. She is a dedicated homemaker who has maintained her traditions and has always done "what every good wife should do" (33). But she is also troubled by doubts about her path in life, the constrained role of the Indian mother and wife. With her sons gone off to prestigious colleges and careers and her husband indifferent, Lakshmi feels isolated. Her isolation alludes to a large proportion of Indian immigrant women obscured by the stereotype of the male tech migrant. As U.S. immigration policy welcomes Indian professional men, it issues a different status to their spouses, who are often highly educated themselves. Behind the H1-B visa is the little-known H4 spousal visa, which restricts its holders from working and solidifies an "economic and legal dependency" on their husbands.[27] The H4 category limits the freedoms of these women to work outside the home and get a divorce. It reinforces a gendered public-private divide and engineers power differences that overlay existing gender inequalities in Indian communities. The disparate rights afforded by the H1-B and H4 visas reflect unequal valuations under neoliberal immigration. Married Indian women are not seen as productive contributors but as the human baggage that comes with recruiting professional men. As Wendy Brown observes, neoliberal valuations cannot acknowledge that women are disproportionately the "invisible infrastructure sustaining a world of putatively self-investing human capitals."[28]

Lakshmi finds some relief from her domestic isolation at the local library where she is friends with the librarian, Elias. The story turns on their sudden intimacy when he falls ill. When Lakshmi calls on him one afternoon she realizes that she's able to open up to him in a way that she can't remember doing with her husband. Her traditions would chastise such freedom with another man, but Lakshmi comes to an epiphany in his company: "she has lived her life always seeking convenience, traveling the safe middle road . . . adjusting herself to every circumstance, challenging nothing and no one, not her traditions, not her husband, not herself" (58). She kisses Elias in a moment of resolve to overcome her fears and challenge the constraints of her position. It's not an affair, but Lakshmi knows she will be judged by her tight-knit community. She commits to facing this judgment.

It's with the weight of all this that Lakshmi appears again as a minor character in the next story. "The Validity of Love" develops parallel themes, centering on Lata, a second-generation Indian American woman who also feels bound by gendered restrictions and the institution of marriage. The story follows Lata and her best friend, Supriya, as they contend with arranged marriages. Lata's parents pressure her to accept a marriage with a bachelor "who was much sought after because he'd placed in an excellent residency program for ophthalmology, which, as everyone knew, was a very lucrative specialty" (72–73). Meanwhile, Lata conceals a long relationship with a white boyfriend. While Lakshmi's story alludes to the ways neoliberal valuations penetrate married life, Lata's story shows how such calculations influence the arrangement of marriages. These values clearly emerge when Supriya's mother lectures Lata about the wisdom of arranged marriage: "Don't you know that all the rich corporate families in America . . . get married like this only?" (81). Supriya also faces an arranged marriage. The two are allies, commiserating over their community's constrictions on young women. But despite her initial reservations, Supriya walks happily into the marriage. Lata feels betrayed, and when she attends Supriya's engagement party, she feels out of place. Reddi captures her rebellion against the proceedings in a contrast between her short haircut and the long sweep of her traditional dress. It's then that she runs into her mother's friend, Lakshmi:

> "So, what do you think of all this, Lata?" Lakshmi Auntie said after giving me a hug. I felt her eyes sweep over my new haircut, but there was no judgment. If anything, she seemed a bit contemplative in the midst of the festivities. "Supriya looks beautiful doesn't she?" she said. . . . "Perhaps soon we will see you up there also. But don't rush, Lata. There is no hurry." (90)

Coming from the previous story, it's difficult to read this passage without sensing how Lakshmi's interiority has been compressed into a tiny character-space. The compression of the full, conflicted person into a few lines charges each detail of this encounter. How can we not read into Lakshmi's acceptance of Lata's hair some of the nagging desire to break with tradition that pulled at her own story? How can we not see in her contemplative mood and her advice to Lata not to rush into marriage her own reservations about passing up the "greatness of life" (33)? As Alex Woloch notes, readers can always construct patterns of attention against the grain of a story's established pattern.[29] But the transposition primes readers to do so in a targeted way. The juxtaposition of major and minor narrative positions in the two stories invites us to make far more of this minor character than the story itself does. Woloch proposes that each minor character incompletely inflected into a narrative has "an orienting consciousness that, like the protagonist's own consciousness, could potentially organize an entire fictional universe."[30] Woloch's model is the nineteenth-century novel. The difference of the transfictional story cycle here is that minor characters do not "potentially organize an entire fictional universe"; rather, they actually do so in separate stories of their own.[31] Henry James argues that a writer's material exhibits a "space-hunger," an "expansive" desire for full expression that struggles against settled form.[32] *Karma*'s structure lets loose this latent instability and disturbs the foundational narrative distinctions between the major and the minor. With transpositions, a minor character points to another distinct story and a different view of the community that would center that character instead. This shift complicates the claim of the protagonist to central attention. When reading "The Validity of Love," we don't lose involvement with Lata when we encounter Lakshmi, but if our attention had been fixed and singularly focused, it becomes contingent and divided. The current pattern of attention hovers against other patterns of attention, ones already encountered and ones yet to be realized.

Of course, many classic Asian American as well as Latinx story cycles of community feature character recurrences flipping minor and major roles. Think of Tomás Rivera's . . . *y no se lo tragó la tierra* (1971), Toshio Mori's *Yokohama, California* (1949), or Rolando Hinojosa's *Estampas del valle* (1973). What distinguishes Reddi's transpositions from this tradition is how their alternative hierarchies of characters highlight the social hierarchies in the community and the moment she depicts. Reddi, and Plascencia too, as we'll see, use transpositions to construct community portraits emphasizing social and economic stratifications. Classic story cycles like Rivera's, Mori's, and Hinojosa's, in contrast, portray communities that are more economically homogeneous. Their depictions of working-class ethnic communities deploy character recurrences not to stress the stratifications between parts of the community but to trace the social ties that link a community.

The key effect of Reddi's transpositions is to make contingent the fixed and unequal distribution of attention in a narrative work. This technique has important implications in a work so attuned to the challenges of stratification and stereotype on community portraits. To understand these implications, we'll need to consider the form of stereotyping, in particular how the unequal positioning of characters is central to the workings of stereotypes.

THE FORM OF STEREOTYPING

Ethnic studies has paid extensive attention to stereotypes, emphasizing the struggle with their content and their contexts of production. I point to a new area of focus that is equally important: the form of stereotyping. We should examine how stereotypes work as discursive structures, how they might be reinforced by patterns in narrative representation. These formal questions point to an underexamined site where minority authors can intervene. At the same time, interventions targeting stereotyping's forms must take into account strategies focused on content and context; stereotyping is multifaceted, and these other strategies have insights to offer as we assess works like *Karma*.

One central strategy has been to counter stereotypes with more realistic and positive images. While crucial to the history of minority cultures, this approach is limited by its focus on reversing content. As Kwame Anthony Appiah explains, revaluing a stereotyped identity into a positive one through which to be recognized is necessary in certain moments of political organizing. But these rewritten identities can introduce restrictive boundaries on who belongs in the community.[33] Many critics in Asian American studies critique an earlier cultural nationalist period for reversing anti-Asian stereotypes through a strongly defined masculine Asian American identity.[34] This problem also arose in Chicano cultural nationalism.[35] Norma Alarcón recalls that there was "a quest for a true self and identity" driving writers in the Chicano movement.[36] This quest resulted in what Renato Rosaldo describes as a "self-enclosed, patriarchal, 'authentic' Chicano culture."[37] Many counterstereotyping efforts effectively produce their own stereotypes, reversing the negative content of a stereotype while leaving its form, its structure of prescriptive oppositions, unchanged. As Tina Chen contends, "stereotyp-ing is, by nature, oppositional," so contesting stereotype "requires more than counteracting it with antithetical representations."[38] It requires engaging with the form of stereotyping.

Another important strategy focuses on satirizing the contexts in which stereotypes are produced. Consider the parallel concerns of Luis Valdez's 1986 play *I Don't Have to Show You No Stinking Badges* and Philip Kan Gotanda's nearly contemporaneous play *Yankee Dawg You Die* (from 1988). Focusing respectively on Latinx and Asian American actors, these comic plays expose the stereotyped constrictions on minority actors in Hollywood. Such efforts stress the importance of the culture industry power relations behind the circulation of stereotypes, a concern that we'll see echoed in Salvador Plascencia's critique of the ethnic literary industry. A third family of strategies has focused on de-constructing stereotypes and revealing their artifice. Scholars such as Juan J. Alonzo, Tina Chen, and Karen Christian have shown how reappropriation, impersonation, camp, and drag undermine the stability of fixed images of ethnic identity.[39] Contextual and deconstructive approaches, though, have their limits. They help to destabilize existing stereotypes, but they do not fill the continuing need for more nuanced representations and understandings of ethnic communities. To address this need in rigorous ways requires wrestling with the powerful form of stereotyping.

Analyzing stereotypes as formal constructions is important because it runs against a fundamental process in stereotyping: naturalization. The capacity to construct social difference while disguising this construction is one of the conundrums of stereotyping. "The recognition of difference is thereby made in-nocent," Michael Pickering observes, "as if what we see and know in the stereo-typical representation is what is simply visible and palpable."[40] Stereotypes slide representation into reality. Edward Said notes that much Orientalist discourse betrays a form of "radical realism"; it uses a "declarative and self-evident" language in which the "copula *is*" is sufficient to designate truths about the Orient.[41] This grammar reminds us that the transparency of stereotyping's signification is linked with a pellucid ontology. "They" can be so readily represented and known because they are so knowable: simple, static. Naturalizing is a process of fixing. As Homi K. Bhabha explains, it's not stereotyping's falseness that makes it a simplification, it's the way it arrests representation.[42]

Among the formal mechanisms that allow stereotypes to naturalize their representations, the relation between stereotyping and characterization is particularly intriguing. We can sense the interplay of the two in the category of the type character. Type characters share much with stereotypes—reductive flatness, conflation with a social group, recognizability—but little has been made of this relationship.[43] Alex Woloch's theory of character-space provides a way to understand how typification becomes naturalized. Woloch theorizes two processes that construct a character's flatness: compression and externality. Compression describes how the narrative abstracts a characteristic from the character, which in turn subsumes the person. Compression helps fit an individual into a delimited space in the discourse.[44] Slotting the character into a socially shared type or stereotype helps facilitate this process. Compression is often reinforced by externality. Flat characters come across as flat in part because they are usually the narrated rather than the narrating, the focalized, not the focalizing. That their exteriors are all we are given contributes to our sense that they are no more than their exteriors.[45] It's not much of a leap from here to the structures of stereotyping. I'm reminded of Frantz Fanon's account of being confronted with "the fact" of his blackness. "I am overdetermined from without," he realizes. "My blackness was there, dark and unarguable."[46] In racist epistemologies, externality is paramount. Stereotypes often unfold through compression and externality. They are usually expressed from an external point of view, and they draw out characteristics that delimit the representation of a minority group. Think of how often stereotypes arise when minority individuals appear as minor characters in stories told from the perspective of the racial dominant.[47]

Compression and externality are powerful formal processes for stereotyping because they compel our perceptions of certain characters as types while covering their own workings. Woloch describes a naturalizing slide. The "descriptive distortions" to which minor characters are subject, which result from their positioning on the narrative margins, seem to emanate from the nature of the characters themselves. The "representational tactics," Woloch observes, "seem justified by the character being depicted."[48] This naturalization makes it seem that the way an individual is represented is justified by the reality of that individual. In narrative representation however the "reality" of a character is a reality effect emerging from the interaction of the reader with the presentation

of that character in the discourse. So what appears to be representation justified by reality is a more complex, self-reinforcing system in which the treatment of a character in the narrative discourse constructs a reality effect of
that character which—and this is the key move—circles back to justify the
discursive treatment of the character in the first place. The naturalizing trick
is for the character effect to come across not as an effect of representation but
as the cause. This inversion is precisely the ideological efficiency of stereotypes,
which veil their distorted constructions of others as a direct apprehension of
"how they really are."

My point is not that the naturalizing capacities of characterization are
inherently stereotyping.[49] Stereotyping is not simply a form (though I have
been training attention on this understudied aspect); forms of characterization
are part of broader struggles over minority images in specific configurations
of power and voice. I am advocating that, as part of wrestling with stereotype,
we need to be aware of the ways its workings converge with fundamental
techniques of narrative characterization. If minority writers are to write against
stereotype without reproducing its forms, these narrative mechanisms are key
areas for intervention.

THE SHIFTING TOPOGRAPHIES OF ASIAN AMERICA

With an understanding of the formal mechanisms of stereotyping, we can
grasp the full significance of Reddi's aesthetics of transposition. *Karma* presents
a transfictional panorama in which distinct stories of the same social world offer
transposed arrangements of characters and divergent perspectives on an ethnic
community. This structure attempts to undo the formal strategies of stereotype
and develop other modes of representing ethnic communities that can recognize
the stratifications they experience under neoliberal immigration. The instability
of major and minor character positions denaturalizes the narrative mechanisms
that stereotyping employs. In transpositions like Lakshmi's, minor characters do
not remain stably compressed or externalized. They oscillate between being marginal and central in different stories. The character recurrences encourage readers
to read transfictionally across the stories and their conflicting arrangements of
characters. This reading experience highlights how characters are positioned
and stresses how powerfully such positioning changes and distorts our sense
of the characters and their places in the community. By highlighting character

positioning and distributions of narrative elements as generating our sense of the "reality" of characters, transposition aesthetics marks a crucial reversal of stereotyping's naturalizations, in which the discursive treatment of minority figures seems to follow from their nature. With multiple arrangements of its characters juxtaposed, *Karma* insists on the many ways minority communities can be described. *Karma* argues through its form that there is no natural point of view on ethnic community.

Reddi, of course, has her own angle on this community. She tends to devote attention to characters marginalized from the neoliberal economy. But she does not present the marginalized as a homogeneous bloc, which would constitute its own stereotype inadequate to grasping the intricate variations of neoliberalism's impacts on community members. Instead, through its transpositions of competing views, *Karma* invites comparison of different characters' positions to grasp the unexpected ways in which people are positioned by stratifications of legal status, economic power, and life chances. This is most evident between the stories "Bangles" and "Karma," back-to-back stories that look at people in opposed positions only to reveal their surprising resonances. "Bangles" focuses on Arundhati, a widow who has come to the United States to live with her son's family. Arundhati finds herself economically dependent and ill-equipped to adapt to a new country. The story also reveals her place in family hierarchies. As a mother and caretaker, she realizes that she has sacrificed her life's ambitions and labor for the good of her son. In each generation of her family, the privileged son—first her brother, then her son, now her grandson—has loomed over the women and other children.

In an intriguing move, the next story, "Karma," centers on a privileged son, Shankar. Reddi motivates a comparison of the two stories with a transposition. Connecting the stories is Prakash who, like Arundhati, lived in the shadow of the privileged son in the family, in this case his older brother Shankar. In "Bangles" Prakash appears as a minor character, while in "Karma" he takes on a major role. With a thematically specific transposition, Reddi guides readers to compare the hierarchies within Indian families across these stories. But having established this link, Reddi complicates things. In "Karma" it's the younger brother Prakash who makes it to the United States as a skilled professional, and he sponsors Shankar to immigrate. Shankar arrives with few prospects, cycles through low-wage jobs, and lives with his brother. But "the home was not

entirely traditional—Prakash was the head of the household although Shankar
was the older brother. Prakash owned the house and the car, and had a lucrative
career" (129). The tension between the brothers comes to a head when Prakash
decides to kick Shankar out of the house. Shankar realizes later that he is cast
aside because he is a liability to Prakash's career advancement. The familial
hierarchies propping up the privileged son are upended in this story when they
meet the distinct hierarchy of human capital in the United States. Is Shankar
the privileged villain in this story, or is Prakash? Reddi offers no easy answers.
Instead she dwells on how Indian Americans navigate the uncharted terrain
when divergent hierarchies intersect in new combinations.

The transposition here is a formal strategy motivating the comparison of
stories that depict the Indian American community with different hierarchies
of characters and from opposed social positions. The resulting image of the
community does not reinforce this opposition. It reveals instead the layer-
ing of distinct social hierarchies that complicate any facile understandings of
centrality and marginalization. From "Bangles" to "Karma," readers shift from
a woman's view of the inequalities tilted toward privileged sons to a privileged
son's experience of being displaced from economic and familial power. Breaking
open the type figure of the privileged son, the linked stories reveal Arundhati
and Shankar to share more than we expect. When gendered familial structures,
immigration categories, and economic hierarchies intersect, they produce com-
plexly differentiated life chances across a community. Reddi's shaping of this
social content highlights the importance of a representational form that does
not take particular hierarchies of character and social position for granted but
submits these hierarchies to dynamic upending and comparison.

Many Asian Americans today navigate a shifting economic geography and
stratified immigration system in ways that defy traditional mappings of ethnic
marginalization and immigrant disadvantage. The terms "oppression," "marginalization," and "resistance," Kandice Chuh notes, need to be redefined in a transnational context where they take on new forms and scattered articulations.[50]
Karma traces the shifting social topographies with an aesthetics of transposition,
which invites readers to question the given hierarchies of an ethnic community
by linking divergent renderings of the community. To grasp the many layers
of class, legal status, and social position within Asian American immigration,
we must move beyond fixed hierarchies of attention and established mappings

of community. And we must investigate how any particular view of ethnic community comes to seem a representative one, whether it's established by stereotypes or put forward by ethnic writers themselves.[51] As transpositions spread across Reddi's story cycle, any single story of this community is unsettled by other stories (and potential stories) that invert our views of the community and our sense of which figures should be central in our perceptions. In an era of neoliberal stratification that has witnessed rising economic power for a substantial echelon of Asian migrants, Asian America can no longer be seen in any simple way as a marginal site. Urgent economic inequalities are increasingly manifesting not against Asian Americans as a whole but within this community. In this moment, the transposition aesthetics Reddi develops is a much-needed tactic for mapping the intricate divisions striating the terrain formerly known as the Asian American margins.

WAR OVER NARRATIVE DISCOURSE IN *THE PEOPLE OF PAPER*

Karma's strategies and the formal mechanisms that power stereotypes reveal that the distribution of narrative discourse, as it intersects with social topographies, is a crucial point of contention in representing stratified ethnic communities. I turn now to a novel contemporaneous to *Karma* that takes the idea of narrative discourse as a site of conflict further than any other work in recent memory. Salvador Plascencia's *The People of Paper* wrestles with the fraught politics of constructing communities out of paper and on paper. The community it depicts includes Mexican American undocumented immigrants, farmworkers, and gang members. These are groups subjected to longstanding stereotypes, which continue to inform U.S. policies including immigration restrictions, detentions, policing, militarization of the border, and the denial of civil liberties. Stereotypes of Latinxs are an abiding concern for Plascencia. In interviews he explains that he was writing within and against the perceptions of Latinxs and of his community of El Monte, a majority Latinx city east of Los Angeles. He explains:

> I remember the first book I read about El Monte, the James Ellroy book [*My Dark Places: An L.A. Crime Memoir*], which completely criminalizes El Monte. . . . Growing up, I loved my neighborhood, I loved my friends, I loved the community, and in a way I wanted to pay tribute to that, to El Monte. . . . [El Monte] was on *Cops* a lot, . . . but that wasn't *my* El Monte.[52]

With this novel, he sought to "play on the stereotypical conception of gangsters, of Chicano youth—or Latinos in general—being in gangs" and to insist that the lives of people in this community "exist beyond stereotypes."[53] Plascencia admits that he's not exempt from the attraction of stereotypes but he insists, "I wanted to complicate it somehow, to make it more parody and operate more . . . in an intergalactic way."[54] For those not familiar with this magical book, this last phrase should give ample warning that he writes against Latinx stereotypes in no ordinary way. *The People of Paper* follows a resistance movement of farmworkers struggling against exploitation. This seems a familiar trope of Chicanx literature except the oppressor here is not U.S. capitalists. It's a planet. The planet Saturn they believe is peering down into their private lives and controlling their fates. Saturn, it turns out, is the omniscient narrator and author of the novel in which they are characters. And they are fighting his narratorial tyranny. If its agricultural context suggests a war over the means of production, *The People of Paper* concerns a war over the means of representation. Saturn and the community fight over the narrative capital of space, voice, and position.

Like *Karma*, *The People of Paper* unsettles narrative hierarchies of major and minor to destabilize fixed representations. But *The People of Paper* makes the struggle over narrative discourse literal in a visible war on the page. It situates itself within a tradition stretching from Lawrence Sterne's *Tristram Shandy* to Mark Z. Danielewski's *The House of Leaves*, novels that experiment with typography and design.[55] The battlefield on which this war is fought is arrayed as three-column, two-page spreads. On the left-hand page is a column of text in which Saturn narrates the story from an omniscient, heterodiegetic position. There are two columns on the right-hand page; the middle is where Little Merced, one of the main characters, narrates, and the rightmost column shows the narrations of rotating members of the community. As the war heats up, this distribution of space is contested.

The parties in the war include a diverse cast of characters from Mexico to the United States in the era of NAFTA, when economic inequalities are intensifying. If *Karma* writes against a model immigrant type that covers over the inequalities in the Indian American community, a related challenge faces representations of Mexican Americans from the opposite end of the economic spectrum: How does one depict communities with growing middle-class strata in the face of a pervasive image of the "illegal immigrant underclass"? Plascencia registers these cleavages. Many of the figures in the resistance movement are farmworkers. The leaders of the resistance include Federico de la Fe and his daughter Little Merced who struggle to find work in the United States because they lack green cards. But the novel is also concerned with those who leave working-class Mexican communities to find professional success, including a fictional reworking of Rita Hayworth, who in this incarnation came from a family of Mexican farmworkers but deracinated herself to become a star. Most intriguing is a metafictional twist that places the novel's position in the literary marketplace within the mapping of inequality. Saturn's real name, we discover, is Salvador Plascencia. Beyond hierarchies of major and minor in the narrative, *The People of Paper* draws our attention to the divisions between author and represented community. As Jennifer Harford Vargas observes, the novel highlights the relations of power in literary production and the literary marketplace.[56] The ethnic author's position is charged in a moment when Mexican American communities are stratifying and part of the upwardly mobile stratum are writers embraced by the marketplace for multicultural literature.

The resistance confronts the ethnic author, challenging his control of the plot and of the three-column battlefield. The members of El Monte Flores (EMF), the gang that leads the war, contest the fixed structure of columns: "EMF's strategy was to envelop Saturn, to surround him, forcing him to concede territory" (210). And indeed, on a spread across pages 210 and 211, we see blocks of text in the voices of community members starting to marshal on the right-hand page. On the next page, they make their move. For the first time, one of EMF's blocks of narration infiltrates Saturn's narrative space on the left-hand page, diminishing the territory Saturn has to narrate. The intrepid invader is Froggy, one of EMF's commanders. Froggy declares, "We were forceful, imposing our presence where it had never been before" (212). Treating discourse as territory that must be won through force, the resistance's struggles make palpable the idea that distributions of discourse are the results of power and sites of contestation. This view forcefully denaturalizes the stable distributions of discursive space that enable stereotyping and calls attention to the unequal representations that ethnic writers themselves might put forth.

As the characters gain the upper hand and break up the strict three-column arrangement, Froggy asserts, "It is an affront . . . to limit us, to relegate us to strict columns and force us to act in one story" (232). The limit that he feels the one story imposes upon the many is a form of the transfictional tension between unified narrative and multiple autonomous stories. The independent stories and voices of the many characters in this novel challenge the unity of the author-controlled narrative. At the height of their revolt, the characters push Saturn into a mere corner of the narrative, leaving him with space for only a single line of narration. Meanwhile, the rest of the narrative space is fragmented among divergent plot lines. The two-page spreads become riotous cacophonies as the stories of minor characters proliferate. A mechanic and a wrestler whose paths the protagonists cross early in the novel return once Saturn's hold on the narration crumbles. Such stories have little to do with the novel's central plot. As narrative control and unity wane, transfictional autonomy waxes. One could even say that the characters are fighting to reshape this novel as a transfictional form, in which their distinct life stories can be independent rather than caus-ally intertwined and forced "to act in one story." As Froggy notes, "our voices bloomed everywhere, like wild unfurrowed flowers" (212). While *Karma* of-fers select transpositions that each open an independent story for a character marginalized within another story, *The People of Paper* at the height of the war effectively offers independent stories to all its characters at once. The exuberant chaos that ensues reveals the destabilizing force of the many narratives contained within any one story of ethnic community. Exploding homogeneous images of ethnic community, the novel's transfictional autonomy insists that to grasp this community requires dealing with a wild proliferation of stories.

For the Chicanx community depicted in the novel, this is a war for control over their lives and representations. "It is a war against the fate that has been decided for us," says Federico de la Fe (53). To illustrate what he means, Federico puts up a map of their battle position, which comically turns out to be a plot diagram of rising and falling action. He warns, "We are being pushed in this direction. Saturn wants to move us into the peaks and then into denouement. And we must stop before our lives are destroyed" (43). Now on some level, the struggles of this community are absurd, dismissible as a rehearsal of post-modern metafiction. But I submit that the metafictional play makes possible an important thought experiment. It asks, what if we took seriously the idea that representations of people had wills of their own, that they have claims to their own lives? What issues of exploitation, commodification, control, and consent would we have to grapple with? Instead of exposing fiction as mere artifice, the metafictional turn of the novel insists on the real stakes of narrative representation for Latinx communities. Stereotypes and stories contribute to the U.S. racial imaginaries that have violent impacts on their lives. Immigrants are forced into life-threatening desert crossings by a militarized border defending against a "foreign invasion." Latino teenagers are profiled and brutalized by the police. The form and metafictional gambits of *The People of Paper* constitute a polemic that once these stakes are taken seriously, the way we tell stories cannot remain the same.

No doubt, taking the politics of representations this seriously has risks. Jodi Melamed and others have powerfully critiqued a multicultural-era focus on representation and culture for distracting from the redistribution politics urgently needed.[57] While acknowledging these critiques, my argument shows the specific ways that struggles of representation and redistribution are intertwined rather than opposed. Redistributive politics needs a representational politics that can change perceptions of ethnic communities to reveal the stratifications within them. So long as we operate with undifferentiated types of the Indian professional immigrant or the Mexican undocumented "underclass," materially vulnerable Indian Americans and class conflicts among Mexican Americans will go unaddressed. Against Melamed's critique of "aestheticizing race issues,"[58] I argue that aesthetic structures can be important sites of intervention. The aesthetic strategies we see in *Karma* and *The People of Paper* are attempts to transform stereotyping modes of representation and settled distributions of discourse to produce portraits highlighting the uneven landscapes of material struggles.

THE INTERTWINING OF ASIA AND LATIN AMERICA IN NEOLIBERAL MIGRATION

Throughout this book, I've argued that tracing socially engaged formal strategies across distinct contexts can reveal broader landscapes of struggle. In Chapter 2, shared forms across Dominican and Vietnamese contexts allowed an interconnected mapping of the U.S. Cold War order. Here it reveals the global scope of neoliberal immigration. Brought together through formal strategies that scramble narrative hierarchies and highlight stratification, *Karma* and *The People of Paper* describe the complex terrain of inequality across Asian American and Latinx populations. This comparison connects the separate conversations on neoliberal migration in Asian American studies and Latinx and Latin American studies to offer a cross-regional and cross-class perspective. Within the migrations from these regions, India and Mexico are especially important; they are today the two countries sending the most international migrants. Though these migrations seem opposite in many ways, our comparison reveals two key insights about their places in an intertwined neoliberal migrant labor system.

First, viewing Reddi's Indian software engineers and Plascencia's undocumented Mexican migrants within the same vision of labor migration allows a more complete view that connects neoliberalism's governing of immigration policies in receiving nations to its effects on the economic conditions of sending nations. At the same time that neoliberal preferences have recruited elite Asian workers to the United States, neoliberal restructuring in Latin America has displaced a valuable and geographically proximate working-class labor force to the United States. Neoliberal globalization and adjustments have devastated Latin America. With the goal of spurring development, the U.S. government, the International Monetary Fund, and the World Bank coerced Latin American nations to lower trade barriers, slash taxes, dismantle the welfare state, deregulate the flow of capital, privatize public assets, and suppress unions.[59] The result was widespread economic crisis and unemployment.[60] Meanwhile U.S. and other foreign capitalists have taken advantage of debt crises and privatizations to acquire Latin American public assets at fire sale prices. Latin America now is the region transferring the most wealth to the financial centers of the global North, with Mexican transfers to the United States the most prominent.[61] The fallout from neoliberal restructuring has induced mass migrations, much of it to the United States. Emigrants from Latin America quintupled from 1980 to 2010. Raúl Delgado-Wise rightly classifies this migration as a "compulsive displacement" as people are forced to "sell their labor" abroad.[62] These displacements have produced an exploitable pool of migrant labor central to the U.S. economy and a restructured global economy.[63] Such vulnerable migrants are a key "reserve army" of cheap labor integrated into globally dispersed production chains.[64] The U.S. economy, itself transformed by neoliberal globalization, is now dependent on this displaced Latinx labor force to fill the bottom of a bifurcated labor market.

The neoliberal period has seen U.S. capital extracting wealth from Latin American nations through economic restructuring while taking advantage of the undocumented labor that restructuring displaces into the United States. This strategy has been less common in Asia because of the rising economic power of many Asian nations. With Asian nations, the United States has adapted a complementary strategy for extracting wealth. While the neoliberal categories of U.S. immigration deny rights to lower-class Latin American migrants to slot them into low-wage sectors, they welcome elite Asian capital and talent to fill the higher tiers of a bifurcated economy. Asian American studies has emphasized neoliberal immigration policy and elite economic migrants while Latinx and Latin American studies has stressed neoliberal adjustments and impoverished migrants. By attending across Asian and Latin American economic migrations, however, we can see these two forms of neoliberal policy as adapted strategies to extract wealth from regions of the world with varying economic power and to draw profitable labor flows into complementary roles in the U.S. economy. These seemingly separate and opposite labor migrations are part of flexible strategies in an integrated neoliberal project to concentrate human and actual capital in U.S. financial centers.

Reading Reddi's and Plascencia's works together reveals a second key insight, that the race-class types of the Asian elite migrant and the Latinx "underclass" are more intertwined than opposed. Recall how in *Karma* transpositions motivate comparison of opposed social positions to unveil the surprising resonances between them. A similar comparison of opposed race-class types in these works shows how they overlap and blur. By neoliberal standards, who are the "contributors" and who are the "burdens" across these portraits of Indian and Mexican American communities? The stereotype of the Latinx underclass suggests the burden would appear among the Chicanxs of El Monte, but the only potential burden to the state across these works is Shankar in the title story of *Karma*. It's a member of the model immigrant community who spends much of his story trying to apply for unemployment benefits, not the Chicanx farmworkers. Shankar arrived under the sponsorship of his brother, one of the Indian professionals coveted by immigration preferences. With this direct relation to professional migration, Shankar immigrates legally and can draw state benefits even when he is not working.

Reddi foregrounds the "underclass" existing within the paradigmatic model immigrant community. She focuses on many unemployed Indian American characters, but these portraits do not reinforce the burdensome underclass type.

In "Karma," Shankar cooks the meals in his brother's household. Lakshmi's and Arundhati's stories show the sacrifices of female homemakers and caretakers who nurture male professionals. *Karma* looks beyond neoliberalism's individualist view and distinctions of value to acknowledge the kinds of labor and communal support that have no valuation in the neoliberal model and yet are essential for the professional workers it values. All these characters enter the United States through family migration or spousal visas; by the standards of neoliberal immigration, they are the human baggage that come with recruiting immigrant workers. But Reddi's attention to multiple realms of labor shows that calculations of human capital cannot account for the full lives of the workers the nation wants. Reddi redistributes narrative attention to an "underclass" within the model immigrant community and transfigures the "underclass" image into unacknowledged but essential care laborers. The "underclass," then, is not a noncontributing figure but rather the fault line between the kinds of contributions the neoliberal economy recognizes and those it disavows.

If Reddi's portrait shows how the model immigrant category obscures an "underclass" doing unacknowledged but essential labor, setting it alongside Plascencia's El Monte reveals the undocumented "underclass" as model immigrant workers essential to the nation. Plascencia describes the crucial roles these workers play in California's flower industry. He introduces them as bearing knives in hands that are full of "splinters and calluses from tilling the land." "It was from these blades and hands that bouquets and potpourri came," he observes (34). Contemporary immigration policies have opened to professional migration from Asia while drastically restricting legal migration from Latin America. Framed as an "underclass" burden and restricted from entering, lower-class Mexican migrants are pushed into illegal immigration. As William I. Robinson notes, immigration restrictions do not stop undocumented migrants from coming so much as ensure that they arrive as a pool of labor without rights.[65] Unable to claim many state benefits and lacking economic power, they must work cheaply under exploitive conditions, with the profits redounding to U.S. capital and consumers. The racialized stereotype of the "underclass" migrant obscures the reality that undocumented workers contribute enormous value to the U.S. economy yet are unable to be a burden on the state. In the comparative perspective of Indian and Mexican American labor, the categories of the model immigrant and the underclass are more intricately intertwined than they appear.

The poles of the model immigrant and underclass cannot sustain their distinctions because the state recruits and gains value from across the different strata of immigrants. Reddi's and Plascencia's complication of the categories of neoliberal immigration make clear that human capital differentiations are not about recruiting the higher tier of immigrants alone. Rather than a system to differentiate those we want to let in from those we want to keep out, the neoliberal hierarchy of more and less deserving immigrants is a system for producing the differentiated immigrant labor forces our economy requires, from high-tech workers to care workers doing reproductive labor to cheap undocumented labor. The hierarchy rationalizes and enacts divergent allocations of legal statuses, economic conditions, and life chances to different immigrant populations to slot them into the labor needs of a bifurcated, globalized economy. To address the range of economic injustices endemic in this migrant labor system, injustices that cut within and across ethnic communities, we need representational means and comparative methods to grasp the differentiated ways that the nation profits from immigrants.

THE LIMIT AND NECESSITY OF REPRESENTING ETHNIC COMMUNITIES

The labor of racialized immigrants has produced enormous value for the United States and global economies, but so too have their stories and images. *The People of Paper* is deeply self-conscious of the economic hierarchies that structure the commercial traffic in ethnic representations. As Jennifer Harford Vargas argues, it foregrounds the fraught position of the ethnic minority author who profits off the stories of his community.[66] The unequal class positions of the author and his community are the direct result of the author capitalizing on their stories. The novel hides nothing of Plascencia's position. It notes the geographic and social distance the author has traveled from his community and the prestigious creative writing program in which he is enrolled. It also reports that Saturn's war is supported by a grant from the "Ralph and Elisa Landin Foundation" (114), an allusion to the financial realities behind *The People of Paper*, which was funded by the Paul and Daisy Soros Foundation for New Americans. Established by Paul Soros, an engineer who made millions developing the port facilities that enable global trade, the foundation supports "the most promising New Americans who are poised to make significant contributions to the nation through their work."[67] The foundation is situated within the global economy and aligned with neoliberal immigration criteria.[68] Plascencia highlights his implication within the global economy while questioning the economic relation he bears to his community. As Federico de la Fe explains, "we are part of Saturn's story. Saturn owns it. We are being listened to and watched, our lives sold as entertainment" (53). Plascencia puts his finger on a thriving center of the neoliberal multicultural economy: the delivery of racialized others through cultural productions. Literature by people of color, Jodi Melamed observes, has become a valuable form of "cultural property" at the same time that global capitalism has embraced the value of diversity in its operations.[69]

The novel's self-critique breaks down any critical pieties about ethnic literature being inherently resistant to racial capitalism and dominant representations and insists that the struggle against damaging community images must scrutinize minority discourse just as thoroughly. Plascencia is as cognizant of fixities that emerge in Chicanx representations as he is of dominant stereotypes: "I play on the stereotypical conception of gangsters, of Chicano youth . . . . I also wanted to challenge our conception of the Chicano-Latino novel."[70] As Ramón Saldívar notes, the novel plays on many classic tropes of Chicano realist protest fiction: the border, immigrant farmworkers, economic exploitation, and resistance movements.[71] But the novel questions this tradition, unsettling "the ethos of belief in the efficacy of realist protest fiction."[72] Most centrally, I argue, it targets this tradition's reliance on a strategy of transparent narration designed to bear witness to the suffering that Chicanx communities endure. As the novel announces, EMF's struggle is part of "the war on omniscient narration (a.k.a. the war against the commodification of sadness)" (218). EMF puts up lead sheets to block the powerful gaze of Saturn, and two of its characters deploy an antitelepathic shield that takes the form of a *Tristram Shandy*–esque black block "cloaking" private thoughts from Saturn and from readers as well (188).[73] This war for control of their private lives questions the strategy of the minority author delivering access to the authentic "truth" of his community.

As Juan J. Alonzo observes, there is a powerful desire for minority groups to correct representational violence with their own more "accurate" images.[74] This is a long-standing impulse in both ethnic literature and critical models, that more exposure and expression is better. We valorize breaking the silence, giving voice to the marginalized, writing back.[75] These ideas have become central protocols of writing and reading in the multicultural era. But this novel's suspicion of omniscient narration pushes us to see that this impulse often relies on a model of transparent access to racialized others that may actually reproduce the problems of stereotype, delivering its own fixities, essences, and types. Jodi Melamed contends that the values of "*representativeness, authenticity, and gaining voice*" celebrated in ethnic literary cultures appear from another angle as technologies of "information retrieval," offering knowledge of minority communities as consumable goods for the cultural market and actionable data for the diversity strategies of global corporations.[76]

The transpositions in *Karma* brought out the tension of marginalized stories struggling for expression against a dominant framing. That tension persists in *The People of Paper* but with an added complication: Is having more expression and discursive space really better? Resisting stereotype may concern not only the distribution of discursive space and position but also the epistemological structure of stereotyping, with its presumption of access to the truth of the other. Saturn's omniscient position is a revealing metaphor in this regard. He is separated from the people he represents by a cosmic distance and able to penetrate their innermost thoughts. In stereotyping the transparency of presumed access to the other is intertwined with separation. For the other becomes an object opened to the subject's powers of knowing, and this power difference ensures separation. Saturn lets us elaborate on Homi Bhabha's notion that stereotyping is "structurally similar to realism."[77] The idea that the minority can be fully other and completely knowable posits an epistemological and representational authority much like the realist narrator's omniscience. There is a clear relation of authority, representation, and truth at the heart of the aesthetics of stereotype whose attraction can be Saturn-like, pulling even efforts pitched against stereotype into its orbit.

Though not as blatantly self-critical as *The People of Paper*, *Karma* too addresses the limitations of more expression and discursive space. Its transpositions unsettle the naturalizing mechanisms of stereotype but this technique is no panacea. Encountering transpositions attunes readers to look for other potential transpositions. We may notice then the minor characters that remain on the margins of Reddi's stories with no corresponding stories of their own.

Transpositions hint at the possibility of opening countless other stories but representational space is inevitably finite. More confounding is that the alternate distributions of narrative resources that transpositions open produce further inequalities of their own. Any transposed story centered on a formerly minor character will contain other persons in the community who remain minor in the new story. There will always be further discursive inequalities produced, other stories, characters, and views to pursue.

Karma and *The People of Paper* point to the limitations of narrative representation while carrying on the attempt to represent the complexities of their communities. Their formal strategies are never quite adequate. *Karma*'s transpositions reveal their own shortcomings. And neither the strategies of refusal nor cacophonous voices in *The People of Paper* can overturn the unequal power of authors and markets over represented communities. These texts sustain transfictional tensions between major and minor characters, discursive centers and margins, and between distinct stories that don't unify into any complete community narrative. Their unsettled forms speak to the unresolved problems of capturing minority community, which stem from the material inequalities that these texts register. The field of power structuring the circulation of ethnic stories compromises the delivery of ethnic knowledge. And neoliberal stratifications cleave these communities so profoundly that legible portraits of them as coherent communities can only be false. The Cold War displacement narratives we saw in Chapter 2 evinced the urgency of mapping refugee routes, while their transfictional forms refused the comfort of filling the gaps in life stories ruptured by war. In a similar fashion, Reddi's and Plascencia's works don't offer aesthetic resolutions to the economic ruptures in their communities even while expressing the urgency of better understanding these stratifications.

There are no easy answers for representation in the face of entrenched stereotype, neoliberal categories, and class cleavage. Minority writers can attempt to satirize and deconstruct these images but that leaves alternative understandings of ethnic communities up for grabs. Counterrepresentations can deliver their own fixed images. Following Plascencia's refusals, one might opt out of the market for ethnic culture, but the market will continue to churn out flawed images on which flawed perceptions and policies will be built. And antiracist struggle doesn't really have the option not to represent. Redistributive politics needs representations that attempt to model the existing distributions to be addressed. None of these options is a clear solution. The unstable forms and portraits in *Karma* and *The People of Paper*, then, may signal a necessarily asymptotic approach. They reveal the stakes of striving for more complete views of these communities so that we can begin to address the material consequences of intraethnic stratification, differential exploitation, and neoliberal allocations of life chances. And they recognize that we have no choice but to use the limited, compromised tools of representation.

PART II

PANETHNIC FICTIONS

CHAPTER 4

FORMING PANETHNICITY
The Book of Unknown Americans *and the*
Comparative Work of Latinidad

THINKING OF an Asian and Latinx America today requires encompassing two communities defined by paradox. Asian American and Latinx communities are more expansive than ever and also more tenuous, more established and more unstable, full of potential power and powerful conflicts. Their paradoxical character is a legacy of the historical transformations that have simultaneously formed and unformed them. The first part of this book explored three of those crucial moments—the post–civil rights era, Cold War displacements, and the neoliberal era of stratified immigration. These moments expanded the scope of Asian American and Latinx communities. They fueled dramatic growth, generating waves of refugees and immigrants that have made Latinxs and Asian Americans central to twenty-first-century America. But in expanding these communities at such a breathless pace, they also introduced and intensified cleavages that threaten to unform the very idea of Asian Americans and Latinxs as unified communities. The uneven opportunities of the post–civil rights period increased class polarization. Cold War conflicts displaced to the United States many new ethnic groups, who brought histories and political outlooks often quite different from others in their racial groups. The stratified immigration system also drew in new ethnic groups while consolidating starkly divergent positions in an economy of human capital.

The transformations of the post-1965 period have culminated in a crisis of unity. Perhaps the most central conflict for Asian American and Latinx politics in the present is whether these groups constitute groups at all, given the incredibly and increasingly diverse peoples and agendas encompassed by each category. The concepts of Asian American and Latinx, having been contested from the time of their origins, are under even greater strain today. Scholars and activists are questioning their principles of unity and political efficacy. Having examined many of the shared challenges and joint aesthetic strategies linking these two groups, this study would be incomplete if it failed to recognize the inherently comparative nature of the groups it places into comparison. The final chapters will probe the categories Asian American and Latinx, as recent transfictional works imagine them, in all their contradictions and possibilities. This moment of uncertainty shows transfictional aesthetics at its most generative, addressing the basic premises for Asian American and Latinx politics. I've argued that the transfictional works developing in Asian American and Latinx communities powerfully model many of the central social conflicts with which these groups are grappling. Here I push that argument further. Transfictional works do more than give form to the social struggles of Asian Americans and Latinxs, they offer conceptual structure and political imagination to the very ideas of these communities.

HAS THERE EVER BEEN A LATINX NOVEL? AN ASIAN AMERICAN NOVEL?

An important part of what the terms *Asian American* and *Latinx* mean is a panethnic formation that brings together many different ethnic groups to pursue shared struggles and collective interests.[1] The political hopes condensed in these terms see them as existent or potential coalitions broader than their constituent parts. For this panethnic sense of the terms, many of the literary works that readers and scholars routinely refer to as Asian American or Latinx present a problem: They focus on a single ethnic group. Representations of cross-ethnic interactions, let alone solidarities, are infrequent.[2] The works that do address cross-ethnic relations largely fall short of a panethnic perspective, with many of them focusing on the interaction between two ethnic groups. Also rare are works that engage the terms *Asian American* or *Latinx*, even though "Asian American" and "Latinx" literatures have ostensibly proliferated. So has there ever really been an Asian American or Latinx novel (or poem, play, story collection, etc.)? The fields of Asian American and Latinx literary studies negotiate an awkward gap between panethnic critical frameworks and the largely monoethnic texts critics analyze through them. To approach such texts through a panethnic framework may involve a synecdochic operation (a text concerning one ethnic group standing in for a panethnic whole) or the imposition of Asian American-ness or Latinidad on texts that do not claim such categories.

Given the historic dearth of panethnic works, the recent fictions I examine in these final chapters are remarkable, because they take on panethnic categories and solidarities as central subjects. Karen Tei Yamashita's 2010 novel or novella cycle *I Hotel* is a historical fiction narrating the formation of the Asian American movement in the San Francisco Bay Area in the 1960s and 1970s. The promises and problems of many ethnic groups coming together as Asian Americans are *I Hotel*'s primary concerns. Cristina Henríquez's 2014 novel *The Book of Unknown Americans* depicts the construction of Latinidad among immigrants from many Latin American nations whose lives intersect in an apartment building in Delaware. Their handling of interethnic differences and support form a major part of the story. It's tempting to hail these works as the Asian American and Latinx novels we have been waiting for.[3] But rather than being the novels that finally fit the panethnic categories, what's important is how they help think through and reshape those categories. They deploy transfictional forms to imagine alternate ways of structuring a collective spanning many ethnicities and differences. The tension of unity and multiplicity is the clearest way that transfictional form speaks to the challenge of imagining panethnicity, but nearly all the features we have encountered converge in these attempts to render panethnic communities: semiautonomous stories, narrative gaps that invite readers to construct links between stories, expansive range and indirect relations, tensions of diachronic progression and spatial expansion, a focus on the individual and attention to the stories of others, narrative borders and crossings. That *I Hotel* and *The Book of Unknown Americans* draw together many of the transfictional features seen in earlier moments is not surprising. The social conflicts of earlier periods contributed to the current impasses of panethnic coalition.

Imaginatively constructing different panethnic collectives but drawing on similar strategies to do so, *I Hotel* and *The Book of Unknown Americans* reveal the shared aesthetic challenges and political contradictions of Asian American and Latinx coalitions. These challenges have been central subjects of debate in Asian American studies and Latinx studies, but the conversations have been separate. The emergence of panethnic narratives with joint aesthetic strategies is an opportunity to bring these conversations together, combining efforts to take on questions central to the very definition of these fields. This chapter opens the dialogue. It reveals that scholars in both fields are struggling with the same questions, which stem from the historical conditions distinguishing the formation of Asian American and Latinx coalitions. I aim to show that ideas forged in grappling with Latinidad can be generative in conceiving Asian American coalition and vice versa. On top of this cross-field dialogue I layer a literary-theoretical conversation, arguing that panethnic fictions are powerful thought partners in the work of envisioning coalition.

THE SHARED IMPASSES OF ASIAN AMERICAN AND LATINX PANETHNICITY

The many factors linking Asian American and Latinx panethnic coalitions have gone unnoticed because of the isolation of Asian American and Latinx studies from each other. Even the emerging body of comparative studies attempting to bridge these fields has not addressed the shared questions of panethnicity that form central debates in both fields. The oversight is striking because these factors distinguish Asian American and Latinx identities from other forms of panethnicity in the United States. Both collectives are recent inventions that are consolidating while trying to absorb explosive population growth and diversification from continuing waves of immigration. Their internal differences have led many scholars to question the coherence of panethnic categories and to critique their tendencies to suppress conflicts within the communities they call up. The stakes of resolving this paradox of growing strength and internal fragmentation have intensified as the categories Asian American and Latinx become more institutionalized. In short, these terms face a crisis of definition.

While I aim to draw out their shared challenges, it's important to recognize differences in the conditions under which Asian American and Latinx coalitions form. Differences in class, linguistic unity, racialization, and interethnic interactions are major ones, though many of these differences become more nuanced in analyses that break down the aggregate blocs to address the diversities within each bloc.[4] Perhaps the most important difference between Asian American and Latinx panethnic organizing, though, is that the Asian American category originated in a radical activist movement in the 1960s while the categories of Latinx and Hispanic did not originate in movement histories.[5] Political Latinidad arose later, in a complex negotiation among political organizations, federal agencies, media, and marketing firms. Historical narratives play important roles in constructing panethnicity,[6] and Asian Americans have a symbolically compelling movement origin story behind their panethnic concept that Latinxs do not have.[7] As we'll see with Yamashita's *I Hotel*, this movement history offers a rich framework for envisioning panethnicity. With its more ambivalent origin story, activists and scholars must find other means to narrate Latinidad. Clearly, Asian American and Latinx panethnic coalitions are not structurally identical. My goal is not to conflate their differences but to bring out the surprising ways that their challenges speak to each other.

Turning to those challenges, both Asian American and Latinx panethnic concepts are recent inventions. The concept of Asian American emerged in the late 1960s, and that of Latinx or Hispanic in the 1970s.[8] This recentness distinguishes the categories from African American panethnicity, which consolidated much earlier through centuries of shared struggle and under different conditions of forcible removal from native ethnic ties. Because they are so new, their artificial nature is starkly apparent; the extent to which the terms *Asian American* or *Latinx* have a lived meaning for the communities they strive to represent is an open question. Many people categorized as Latinx or Asian American don't identify with these labels, identifying instead with their ethnic and national origin groups.[9]

Lacking long histories of circulation, interethnic relation, and lived experience, the sense of Asian American and Latinx communities is unstable. Continuing waves of immigration add to this instability. An influx of Asian immigrants and refugees in the decades following the 1965 immigration reforms and the end of the Vietnam War intensified intergroup conflicts by bringing different ethnic, cultural, national, and class experiences into the Asian American community.[10] During this same period, multiple streams of Latin American immigration and Cold War displacements resulted in a "huge demographic increase and the dispersal and diversification of Latina/o communities."[11] Mass immigration distinguishes Asian American and Latinx panethnic categories from other recent formations such as Native American pan-tribalism. And it creates particular challenges for organizing. The continuous stream of new arrivals reinforces ties to ethnic groups and nations of origin and dilutes connections across ethnic groups; renewed diasporic ties can also keep interethnic strife from the "home" region fresh in the minds of communities in the United States.[12] New arrivals often have different needs that established panethnic coalitions may not recognize.[13]

Latinx and Asian American panethnic coalitions face the distinct challenge of forging political unity at the same time as their populations undergo explosive growth and flux. They face a political paradox. As Yến Lê Espiritu says of Asian Americans, "the very force that has boosted Asian American political clout—immigration—has also produced a population more divided along ethnic, class, and generational lines."[14] For both Asian Americans and Latinxs, continuing immigration feeds the enticing prospect of politically powerful panethnic coalitions while making the realization of these coalitions that much more fraught.

Recognizing this paradox, scholars are scrutinizing panethnic categories. For many in Asian American studies, the organizing term of the field verges on incoherence.[15] In Latinx studies, many question the analytical usefulness of the terms *Hispanic* and *Latinx*; their purported strength, their inclusivity, is also their weakness. They are so comprehensive that they lose meaning.[16] Some argue that analysis of Latinxs as a collective must proceed with caution and full recognition of the "contradictions, tensions, and fissures" rending this collective.[17] Others are skeptical of even that, seeing the panethnic term as an empty category lumping vastly different peoples into a nonexistent population.[18] More problematic than a lack of analytical rigor is the possibility that the panethnic category covers over the inequities within communities. Latinx unity can conceal intra-Latinx colorism, racism, and discrimination against indigenous populations.[19] Equally serious cleavages lie beneath the surface of Asian American unity, from the labor exploitation of new migrants by established groups to the legacies of imperialism between Asian groups. Since the 1990s, Asian American and Latinx studies have undertaken a cataloging of such cleavages. The emphasis on differences has undermined the idea of panethnic identity, casting doubt on the theoretical premises of the fields. Any attempt to rethink panethnicity must contend with a tangle of differences.

Most directly, prospects for Latinidad falter in the face of the ethnic diversity brought by migrations in the past few decades. Migrants from across Latin America have joined the three largest and most established Latinx groups, Chicanxs, Puerto Ricans, and Cuban Americans. Latinx ethnic groups occupy widely differing positions in the United States, which result in large part from their different histories of entering the nation.[20] Different relations with the United States determine how the nation receives Latinx groups. The first wave of Cubans arriving in the 1960s, for example, received a warm welcome as they were considered political refugees from a communist regime.[21] In contrast, as Chapter 2 discussed, the U.S. government labeled Dominicans fleeing to the United States in the late 1960s as economic immigrants, which amounted to a disavowal of the U.S. invasion of their country. Different trajectories contribute to wide variation in citizenship. Whereas Cuban refugees and Puerto Rican colonial subjects bear citizenship rights, a significant proportion of immigrants from other Latin American nations do not. This divergence belies the popular idea that immigration reform is a unifying issue for Latinxs. The comparison of Cubans and Puerto Ricans raises another crucial cleavage: class. The wide socioeconomic variation between and within Latinx ethnic groups compromises the ability of the category Latinx to name an economically disadvantaged minority group. The label might even allow affluent immigrants to "pass, statistically, as members of an oppressed group."[22]

That Latinxs are a minority group struggling with racial and economic oppression is one principle of unity among several that purports to cut across Latinx differences to secure the coherence of the category. Under scrutiny, however, these principles are not airtight. Some scholars question racial and economic oppression as a unifying factor, arguing that some Latinx groups should not be considered minorities because they are not economically marginalized.[23] Positing racial oppression as a shared condition is also problematic, given the complex mixtures of racial identities among Latinxs.[24] The idea of Spanish as a shared language is also tenuous as many Latinxs do not speak it.[25] And common culture, many argue, is little more than a stereotype.[26] Finally, if Latinx designates a political formation then political orientation should unite Latinxs. Marta Caminero-Santangelo observes that Latinx studies has too often taken for granted a specific form of oppositional left politics as a banner under which Latinxs come together. But this presumption founders on the anticommunist and conservative politics of a significant portion of Latinxs.[27] There may be no such thing as a unified Latinx political community with a common agenda, despite the recurrent imagery of the "sleeping giant" of Latinx electoral power that pundits evoke in every election cycle.[28]

Asian American panethnicity shares many of the same difficulties. As with Latinxs, growing ethnic diversity and demographic changes have defined the past few decades, shifting the community from the East Asian groups that dominated the population during the rise of Asian American coalitions. Likewise, Asian Americans have come to the United States under vastly different conditions, with consequences for their social positions and politics. As discussed in Chapter 2, many were displaced by Cold War conflicts and their aftermaths (many Southeast Asians and Koreans, for instance). Others were driven by global economic inequalities to seek opportunities abroad.[29] Relations between the United States and Asian nations have framed migrations and also the precarious place of Asians already in the United States. Contingent on these relations, the United States has excluded or recruited, vilified or rehabilitated various Asian ethnic groups at different moments. The shifting fortunes of Chinese and Japanese Americans from World War II to the Cold War are examples of this contingency.[30] The vicissitudes of U.S. warfare, foreign policies, and immigration regulations have resulted in highly variant citizenship statuses among Asian Americans. Today, the category encompasses refugees, American-born citizens, naturalized citizens, undocumented immigrants, professionals with sponsored visas, and a managerial class of "flexible citizens" who cross borders freely.[31] Latinxs dominate public discussions of "illegal" immigration, but it's worth noting that the Asian American population includes a significant stratum of vulnerable undocumented immigrants. As this range shows, stark class divisions complicate not only Latinx unity but Asian American coalition as well.[32]

Like Latinxs, Asian Americans strain principles of unity. If the question of common minority status troubled Latinx panethnic unity, it is only more problematic for Asian American collectivity, given the high class position of many Asian Americans. "The twenty-first-century Asian American," Colleen Lye observes, "figures the racial instance where the associated links between cultural marginalization and economic disempowerment are the most blatantly attenuated."[33] To unify Asian Americans as a minority group raises questions about whether and how affluent Asian Americans are disadvantaged minorities. At the same time, this general image of affluence covers over the many groups who are struggling. While minority status raises many questions, shared politics seems more promising, given the concrete history of coalition in the formative years of the Asian American movement. But even at that time, the movement's causes of Third World solidarity, antiracism, and anti-imperialism did not speak to large portions of the Asian American community that it purported to represent.[34] Such radical politics remains vital to Asian American studies, but it runs into the same problem that we saw in academic claims for Latinx politics. In a critique that parallels Marta Caminero-Santangelo's assessment of Latinx studies, Viet Thanh Nguyen exposes the uniform resistant politics the field has used to define the boundaries of proper Asian American politics. This rigid definition cannot deal with the ideological diversity of Asian America.[35]

The panethnic coalitions that do manage to form across all these differences struggle with distributing power and setting agendas within organizations full of internal hierarchies. Which ethnic group dominates the panethnic category is a continual problem. Mexican Americans significantly outnumber other Latinx groups while the Asian American movement was plagued by the sense that Asian American interests meant Chinese and Japanese American interests.[36] The potential of the panethnic category to cover over the complex internal architectures of coalitions can lead to forms of emblematizing, with one group standing in for the whole. An idealized Latinx identity can emerge that excludes many who could be involved in the political movement.[37] Ethnic nationalist movements tended to stress a masculine subject of resistance, which scholars and activists in both fields have extensively critiqued.

Both Asian American and Latinx coalitions face increasingly tangled fields of conflict and unifying platforms that strain to bear the weight placed on them. But the specific contradiction of these coalitions today is that their internal conflicts are undermining the prospects of unity at the very moment that the concepts of Asian American and Latinx have taken on institutionalized lives across state, nonprofit, media, and commercial domains. This contradiction extends to the academy, where scholars theorize the fictionality of panethnic categories while participating in expanding curricula and programming under these labels.[38] The increasing power of these categories makes it even more imperative to address their internal tensions.[39] The challenge of panethnicity today is not constructing coalitions from scratch but assessing and reconstructing already entrenched ones.

The troubling consequence of institutionalization is that it reifies constructed categories, making it even harder to address the diversity and flux of the communities they represent. Over the decades, stakeholders across many fields have reinforced the concept of the Hispanic community.[40] These stakeholders have vested interests in making the idea of a unified community of Hispanics appear natural. The more self-evident and unified the community, the more easily resources can be claimed. While naturalizing is the cost of laudable efforts to gain resources for disadvantaged communities, it also allows panethnic organizations to bolster their own growth. Many careers are dependent on panethnic categories. Latinx and Asian American political organizations have become professionalized, joining the "nonprofit industrial complex."[41] Under the pressures of institutional growth, resource chasing, and invested parties, the constructed nature of the panethnic concept ebbs away.[42] Academic institutionalization creates similar pressures. In the struggle to legitimate Asian American studies, change curricula, and secure resources for marginalized subjects, it's tempting to point to a legible, coherent object of study. The effect can be to make Asian America "ahistorical, self-evident, and transparently knowable, thus effacing the dynamic complexity of Asian-raced peoples."[43] Even more troubling, institutionalization can undermine the political impulses that justified panethnic organizing in the first place. Incorporation into political and nonprofit infrastructures can come at the cost of moderating the radical social justice goals of earlier movements.[44]

It is not a stretch to say that the contradictions of the Asian American and Latinx categories have reached a crisis point. Some question whether the categories should be kept at all.[45] The established methods of sustaining the terms are no longer adequate. Strategic essentialism—being aware of differences but bracketing them off in the strategic interest of unity—has come under fire. Scholars in both fields warn that the instrumental use of essentialist categories can slide into naturalizing those categories.[46] Moreover, bracketing off differences postpones the work of addressing the conflicts within identity categories.[47] Also tenuous is the model of additive inclusion, whereby the panethnic category continually expands to include other groups. This model can become a facile celebration of diversity that does not address the "contradictions and heterogeneities" that the inclusive category attempts to encompass.[48] Unless it sees the inclusion of other groups as requiring fundamental restructuring of the panethnic category, additive inclusion amounts to little more than marginal window dressing.

With panethnic concepts in crisis and established models inadequate, scholars in Asian American and Latinx studies are venturing new concepts of panethnicity. The proposals across these fields complement each other in compelling ways. Not only do Asian American and Latinx coalitions face shared problems, they are converging on similar solutions. These proposals open exciting possibilities, but scholars are not alone in struggling to rethink panethnicity. Fiction writers too are offering imaginative responses to the impasses of panethnicity. The very ideas of Asian American and Latinx and the political hopes invested in them are at stake, so it's not surprising that thinkers across multiple domains are wrestling with these questions. Recognizing theory and fiction as complementary modes of conceptual invention and two vantage points on the same debates, I will avoid an isolated survey of the scholarly proposals. Instead I will interweave them with the new paradigms imagined in panethnic fictions. This structure aims to show that panethnic fictions are co-theorizers of coalition. They are provocative interventions in the effort to reshape panethnic coalition for the future. I'll begin with Cristina Henríquez's novel of Latinx migrants, *The Book of Unknown Americans*, which offers a comparative vision for perceiving emergent forms of coalition. It considers how Latinidad can form as part of broader solidarities with Americans and minority groups more generally. In the next chapter, we'll see the radical potential of this idea of panethnicity as both specific and unbound as we follow the expansive imagination of Karen Tei Yamashita's *I Hotel*.

THE BOOK OF UNKNOWN AMERICANS, LATINX NOVEL

Cristina Henríquez's 2014 novel *The Book of Unknown Americans* follows a group of Latin American immigrants in a multiethnic neighborhood near Wilmington, Delaware. Forming the major plot of the novel are the gradually intertwining lives of the Rivera and Toro families, Mexican and Panamanian immigrants respectively. The Riveras moved to the United States to seek medical and educational care for their daughter Maribel, who suffered brain trauma in an accident. The two families are drawn together by a budding romance between Maribel and Mayor, the Toros' teenage son. The story takes a melodramatic turn when Mayor is forbidden to see Maribel. Defiant, Mayor takes his father's car and takes Maribel to see the ocean. This reunion of star-crossed lovers sets off a tragic chain of events when Maribel's father, Arturo, goes looking for her and accosts a neighborhood boy who has been taunting Mayor with nativist slurs. In the confrontation, the boy's father shoots and kills Arturo. The community is devastated and the novel ends with the Riveras returning to Mexico.

The novel, though, extends much further than this plot, because the central narrative is surrounded by the life stories of the many other migrants in this neighborhood. The main plot is alternately narrated by Mayor and by Maribel's mother, Alma. Interspersed with their narrations are first-person testimonies from the other community members describing their journeys to the United States and their struggles making a life here. Though minor characters in the drama of the Riveras and Toros, their stories are crucial to Henríquez's project of writing a book of unknown Americans. They expand what would be a cross-ethnic narrative of Mexican and Panamanian families into something approaching a panethnic Latinx novel. Given the hierarchy of visibility among Latinx ethnic groups, it's fitting that an author identifying with a less visible group, Panamanian Americans, would craft a novel sensitive to a broader range of Latinx ethnic groups. The characters hail from Mexico, Panama, Guatemala, Venezuela, Nicaragua, Paraguay, and Puerto Rico.

The novel doesn't presuppose this group of migrants as a Latinx community. Whether its many stories form a unified whole remains an open question in this transfictional work. The novel uses this form to register the characters' differences and show the relationships that they must build. At the same time, it observes the conditions in the United States that drive different peoples to come together. In doing so, it makes important contributions to the debates on panethnicity. Most interesting is a proposal that Latinidad can form in the process of claiming broader solidarities while maintaining its specificity. But even more intriguing than the specific expressions of panethnicity the novel offers is how it encodes key problems and processes of panethnic construction into its form. The novel's transfictional tensions and separations illuminate the conflicts among different visions of Latinx struggle and invite readers to practice the comparative work necessary to bring new Latinx solidarities to life.

RECOGNIZING DIFFERENCES, PROPOSING LATINIDADES

The Book of Unknown Americans is attentive to the many differences among its cast of migrant characters. It's especially cognizant of divergent experiences of migration. The novel's structure of many semiautonomous stories highlights these distinctions by suggesting that the many variations on the Latinx immigrant plot cannot be told in any one story. Exploring what drives Latin Americans to the United States, the novel sketches a range of factors from warfare and displacement to the draw of American opportunities. One character, Gustavo Milhojas, fled war-torn Guatemala, a nation transformed by a U.S.-backed coup. Warfare also displaced the Toro family; the U.S. invasion of Panama in 1989–1990 devastated their home city. Benny Quinto fled the poverty and destruction left in the wake of war in Nicaragua. His testimony speaks to the economic inequality in the Americas that draws migrants from Central America. "Leaving the poverty of Nicaragua to go to the richest country in the world didn't take much convincing," he admits (44). The paths of other characters evoke the American immigrant myth. Fito Angelino traveled from Paraguay to train with a famous boxing coach, while Nelia Zafón left Puerto Rico with hopes of becoming a Broadway star. Despite these dreams, they end up like many of the others upon arrival, scraping by on low-wage jobs. Other stories oppose the immigrant narrative. The Riveras did not come to the United States to seek opportunity. Arturo had a good job managing a construction company in Mexico. He reflects on the immigrant desire for a better life and pushes against it: "it wasn't like that for us. We had a good life, a beautiful life" (285). Instead, they came to seek support for their disabled daughter. These stories form a nuanced panorama of experiences that breaks open any singular image of the Latinx migration experience.

Across these differences, the characters develop several senses of Latinx solidarity. One powerful kind forms under shared threats. It recognizes the nativist violence that lumps Latinxs together, making a unified response imperative. But these instances do not call up Latinx solidarity in isolation. They evoke this solidarity in relation to other racial groups. Mayor's father, Rafael, identifies growing nativist violence that draws Latinxs together but also links them to Asian Americans and Arab Americans. "They're targeting people who look like us," he warns. "It used to be the Orientals, but the style now is to pick on the

Latinos. And the Arabs" (207). As Yến Lê Espiritu argues, the threat of racist violence that does not distinguish among ethnicities can be a powerful spur to panethnic solidarity.[49] Rafael's warning adds that nativist violence can unify a panethnic group while linking it with other minority groups.

Political Latinidad in this novel brings Latinxs together at the same time as it aligns them with other people of color. The novel proposes that panethnic identity does not necessarily precede alliances with other racial groups; instead, it is through relational racialization and cross-racial affinities that Latinx as a political identity consolidates. The novel traces this process in one chapter that shows the neighborhood responding to the 2008 presidential campaign of Barack Obama. The chapter captures the political hopes Obama's campaign sparked for many communities of color. The residents in the building are excited. They plant Obama signs and follow the news eagerly. Micho Alvarez goes around making sure that everyone who can vote is registered. He tells everyone "how important it was that Obama, a black man who looked like no other U.S. president and who had family that came from different places, could possibly lead our country. It meant that we, who also resembled no other U.S. president and who also had family from faraway places, could one day rise up and do the same thing" (76). The "we" here, and the Latinx political solidarity it evokes, forms in the process of identifying with other minorities who are marginalized from the U.S. body politic by race and perceived foreignness.

The Book of Unknown Americans shows how Latinx coalition can form within broader solidarities with other communities of color. It may be that the struggles to define Latinidad have reached impasses because they have too often tried to define Latinx in itself as a subject whose isolation could justify the particularity of a field of study and an arena of politics. The need to justify Latinx studies on an institutional level only intensifies this impulse. These debates of definition have proceeded as if it were possible to identify the characteristics that would unite all Latinxs, and just Latinxs. There is a maddening knife's-edge balance to this attempt, to try to conceive Latinidad as capacious enough to encompass all Latinxs and yet particular enough to apply only to Latinxs. Henríquez outlines a less fraught way of proceeding, to see how Latinidad can arise as part of multiple broad political formations.

The broader solidarities in which Latinxs play a part need not subsume the specificity of panethnic Latinidad. This point is especially clear when the novel addresses the events of 9/11 to argue that claiming U.S. national identity can be a process of articulating Latinidad. The novel shows the community processing 9/11 together. Doors open, people comfort each other, and many are "standing around stunned and shaking with fear" (84). It could be a scene from anywhere in the country on that date. This is part of Henríquez's point, that Latinxs, although they were missing from national narratives of 9/11, experienced this traumatic event as Americans too. Patriotism surges among some of the residents, as was common throughout the nation at the time. But in the midst of the commotion that draws Latinxs into a national identity, Celia Toro asks a question that recalls their particular perspectives: "We moved here because it was supposed to be safer! Where can we go after this?" (84). It's a wonderful moment of concentric identifications. The community is drawn together by fear and worry as all Americans are, but within this national identification there are also specific fears stemming from the histories many in the community bear with them. Americans as a whole feel linked by political violence shattering the sense of security in their homes. But these Latinx Americans are also brought together by memories of political violence in their home nations. They have known political violence all too intimately; their home nations did not enjoy the hegemonic power that allowed several generations of Americans to avoid the trauma of a major political attack at home.[50] As Latin American migrants, they bring particular forms of knowledge to processing this national trauma. Henríquez pulls off an intricate move in this scene, situating Latinxs as an integral part of the United States without dissolving the specific histories that form who they are.

These instances of Latinidad lay the conceptual foundations for the final and most expansive image of solidarity in the novel, the community of people that come together in the aftermath of Arturo's murder. This image of community draws out a corollary to the idea of broader coalitions: If Latinxs unite as part of larger formations, in some cases these larger formations should be seen as Latinx themselves. The novel explores whether Latinx coalitions can extend beyond those who identify as Latinx. Henríquez builds the case for such a coalition by tracing a network of institutions and people who interact with and support Latinx migrants: a Spanish translator at the school district, a community services center for immigrants, the bus drivers and English Language Learner teachers to whom Alma entrusts her daughter each day. The extent and shape of this network of support only become clear with Arturo's death. In the aftermath, Alma grieves and wonders how she will afford the five thousand dollars it will cost to transport Arturo's body to be buried in their hometown of Pátzcuaro. Meanwhile, her close friend Celia takes up a collection to come up with the funds. The community this collection expresses is expansive. All the people in the building contribute, as do Arturo's coworkers, and the manager at the local Mexican grocery store. These donors may see their contributions as tribute to an acquaintance and fellow Latinx, but the collection moves beyond ethnic identification. It includes a translator and the teachers at Maribel's school, a receptionist at the school district office, teachers at the immigrant community center, an Irish Catholic priest and his congregation, and interpreters and nurses from the hospital where Arturo was treated. This network extends beyond the bonds fostered by neighborly interaction or ethnic identifications. Much like the networks surrounding Vietnamese child refugees discussed in Chapter 2, this shape of interconnected responsibility can best be described as a "community of shared fate," a set of ethically significant social relations whose binding force is not shared identity but rather "a system of social interdependence."[51] But even as shared identity is not the primary force in this collective and even though it includes many who would not identify as Latinx, I argue that this community of fate is a Latinx one. This is a community centered on Latinx migrants and encompassing the many people and institutions whose lives and work are intertwined with Latinxs and the struggles they endure in the United States. And it's a body of support that responds to the needs of Latinx communities torn open by anti-Latinx violence. The novel presents a fascinating shape for Latinx coalition that includes panethnic identification but does not end there. As it shows with the 2008 election and 9/11 episodes, Latinx lives are deeply embedded in American communities. To take this idea seriously means seeing Latinx struggles as the concerns of many other Americans as well, Americans whose lives, communities, and fates are intertwined with those of Latinxs. The constituents of a Latinx coalition need not be Latinx themselves.[52] As we'll see in the next chapter with *I Hotel*, this refusal to view panethnic minority coalition as a bound and particular movement opens possibilities for insisting on the broader stakes of Latinx and Asian American struggles.

The collection for Alma and Arturo exemplifies the solidarities that flare up from specific moments and urgent needs. This conditional sense of coalition dovetails with current proposals to abandon the idea of a grand, unified, and enduring panethnicity. Formulating an overarching agenda that will speak to all the peoples gathered under the panethnic umbrella may be futile.[53] Instead, scholars are considering the power of situational panethnicity. This proposal sees panethnicity not as a fixed and stable unity but as a collective identity that people construct in specific situations and around particular issues.[54] Examples of Latinx coalition bolster this view and show the tactical advantages of situational panethnicity. National Latinx political coalitions centered on specific issues can be temporary and ad hoc. More than institutionalized coalitions, these ad hoc alliances can respond with urgency on specific issues and take advantage of evolving political conditions that throw groups together.[55] Panethnic identity then emerges through specific mobilizations. The solidarity called up by Arturo's murder shows the situational emergence of a panethnic community. But it also reveals a larger scope. Urgent issues can draw Latinxs together, but a broader view of situational panethnicity would see that the issues that rally Latinx coalition can reverberate widely beyond those who identify as Latinx.

The Book of Unknown Americans presents versions of Latinidad that push debates on panethnicity further. They spur recognition of the broader formations within which Latinxs come together. The novel posits Latinx coalition as a potentially unbound designation. These proposals for panethnicity are illuminating, but the most powerful contributions the novel makes may be the ways it encodes panethnic thought into its reading experience.

PULLING AGAINST THE COMPELLING NARRATIVE OF LATINX STRUGGLE

The discussion of Sandra Cisneros's *The House on Mango Street* in Chapter 1 revealed a transfictional tension between the diachronic progression of a major plot and the expansive spatial attention to other stories that don't progress in the same ways. Cisneros used this tension to unveil the contradictions of individual mobility and collective obstacles and to stress how unrepresentative the protagonist's story is. Henríquez deploys this tension to related ends, to challenge the representativeness of any singular narrative of Latinx struggle for the many other circumstances in this community. The novel uses the diachronic/spatial tension to model the conflicts between competing narratives of Latinx struggle.

By acknowledging competing versions of Latinx politics, *The Book of Unknown Americans* aligns with scholars advocating for multiple panethnic identifications. This idea follows from the movement to let go of an all-encompassing account of panethnicity. Marta Caminero-Santangelo makes a compelling case for this shift. "A single, monolithic *Latinidad*," she observes, "must continually make the case for overarching commonalities among all the groups—a case which inevitably fails." In a model of "multiple latinidades," though, each form of Latinidad can "reach across national-origins lines but need not account in some comprehensive way for all."[56] The multiple approach allows for panethnic politics to address the different struggles that members of the community confront. The realities of Latinx organizing bolster this idea. Latinx social movements and political organizations are diverse, addressing a range of issues.[57] A single comprehensive coalition may not meet the many needs of the Latinx population. This approach may also address issues of political hierarchy. Scholars argue that multiplying panethnic politics can be a way to guard against one form of politics dominating others within the community.[58]

While taking up the idea of multiple panethnic collectives, *The Book of Unknown Americans* troubles the notion that multiplicity can alleviate political hierarchies. It suggests that dissolving these hierarchies may not be so easy by highlighting how multiple narratives of Latinx politics compete. A key challenge of panethnic coalition is that certain idealized subjects and visible groups can dominate the collective conversation. With the transfictional tension between major plot and other stories as well as a collision of different genres, Henríquez's novel dramatizes how certain narratives can sideline others in perceptions of the Latinx community. The novel pushes the conversation on multiple Latinidades to confront the hierarchies of visibility between different versions of Latinx politics. It asks which versions of Latinidad seem to make more compelling narratives, and why?

Some readers might view the novel's main plot as young adult sensationalism: teen lovers, bullying, parental ultimatums, a romantic excursion that results in murder. But recall that this plot does not account for all of the novel. Henríquez stages the novel as a conflict between the propulsive drive of this central plot and the many migration stories that interrupt its momentum to detail the lives of other characters not centrally involved in the main plot. We could see these interruptions as aesthetic flaws, distractions, or pieces that aren't fully integrated into the novel. But that judgment relies on a standard of unified wholeness that is ill-suited for an unruly novel like this. Transfictional form as an alternative narrative paradigm that doesn't prioritize unity makes it possible to interpret the unruliness as a deliberate strategy. I read the interruptions as a provocative formal choice forcing readers to confront how readily we get involved in a dramatic plot at the expense of other stories of "unknown Americans."

The characters in these other stories do not exude the aura of sympathetic innocence that suffuses the portrayal of the young protagonists, Mayor and Maribel. The story of Benny Quinto offers a good example. Eager to leave the war-scarred nation of Nicaragua, Benny steals money from a local church. He endures a harrowing smuggling experience and has to take up drug dealing to pay off his debts. Eventually he makes his way to Delaware. By the story's end, he is working at a Burger King. "I feel settled here," Benny reflects, "I took a couple nasty turns, but I ended up all right" (47). His narration is frank, whitewashing little. In these stories, Henríquez is not interested in portraying model immigrants or bolstering mythologies of immigrant success. In another testimony, readers meet Gustavo, a father working two jobs cleaning movie theaters all to send money home to support his children. These outcomes are middling, neither triumphant arrival nor the violent victimization that drives the main plot. These are sober accounts of making do. Forthright and unembellished in style, they do not emphasize gripping suspense and pathos-evoking character (Henríquez even minimizes the drama of Benny's potentially gripping smuggling story, writing it in matter-of-fact language). The stories immerse readers in the ongoing grind of immigrant life. The novel places such testimonies against the compulsively readable melodrama of the main plot. With this generic tension, the novel acknowledges how some Latinx stories of struggle come across as more compelling and urgent than others.

The final interrupting story, Micho Alvarez's, most fully reveals the function of these stories. They insist on the less digestible subjects that the public must confront in addressing Latinx struggles. Micho's story comes at the height of the main plot's suspense, after Mayor steals Maribel away to see the ocean. It could feel perverse to pull away from the main plot at this heightened moment, but Micho's story is no mere interruption. His testimony, in fact, gives the novel its title. This title story confronts readers with a combative political voice that contrasts with the sympathetic young immigrants in the central plot. Micho indicts anti-Mexican racism and confronts the U.S. public with its failure to recognize an entire swath of the nation. "We're the unknown Americans," he asserts, "the ones no one even wants to know, because they've been told they're supposed to be scared of us" (237). Micho insists that American perceptions of migration do not encompass the full scope of Latinx migrant stories. As the discussion of the bifurcated immigrant chronotope showed in Chapter 2, stories of American opportunity preclude a transnational view of the conditions in Latin American nations that drive people to migrate. "Does anyone ever talk about *why* people are crossing?" Micho asks. "People are desperate" (237). He goes further to implicate Americans in the conditions: "No one here wants to admit it, but the United States is part of México's problem. The United States is feeding the beast" (238).

Enabled by transfictional form's refusal to fully unify around a central narrative, Micho's story makes a critical interruption that exposes inequalities in who gets to appear as the face of Latinx struggles. Pulling readers away from the compelling plot about young immigrants that are easy to idealize, Micho's testimony calls Americans to the difficult political work we must undertake in addressing the issues of immigration. It is not as simple as advocating for the most sympathetic migrants. Projects of immigration justice must extend beyond the most acceptable faces of the Latinx community to recognize the injustices endured by all types of migrants.

Pulling against the narrative drive and consumable generic impulses of the main narrative, the stories of Micho and the other migrants expose the ways that sympathetic representations of Latinxs can result in a myopic focus on particularly tragic plots of victimization and idealized figures. In this context, Henríquez's choice to center child migrants is perceptive. The bulk of the action of the novel unfolds in 2008–2009. Legislative attempts to address the flaws in the U.S. immigration system in this period and more broadly in the twenty-first century have made little progress. In lieu of comprehensive reforms that seem impossible to pass, the national debate has circled back time and again to addressing the more specific plight of DREAMers, undocumented immigrants who were brought to the United States as children. In the novel, Maribel falls into this category; she becomes an illegal alien when her father is laid off and her family's work visa expires. The appeal of amnesty for DREAMers as the most palatable form of immigration reform testifies to the rhetorical power of placing innocent children as the face of the issue of "illegal" immigration. (We might think as well of how the separation of migrant children from their families became the dominant immigration issue of 2018.) The plight of DREAMers is an important cause but in its power to command moral and media attention, the DREAMers narrative risks eclipsing the much broader injustices and impacts of the U.S. immigration system. Addressing these broader injustices would demand more fundamental changes, more committed political will, and more material sacrifices from Americans than addressing the needs of the innocent children supported by the DREAM act. As Micho's narration asserts, Americans would need to dismantle entrenched nativism, confront cherished myths of immigration, and reckon with U.S. responsibilities for the conditions in Latin America. Focusing on the compelling cases of Latinx suffering can mean focusing on the easier cases. It can be an alibi for narrowing the scope of justice and eliding the challenging political work ahead.

Presenting a narrative of sympathetic migrants but at the same time pulling away from it with the perspectives of many other migrants, *The Book of Unknown Americans* recognizes the power of the idealized Latinx subject of injustice while challenging Americans not to invest completely in any one Latinx narrative, no matter how compelling. Interrupting the main plot to attend to the stories of other Latinxs, the novel's form foregrounds the question of how we distribute attention in narratives of the Latinx community and in our political consciousness. Much like Salvador Plascencia's *The People of Paper*, whose transfictional form dramatizes the conflict over narrative attention, *The Book of Unknown Americans* questions which images and figures are most central to the understanding of Latinxs. The answers have direct political implications, for the narratives we center in our depictions of Latinx struggle orient our political efforts. As scholars push us to recognize multiple forms of Latinx politics, this novel insists that we must also confront the inequalities of rhetorical power and moral compulsion that make some cases of Latinx struggle seem more worthy than others.

COMPARATIVE FORM AND THE WORK OF SOLIDARITY

Central to the effect of the stories of other migrants in this novel is their semiautonomous relation to the main plot, the way they stand apart from it. These testimonies make no mention of the main events of the novel and most of these characters play only minor roles in the central plot. Their position is similar to the semiautonomy of the stories of community members that we saw in *The Woman Warrior* and *The House on Mango Street*. The relations of these other characters to the main narrative and to each other, beyond neighborly proximity, is somewhat distant and often implicit. And yet, in important instances these characters enact forms of panethnic Latinidad. Using transfictional semiautonomy to depict panethnic community, *The Book of Unknown Americans* makes an aesthetic argument that the lives of Latinxs need not converge into a single story and their outcomes need not intertwine directly for Latinx to be a salient collective identity. As in other transfictional works, this novel does not link many of its stories with direct causal connections. Their juxtaposition in the same storyworld invites readers to draw out other possible relations across distinct stories. Are these people simply neighbors or are there more substantive resonances among their lives? This reading experience activates an important mode of political imagination for Latinx panethnicity. The grounds for political Latinidad may not always be apparent in overt similarities among groups. The novel's form asks readers to compare stories and draw out latent relations of consequence and solidarities across different lives and groups. To the debates around panethnic unity, this novel offers an aesthetic form that structures the thinking process so crucial to building panethnic solidarities, yet another argument for why ethnic studies fields should care about literary form.

The transfictional form of Henríquez's novel is inherently comparative, compelling readers to distinguish and relate many narrative pieces.[59] This quality makes it powerful for addressing panethnicity, which, as many scholars note, is a framework dependent on and generative of comparative analysis.[60] The nuanced comparative work that the panethnic framework enables is one argument for retaining panethnic categories. If scholars eschew "a priori notions of homogeneity," Silvio Torres-Saillant proposes that the panethnic category can be an opportunity to analyze "the material conditions, the social forces, and the political dynamics that frame the experience of Latinos."[61] Latinidad can enable cross-ethnic comparative analysis, producing more intricate understandings of each ethnic group than would be possible in isolated studies of these groups.[62] The panethnic ambitions of *The Book of Unknown Americans* illustrate this benefit. For example, by encompassing many different ethnic migration stories, the novel lets readers tease out the complexities of Latinx migration experiences. It's important, though, that the novel does not perform this analysis for readers. Much like Aimee Phan's *We Should Never Meet*, this novel does not clarify all the relations among its stories. It places the stories of individuals from different ethnic groups together for comparison but does not offer an overarching authorial perspective of how to understand the sense of collectivity that draws these disparate pieces together. This choice echoes Juan Flores's contention that Latinidad must be constructed relationally in the interstices between groups because there is no meaningful overarching perspective "that is simply 'Latino.'"[63] The novel invites readers to question what links these different stories. From these links, models of Latinidad may emerge.

One urgent case for Latinx solidarity that emerges across these stories is the economic precarity that links people from different ethnic groups. Through a combination of factors including migration, language, race, education, and citizenship status, many of the Latinxs in this novel labor in vulnerable, low-wage positions. Maribel's father, Arturo, resigns himself to brutal working conditions at a mushroom farm in Pennsylvania. "I'm not going to make waves," he tells his wife (25). The farm sponsored his work visa. Without citizenship, Arturo is one of the many Latinx temporary workers who have few protections or leverage to contest abusive conditions. As Chapter 3 discussed, such vulnerable workers from Latin America are pivotal to the low-wage sector of the American economy. This precarity recurs in other stories, linking very different lives. Benny Quinto, unlike Arturo, is a refugee. But after fleeing war-torn Nicaragua he also ends up in the low-wage sector, cooking at Burger King. Having citizenship does not necessarily improve this position, as the case of Mayor's father shows. Rafael is a naturalized citizen but, like his undocumented neighbors, he worries about his tenuous grip on employment. Having worked his way up at a local diner, he still has no job security: "even after years of being there. . . . He could be replaced in a heartbeat" (79). Reading these stories side by side reveals the same economic precarity cutting across seemingly strict dividing lines in the Latinx community, such as ethnicity, citizenship, and migration history.

Through the parallels that emerge among its distinct stories, the novel adds nuances to our sense of Latinx divisions. Arturo's story complicates the category of legal employment. Unlike Benny, Arturo came to the United States legally under a work visa, but he is nevertheless laid off. "The only reason they sponsored our visas was because the government was pressuring them to

hire workers with papers," Arturo observes (181). After this gesture of compli-
ance, the employers go back to hiring undocumented workers to save money.
When low-cost, undocumented labor is a foundation of the contemporary U.S.
economy, those who "follow the rules" like Arturo cannot distance themselves
from its impacts. The bright line between legal workers with visas and illegal
workers is obscured in the shadows cast by the unacknowledged presence of
illegality at the heart of the U.S. economy. "We're not like the rest of them,"
Alma insists, but after Arturo is laid off his work visa lapses and the Riveras do
become some "of them" (189). While the exploitation of illegal workers continues as a bedrock principle of the U.S. economy, it affects the prospects of both
documented and undocumented Latinxs. The juxtaposition of distinct cases in
this novel reveals the deeper problem of the U.S. economy's labor dependen-
cies; this problem spans the division between "legal" and "illegal" Latinxs that
many scholars see as splitting the political interests of Latinxs. The novel also
blurs the class differences so often evoked as blockages to panethnic solidarity.
Quisqueya Solís's story stands out because she comes from a rich family and an
ethnic group, Venezuelans, who in aggregate are affluent. Yet Quisqueya too,
after surviving sexual violence and running away from home, ends up in the
low-wage sector. Making narrative space for the specific circumstances of each
character much as Sandra Cisneros's or Gloria Naylor's fictions do, Henríquez
recognizes fine-grained variation at every scale of analysis. Her novel registers
the play of intersectional differences and structural realities that shape lives and
bring them into unexpected alignments that defy the aggregate measures by
which we parse Latinx differences. The class differences among different ethnic
groups are important, but the class variations within each group are equally
important, because they show that the class experiences of many individuals
from different ethnic groups still overlap. The aggregate socioeconomic measures
of each ethnic group mask the stratum of vulnerable laborers spanning ethnic
distinctions. Transfictional form is suited for drawing such unexpected relations
across groups, because it can refrain from prescribing the links between different
stories and the groups portrayed in them. It leaves these relations open for readers to construct. Out of this comparative reading experience a case emerges for
a Latinx coalition addressing the shared challenges of vulnerable workers. This
coalition would call on the nation to reckon with the integral role of Latinxs as

a racialized labor force and to confront the intertwining of economic precarity with differences of race, migration, language, and citizenship.

The economic vulnerability of characters like Gustavo and Benny results in part from the circumstances of their migrations to the United States. Members of the Latinx precariat, these characters fleeing war-torn nations also belong to a second major axis of Latinx solidarity that emerges across the stories. This is an axis that we touched on with Junot Díaz's *Drown*: displacement by U.S. forces in their nations. The story of Mayor's family, which migrated after the U.S. invasion of Panama in 1989, clarifies a cruel irony linking several of the stories. Latin Americans displaced by U.S. interventions had little choice but to flee to the nation that displaced them. Histories of U.S. intervention lie implicitly behind the stories of many of the other migrants. Gustavo fled from Guatemala to Mexico in 1980 and from there moved on to the United States. His narration begins elliptically with a series of dates and locations: "I was born in Clinique, El Quinché, Guatemala, in 1960, the year hell came to that country. I arrived in the United States on November 14, 2000. Before that, I resided in México" (87). Condensed in the interstices of this list is the violent history of a six-year civil war starting in 1960, followed by military dictatorships in the 1970s, all of which resulted from a U.S.-backed coup in 1954 that toppled a popularly elected left-leaning government. The forcible displacements linking many of the lives in this novel come across in Fito Angelino's description of the Latinx community he is sheltering in his apartment building. He sees the building as "an island for all of us washed-ashore refugees" (146). The word choice is telling. Fito sees a band of Latinx refugees, not immigrants. They are a community of the displaced.

As U.S. forces cross the borders of their nations with impunity, U.S. borders constrain the movements of these characters. From Benny Quinto's traumatic border crossing at the hands of a smuggling operation to Gustavo's anxiety about crossing the border to the many characters who worry about their legal status in the United States, the disruptive force of the border acts on their lives not only at the point of crossing but before and after as well. This enduring power comes across most memorably in the case of Arturo's body. Even in death, the border acts on him. When Alma tries to transport his body back home to Mexico, she is told that his body cannot legally cross the border in the car with her; it can only be transported by plane at a cost she cannot afford. U.S. power moving across borders to displace populations while constraining the movements that follow from these displacements—this conundrum links distinct stories across the novel. The novel sketches the contours of a Latinx solidarity, addressing the connections between U.S. policy in Latin America and migration policies affecting the lives of displaced Latin Americans in the United States.

A coalition of the Latinx precariat and a coalition of the Latinx displaced are latent solidarities that are never explicit in the novel's discourse; they emerge only through the comparisons and affiliations that the novel's form fosters. Transfictional literature offers guiding form for the conceptual work of constructing panethnicity. Activating the relations between the distinct stories and ethnic groups that Henríquez surveys, readers are effectively thinking through principles of Latinidad that can draw these groups together. The solidarities emerging in this process cut across many ethnic groups and demographic divisions, suggesting shared challenges that can align groups that might otherwise see little affinity with each other. In the end, what I find most compelling about the latent solidarities in this novel is the perceptive work readers must put in to uncover them. With the transfictional autonomy of its pieces, the novel does not explicitly present these different characters as sharing a unified story. We must perceive and build the shared stories of struggle that link them. This emphasis on the process and work of coalition is this novel's most important contribution to thinking on panethnicity. Solidarities are not readily apparent in the panoply of Latinx differences the novel's stories lay out, and yet they are there, waiting to be brought out. This reading experience conveys an important political point. Readily apparent issues and clear connections of outcomes can delineate Latinx coalition, but relying on them may narrow the potential scope of Latinidad. To extend the political promise of Latinx coalitions, we need to consider relations beyond the immediate, probing beneath given measures and categories of analysis to activate the potent solidarities that we have not yet mobilized and to imagine solidarities that we have not yet envisioned.

Given the current impasses of Latinidad, one might expect the panethnic ambitions of *The Book of Unknown Americans* to be modest, trying to pick out some threads of solidarity in the tangled web of conflicts and divisions characterizing

contemporary Latinx communities. Instead, the novel has more expansive ambitions. The novel doesn't narrow, but rather widens, the horizons for Latinx
coalition by envisioning solidarities that aren't constrained to ethnic identification alone. Through its form, the novel also calls Latinx politics to confront the
rhetorical inequalities that position different stories of Latinx suffering in the
public imagination. Most significantly, the novel involves readers in the work
of drawing affiliations across distinct histories and life paths. The novel shows
the affinities between transfictional thinking and the perceptive work involved
in constructing coalition across differences. In doing so, the novel outlines a
process for envisioning future Latinidades.

But we should note that Henríquez's ambitions come with limitations. One
of the primary challenges of panethnic solidarity is confronting the conflicts
within communities. Henríquez's novel does not stress the conflicts among
Latinxs as fully as it could. Different stories of Latinx struggle compete for
narrative attention. There are passing references to interethnic prejudices and a
memorable Christmas scene that addresses the domination of one ethnic group
over others. But beyond these instances, the novel registers differences among
Latinxs more than the charged conflicts that they give rise to. Transfictional
form, characterized by multiple tensions, should offer a powerful aesthetic for
rendering these antagonisms. The next chapter shows how Karen Tei Yamashita's
novel *I Hotel* uses transfictional tensions to place conflict at the heart of the
story of panethnicity. This novel too is not cowed by the impasses of panethnic
coalition. It responds to the crisis of Asian American unity with expansive
possibility, running with Henríquez's unbound sense of coalition toward a
utopian horizon.

CHAPTER 5

IMAGINING UNITY

I Hotel *and the Utopian Horizons of Asian America*

THE CHALLENGES OF Asian American and Latinx pan-ethnic coalitions today are daunting. These rapidly expanding communities hold out the promise of transformative solidarities, but they also strain the idea of community, encompassing deep divisions and a nearly incoherent range of experiences. Constructing forms of political alliance that do justice to their myriad differences and transformative ambitions is a challenge that demands their fullest imaginative energies. The necessity of creative work in meeting the impasses of panethnic coalition should lead all those concerned with Asian American and Latinx politics to consider the remarkable fictions being produced in these communities. As in the rest of this book, I credit imaginative works as contributions to the political debates with which Asian Americans and Latinxs are grappling. If the concepts of Asian American and Latinx are complex political fictions that scholars and activists are struggling to give shape to, then we should consider how literary fictions are giving form to these concepts. The gambit is to think through the fiction of panethnicity with panethnic fictions. As the last chapter argued with *The Book of Unknown Americans* and as this chapter will further argue with Karen Tei Yamashita's *I Hotel* (2010), panethnic fictions offer new conceptual forms and modes of political imagination to the ideas of Asian American and Latinx coalition. This chapter traces how *I Hotel*'s fluid form and embrace of conflict intersect with current proposals for flexible panethnicity and the powers of dissent. At the same time, the novel pushes on the limits of an anti-identitarian consensus that has turned away from unity, identity, and closure as political values. These limits cannot contain the novel's ambitions for the Asian American idea. Following these ambitions, we will meet a utopian form of panethnicity that reconfigures the place of identity in movements and expands the scope of Asian American politics.

I HOTEL, ASIAN AMERICAN NOVEL

I Hotel may be the most Asian American of Asian American novels. In contrast to the monoethnic works that comprise much of what critics categorize as Asian American literature, *I Hotel* is explicitly panethnic in scope. The issues raised by panethnicity are central to the novel's narration of the Asian American movement centered in the San Francisco Bay Area in the 1960s and 1970s.[1] As it follows the numerous branches of the movement that intersected in the anti-eviction struggle at the International Hotel in San Francisco's Manilatown, the novel accommodates stories from many different ethnic groups: Chinese, Japanese, Filipina/o, Indian, native Hawaiian, Korean, and in its final chapters, the diverse new waves of immigration after 1965. And it explores the interactions and conflicts among these groups as they fitfully coalesce into a movement. It shows students at the University of California at Berkeley inventing the Asian American category and mobilizing to make it a legitimate object of study. When they succeed in establishing Asian American studies, they realize they "had to find out what that was."[2] The leap of invention is exciting and daunting because *Asian American* is not a known quantity. Throughout the novel it is still forming.

Even though *I Hotel* looks back at this period with the retrospective clarity of forty years, it doesn't resolve the meanings of Asian American. Instead it takes up the unsettled spirit of that period, on the content level, by immersing readers in the fights over the Asian American idea, and on a formal level, with a restless form that takes pleasure in the many shapes the Asian American idea might take. Describing this form is difficult. Several critics have identified important features, but analyses of the novel have limited themselves to short excerpts, understandable given its massive scope.[3] Transfictional form offers a framework that can grasp the novel's macro structure.

A good place to start is Yamashita's own theorizations of the novel's form. In the afterword to the novel, Yamashita says she was drawn to the possibilities of the International Hotel as a narrative form. She tried to encompass the "multiple perspectives" within the Asian American movement with a work "divided into ten novellas or ten 'hotels.'" She reflects that "multiple novellas allowed me to tell parallel stories, to experiment with various resonant narrative voices, and to honor the complex architecture of a time, a movement, a hotel, and its people." In the extensive research she did to reconstruct the movement's stories, Yamashita found that her research was "scattered across political affinities, ethnicities, artistic pursuits—difficult to coalesce into any one storyline or historic chronology." What Yamashita has developed is a transfictional form, a novella cycle in which semiautonomous novellas follow parallel trajectories that do not coalesce into a single story, voice, or perspective. This form allows her to do justice to the multifarious threads of the movement. But recall that transfictional form does not resolve the tension between multiplicity and unity. Accordingly, Yamashita does not give up on the idea that this divergent outpouring of political energies should be understood as a movement. "The people I spoke with," she observes, "had definitely been in the movement, but often times had no idea what others had been doing. Their ideas and lives often intersected, but their ideologies were cast in diverse directions. Their choices took different trajectories, but everyone was there, really *there*" (610). Instead of rejecting the idea of a single movement, Yamashita sketches a fascinating image of what a movement can look like. This movement resists clear narration. It accommodates divergent directions of action and multiple ideologies. Instead of unified values and concerted actions, it is linked by people being "there," colliding in a common space as they pursue their activism in their own ways. The Asian American movement, in this view, did not possess a clear sense of its totality; the people involved had "no idea what others had been doing." And yet, the movement flourished, its energies flowing in myriad directions. In this model, political energy is not dependent on aligned efforts. Yamashita's image squares with many of the proposals scholars have put forth to rethink panethnicity. It is multiple, resists unification, and operates without a totalizing idea of panethnic politics and identity. But the novel doesn't just propose these ideas. As it organizes the pieces of the movement into a palpable storyworld, it renders these abstract ideas into aesthetic forms.

If the concept of panethnicity needs reshaping, the novel tries to work out what that shape could look like.

CONVERGENCE AND DIVERGENCE

Yamashita's description contends that the convergence and divergence of multiple political trajectories defined the Asian American movement. The novel models this sustained duality with transfictional form. While overlapping settings, intersecting characters, and other storyworld elements gesture toward convergence, its form also sustains a divergent impulse of stories following separate paths. Rethinking the Asian American movement with this duality, *I Hotel* proposes that the strength of a movement does not come from the convergence of actors into a unified body but rather from a continual flux: distinct actors and directions of struggle intersecting at moments and diverging at others. This proposal challenges assumptions about the beginnings and endings of movements and it revalues periods of disunity. While our thinking about movements usually emphasizes convergence and unity, *I Hotel*'s form reveals the potential of alternate forms that also embrace divergence and multiplicity.

Coalition as an ongoing cycle of convergence and divergence is a structuring principle across the novel. A chapter in the novella "1969" tells the story of the J-Town Collective (JTC), a group of activists serving San Francisco's Japantown. The chapter follows the collective's tumultuous story as they take up many causes. It climaxes with a major schism between the JTC and a more moderate group, the Committee Against Nihonmachi Evictions (CANE). The expulsion of the JTC's members from CANE spells the end of the JTC's formal efforts. The chapter ends with their offices shuttered. This moment of political divergence seems to be the end of their story. But in a transfictional crossing of narrative borders, the JTC story continues in a separate novella. The chapter "Iron Ox" in the novella "1971" focuses on a new Asian American art collective that sets up shop in the offices vacated by the JTC. The narrator qualifies this ending for the activist group: "It isn't that they're giving up the radical life, mind you. . . . Maybe they are going underground or merging with another radical formation. It's like that these days. . . . They come, give you a line, then join some other line" (288). The displacement of the ending of the JTC into a separate novella is a fitting formal instantiation of the principle that the ending of one strand of a movement can in fact be a link to another strand of the movement. In this case, the ending of the JTC allows for a new art collective to emerge. That one line of the movement frequently shifts to "join some other line" suggests how political divergence can open possibilities for new convergences. The coexistence of parallel lines of political action allows for dynamic reconfiguration that keeps political momentum rolling even as the groups within the movement shift and dissolve. Momentum is not dependent on a single line of continuity. Some lines carry on as others come to an end. Some lines seem to dissolve only to reemerge with other lines. The novel reenvisions the temporality of political movements not in terms of beginnings or endings, clear duration or fixed structure, but as a flux among the many possible configurations a movement can take.

This flux reinforces a recent wave of proposals in Asian American and Latinx studies that argue for flexible forms of panethnicity. Flexible panethnicity challenges assumptions that political power comes from stable, long-term coalitions. In line with the ideas of situational panethnicity discussed in the last chapter, flexible panethnicity does not claim to be an overarching unity. Felix M. Padilla notes that the panethnic Latinx framework can be powerful in certain situations and irrelevant in others.[4] Panethnicity "waxes in periods" when it can best advance the needs of those that take it up.[5] Flexible panethnicity can wax and wane as needed much as the converging and diverging rhythms of coalition in *I Hotel*. This idea reframes the instability plaguing Asian American and Latinx coalitions as a potential strength. As Marta Caminero-Santangelo argues, "the shifting and fluid nature of various Latino alliances and coalitions does not need to signify the 'failure' of latinidad but might instead suggest its flexibility, its adaptability to new and changing circumstances."[6] The instability of Latinx and Asian American coalitions can be a form of agility to respond to changes within each community and to the shifting contexts in which they struggle for justice. While it can create challenges for working within establishment politics, which recognizes solid interest groups, flexible panethnicity is a compelling model.

It's common to lament how short-lived movement unity can be. Movements at full strength don't seem to last. By refiguring movement endings, *I Hotel* shifts this view. Attuned to the new cycles of solidarity that can follow from coalitions breaking apart, it claims dissolution not as the end of coalition but as an integral part of a coalition's dynamics. It sees a movement as carrying through periods of waning and reconfiguration.[7] As Asian American and Latinx politics today become increasingly institutionalized, *I Hotel* pushes against this development. The novel does not worry that moments of unified coalition are impermanent. The divergence of a movement into separate directions can sustain the momentum for future reconvergence.

I Hotel goes further to embrace the powers of political divergence not just as the precursor for future unities, but as a way that movements spread into the world along multiple lines of action. The novella "1973" is the novel's clearest argument for the powers of divergence. "1973" traces the lives and work of three Japanese American activists, Ria Ishii, Stony Ima, and Wayne Takabayashi. Their stories unfold across five chapters that outline a full cycle of the convergence-divergence-reconvergence process. In the first chapter, "Turtle Island," the three meet for the first time in 1969 on a boat heading to Alcatraz. They hail from different parts of the Asian American movement and are bringing supplies to support the occupation of Alcatraz by the Indians of All Tribes, a pan-tribal movement reclaiming native lands. This chapter narrates an important moment of ethnic and cross-racial coalition in their lives. Indeed, the chapter's opening describes it as a potentially transformative, if daunting, turning point: "It's not easy to get into a boat with three people you don't know and go rowing off toward your destiny" (373). Their moment together on Alcatraz lasts only a few days, but it is transformative. As part of the occupation, they experience a sense of energy and purpose that stays with them. By the beginning of the second chapter, they are going their separate ways, but their divergent paths bear the imprint of their experience on Alcatraz: "Stony drove everyone home to the beginnings of their separate destinies. Or, you could say their separate quests but same promises" (383). As with the closing of the JTC offices, the ending of a moment of coalition in this novel is never simply an ending. In *We Should Never Meet*, we saw stories reach apparent closure only to be opened again by later stories. *I Hotel* develops this transfictional dynamic to show that moments of political intersection create relationships that endure to be reactivated later.

"1973" and the novel more broadly are fascinated by the ways that even brief moments of solidarity can change people and propel them into the world to pursue different directions of struggle. The novella devotes its middle three chapters to the "separate quests" the young activists undertake after Alcatraz. In "Crane," Ria throws herself into improving the working conditions of Chinatown seamstresses by helping them organize a collectively owned venture. In "Cormorant,"

Stony travels to Japan to join the students protesting the construction of Narita Airport and through several turns of fate ends up meeting his father's side of the family for the first time. Wayne's story in "Muskrat" carries him from the nuclear disarmament movement to an encounter with a Quaker activist who taught at the same internment camp where his family was imprisoned. While a moment of alliance may be impermanent and its direct effects limited, its indirect impacts reverberate along lines of action fanning outward. The usual schemata for understanding movements emphasize concentrated action. They overlook the larger continuum of movement forms. To describe the reverberations emanating from important nexus points we need a different architecture, a movement as a kind of explosion of energies. In this view, the divergence that succeeds moments of unified action is welcome when it unleashes the energies of those moments into expansive impacts across a range of struggles.

The transfictional form of "1973" illustrates the practices of the novel as a whole. The political destinies of multiple ethnic groups converge and diverge across the novel. The International Hotel acts as a powerful "beacon" drawing in different parts of the Asian American movement (579). At the hotel they intersect, interact, and go out into the world to pursue many directions of struggle. In the final novella, Yamashita offers an image of the four doorways of the hotel. People find their way into the movement through different doors and they go out through different doors to pursue their work. Though she acknowledges the conflicts that arise from these differences, Yamashita sees exciting possibility in the proliferating directions of Asian American politics in this period. In the afterword, she offers a Whitmanesque list of the projects sparked by the movement: "communes and cooperatives, drug rehabilitation programs, bookstores, newspapers and journals, theaters, filmmakers, cultural centers, artists, musicians, politicians, law cooperatives, educators, historians, underground Marxist-Leninist-Maoist collectives, and literary and political movements." "For the Asian American community," she concludes, "this was a flourishing time of new creative energy and political empowerment" (610).

TRANSETHNIC SLIPPAGES AND UNLIKELY ALLIANCES

I Hotel's play with convergence translates on a plot level into a preoccupation with chance meetings. These meetings are crucial narrative devices, engines of story generation. But they also offer a further narrative structure through which to rethink panethnic coalitions. Chance encounters are opportunities to examine connections that might be overlooked and to find allies in unlikely places. They reconceive panethnicity as a stranger creature, transethnicity, which emphasizes slippages across seemingly fixed ethnic lines. Accounts of Asian American differences paint a fractured picture of Asian America, divided especially along ethnic lines. *I Hotel*'s transethnic crossings complicate this picture by calling attention to the unpredictable alliances that emerge from Asian America's proliferating differences.

I Hotel opens a fictional space to wonder, what could happen if we saw the ethnic differences obstructing panethnicity as less rigid than they seem? Scholars in both Asian American and Latinx studies emphasize situational solidarities forming between specific ethnic groups. *I Hotel* makes a more radical move. It figures ethnic groups transforming into one another and blurring ethnic boundaries. This fluidity is apparent in the last novella when the narrator gives voice to the new Asian immigration:

> we surged forth, in a post-1965 wave. . . . We were Chinese from Taiwan, Hong Kong, Singapore, Malaysia. We were Filipinos, Koreans, Thai, and Japanese. In another decade, our wave crested again higher, as we Vietnamese, Laotians, Cambodians, Hmong, Nepalese, Burmese, Indonesian also joined our distraught destinies to life across the Pacific. . . . we Indian, Pakistani, Bangladeshi, also entered as *Asian* Americans. (602)

The collective "we" narration inhabits one and then another ethnicity. This is not a panethnic "we" that stands "above" these ethnic groups. Rather, in each syntactical moment the "we" *is* each of these groups. Instead of panethnicity, passages like this explore the possibility of transethnicity, in which the collective category continually transforms from one constituency to another. In narrating the migration that made ethnic differences an acute problem for Asian American unity, Yamashita develops a collective voice that slips across those differences.

Transethnic slippages produce illuminating confusions of seemingly separate stories and experiences. The narrative units of chapters and novellas that make up *I Hotel* each tend to focus on a single ethnic group. Meanwhile, transethnic slippages and character relations prod readers to perceive the links among these groups. In *Drown* and *We Should Never Meet* we saw how the transfictional gaps between stories could map the borders separating nations while challenging readers to construct transnational forms of relation across those borders. *I Hotel* takes up this feature to spur the imagination of solidarities across ethnic boundaries. A fascinating example occurs between the first two novellas, "1968" and "1969," which focus on communities of Chinese Americans and Japanese Americans, respectively. The central chapter of "1969" is a transcription of a documentary film that chronicles Japanese American groups as they try to prevent evictions in San Francisco's Japantown. But the credits reveal that the film has been an act of transethnic narration. The filmmaker is Judy Eng, a Chinese American documentarian who was a major character in "1968." A Chinese American perspective takes on a Japanese American struggle to the point where the ethnic identity of the filmmaker is a surprise. Character recurrences here enact a transethnic narration that links two novellas focusing on different ethnic groups. With a major-minor transposition recalling Rishi Reddi's *Karma*, these novellas show how the activists are involved in struggles beyond the ones in which they figure as central. *I Hotel* formally enacts the myriad cross-ethnic relations and identifications that made up the Asian American movement.

While Chinese American perspectives emerge within a Japanese American story in "1969" the opposite crossing occurs in "1968." The chapter "My Special Island" recounts the flare-up of Chinese-Japanese tensions over the takeover of the Tiao Yu Tai islands by Japan. These tensions spill over to Chinese American and Japanese American communities. Interethnic conflicts in home regions can endure among migrant communities in the United States, complicating panethnic coalition. "My Special Island" is followed by a chapter titled "We" that includes moments of transethnic narration cutting across the image of division. "We" opens with a story of arrival in the United States and detention at Angel Island, the West Coast facility where many Asian immigrants were imprisoned. The narration describes the challenging adaptations and hard labor these immigrants took on. Given the novella's focus, readers might assume that the narrating "we" is Chinese American. But further along, it becomes clear that this is a Japanese American "we": "We gave our adopted towns names like Li'l Yokohama and Nihonmachi" (58). The opening of the chapter performs a transethnic bait and switch that becomes more convoluted as the chapter proceeds. Once the Japanese American identity of this "we" appears settled, it begins to blur again. The "we" visits Angel Island and muses, "Angel Island felt like it might be our island; so much of our history was here" (62). For readers, the claim of ownership might resonate with the Chinese-Japanese dispute over the Tiao Yu Tai islands. Angel Island and its history too might be contested between these groups. But the chapter gradually shifts to the stories of Chinese suffering on Angel Island and the identity of the "we" wavers, seeming to encompass a Chinese American standpoint as well; the "we" listens as the famous Angel Island poems, carved by Chinese detainees on the walls of their prison cells, are discovered and read aloud. Yamashita juxtaposes a chapter narrating interethnic discord and the hardening of ethnic lines with this chapter in which the ethnic identity of a collective "we" blurs repeatedly. Her transethnic confusions open a space to consider the historical links between the disputing groups: the detention, exclusion laws, and racialized labor exploitation they both endured in the United States. Transfictional form, which invites connections among distinct stories, reinforces these confusions by throwing the stories of different ethnic groups together in the same storyworld. This recalls the cross-ethnic links in *The Book of Unknown Americans*, which also juxtaposed stories focused on different ethnic groups to spur interethnic comparison. In Yamashita's hands, transethnic narration is an intentional slippage, a thought experiment to consider the solidarities that might emerge when we do not take ethnic separations as given.

Transethnic narration opens possibilities by suggesting that ethnic groups are not completely contained by their group boundaries. This idea diverges from the tendency to treat ethnic groups as the discrete "building block[s]" of panethnic coalition.[8] In her influential account, Yén Lê Espiritu defines a panethnic formation as "a politico-cultural collectivity made up of peoples of several, hitherto distinct, tribal or national origins."[9] Distinct ethnic groups come first and panethnic collectives are constructed from them. This model works as a historical description, but it doesn't account for situations like the present when panethnic categories are already established and coexist in dynamic relations with ethnic categories. Moreover, the model can imply that ethnic groups are somehow more "real." Martha E. Gimenez, for instance, rejects the Latinx category as a fictional collective composed of "populations that ought to be publicly named by their real historical names."[10] For her, these "real historical names" are primarily ethnic and national origin labels. "Each national origin aggregate," she insists, "is different from the others" in terms of class, history, and many other variables.[11] In the laudable effort to resist the homogenizing effects of a panethnic category, scholars use ethnicity as fixed blocks of difference, which overlooks the instability of ethnicities themselves. Complicating panethnicity can come at the cost of reifying ethnicity. It's important to recognize ethnic differences and the challenges they pose for coalition, but, like panethnic groups, ethnic groups are not self-evident or homogeneous. They are constructed continuously, particularly in interaction with other ethnic groups. Variation and category overflow occur at every scale.

The unlikely convergences and transethnic slippages of *I Hotel* push against a poststructuralist turn in both Asian American and Latinx critique. This turn emphasizes a politics of irreducible difference in contrast to the values of unity and identity in traditional identity politics. Kandice Chuh's influential proposal that Asian American studies should be a "subjectless discourse" is representative of this turn. Chuh contends that "there is no common subject of Asian American studies; there are only infinite differences."[12] In Latinx studies, Cristina Beltrán makes a similar push for a Latinidad that "celebrates specificity."[13] Consider as well the extensive cataloging of differences that have fed into the crises of the Asian American and Latinx categories. *I Hotel* helps rethink this emphasis on irreducible difference. Prioritizing infinite differences can paint a one-sided image. Breaking open images of homogeneity to stress differences is an important step toward recognizing social complexity but only a step. A more complex view of a panethnic community would acknowledge not only underexamined differences but also unexpected alignments among people. *I Hotel* features many different peoples within the panethnic category, but as they follow distinct personal and political paths, their routes do not lead inexorably away from each other. Instead the proliferation of different trajectories results in a tangled web; their paths and stories cross and converge in unpredictable ways. The differences within a panethnic collective do not lead only to conflicts and divisions but to shared situations and alliances. Yamashita's portrait of the Asian American movement shows a generative interplay between difference and commonality, divergence and convergence.

We need to examine the inadequacy of the categories of social difference we use to parse the Asian American community. *I Hotel* takes pleasure in the ways social and political life overflows category boundaries. Embracing this overflow opens political visions to alliances across established lines. The first novella stresses this point with a story of two Chinese American writers, Edmund and Paul. Paul comes from an affluent family; Edmund, from a working-class family. Their stories seem tailor made to recognize the class differences within the Chinese American community. At a meeting Paul and Edmund attend, a speaker exhibits the earnest impulse to acknowledge class difference: "Fact is the restaurants are staffed by illiterate Chinese who work fourteen hours a day, six days a week. Fiction is Chinese businessman is doing good business. Fact is this is exploitation of Chinese immigrants who can only find work in . . . Chinatown" (14–15). Edmund is confused: "I'm not illiterate. What's he talking about?" Paul clarifies, "It's not about you. It's about the others." Edmund replies, "I am the others" (15). Yamashita's most thought-provoking moments are often these comic ones. The attempt to recognize class differences within the community ends up fixing the boundaries of class, leaving no way to see a figure like Edmund, a scholar literate in multiple languages who also works constantly to make ends meet. An unlikely pairing by demographic standards, Paul and Edmund are brought together by their shared love of literature and their struggles with the vocation of writing in a moment of political activism. We saw how *The Book of Unknown Americans* elaborates a solidarity of the Latinx precariat across seemingly fixed ethnic lines. This episode makes a related move, surpassing established categories of difference to bring out political and artistic solidarities. Together, these novels suggest that insisting on difference in the community, an attempt at acknowledging complexity, can become its own form of reductive thinking. It can paint an atomized picture of irreconcilable divisions that leaves little space for the ways that lives cross divisions.

Ethnicity, class, gender, sexuality, ideology—these differences are crucial to acknowledge in coalition building, but they cannot fully account for the relations that make up political life. Assessing the prospects of panethnicity, Marta Caminero-Santangelo argues that no one form of identification can determine the possibilities for coalition. Each person and group holds multiple identifications that intersect in unpredictable ways.[14] Ethnicity or any other category is neither the unassailable ground for nor the insurmountable obstacle to solidarity. *I Hotel*, David Palumbo-Liu observes, is a sympathetic account of human messiness, "the human motivations—good, bad, honorable, egotistical, wise, naive" behind the Asian American movement.[15] The novel delights in showing us how categories of difference do not contain the messy entanglements of the lives that drive a movement. And its transfictional form thrives on unexpected links across the stories of different groups. If a panethnic coalition is a constructed fiction, then its writing is an opportunity for imaginative work. Why let our current containers of difference bind our political imagination?

THE FORCE OF CONFLICT IN THE NARRATIVE
OF ASIAN AMERICA

With attention to unpredictable alliances emerging from proliferating differences, *I Hotel* extends the idea of multiple panethnicities proposed in Asian American and Latinx studies. It is important that *I Hotel* does not shy away from the conflicts among these groups. Its narrative strands thrive on the antagonisms within the Asian American movement between the personal and the political, art and politics, intellectualism and activism, local and international struggles, revolutionary ideals and pragmatic tactics. These arguments were not always productive. In the final novella, Yamashita devotes a chapter to surveying the many activist groups around the International Hotel that often worked at cross purposes, fighting each other rather than a shared enemy. While the novel registers the limitations of argument, on the whole, it proposes that panethnic coalitions should see dissensus as a positive good.

Instead of seeing conflict within panethnic coalitions as a liability, recent scholarship calls for embracing it. This reevaluation is connected to a politics of difference, which critiques the idea that unity and consensus are prerequisites for effective politics. While some voices acknowledge the challenges of solidarity but hold onto the idea of panethnic unity,[16] others go further. "I have no wish to create unity out of diversity," Cristina Beltrán declares.[17] Beltrán is a sharp critic of the idea that Latinidad is most powerful when united behind a single agenda. This assumption, she argues, conflates political power with consensus, with troubling consequences for those in the community who don't fall in line.[18] For her, the ideal of unified power works to deny differences, exclude marginal groups, and turn dissent into a betrayal of the collective cause.[19] The charges of betrayal lodged against feminist and queer Latinx groups that critiqued the sexual politics of Latinx movements is well documented and parallel cases in Asian American politics abound.[20] Lisa Lowe insists that minority groups must examine whether they have reproduced structures of domination and assimilation within the movements they forged to fight racial domination and assimilation.[21] These critiques of unity are generative. They question basic assumptions about political coalition and call on movements to practice principles of nondomination within their structures.

Doing away with the rallying cry of unity might seem to entail a loss of political energy, but critics of unity point to the powerful energies of conflict. Beltrán argues that Latinx movements should embrace the powers of disagreement.[22] Debate can help ensure that Latinx coalition is a just and democratic structure.[23] Debate is also a transformative force that can keep the panethnic category responsive to new developments and marginalized constituencies.[24] Kandice Chuh concurs, seeing disagreement as the lifeblood of politics.[25] She argues for re-envisioning Asian American studies as "a field of *collaborative antagonisms*," an intriguing phrase that implies that conflict can generate attachments not just divisions.[26] By viewing conflicts as a binding force for panethnic collectivity, we can revalue friction and difference as integral features of coalition. This call to embrace the conflicts within Asian American and Latinx politics opens exciting possibilities by turning a seeming weakness into a strength.

Yamashita's novel joins these scholars to make a strong case for conflict. As Nathan Ragain observes, *I Hotel* takes the antagonisms between different pieces of the Asian American movement as a creative force.[27] This creative energy is a major theme of the novel. But more intriguing is the novel's medium-specific contribution to the critical debate. Through its narrative form, the novel demonstrates not just how conflict can foster dynamism and democracy within movements but how it can expand their political horizons.

I Hotel offers narrative as a generative model for thinking through the productive force of conflict. Narrative, after all, thrives on conflict. *I Hotel* sees movements not just as political groups but as dynamic narratives of formation and social transformation, stories driven forward by the conflicts within. The novel invests consistently in this analogy. The novella "1970" opens with a member of the Red Guard Party, a radical Asian American youth organization, chatting with a fictionalized Eldridge Cleaver. The Red Guard member asks Cleaver how Mo Akagi came to be part of the Black Panthers (Akagi is a fictionalization of Richard Aoki, the Japanese American who famously armed the Panthers). "Now that's a story," the narrator interjects as the novella immerses us in a narrative of intersecting lives in West Oakland (198). Later in their conversation, the storytelling turns to how some Chinatown street kids became radicalized into the Red Guard Party. Their exchanges show that narrative is a crucial part of how these movements understand their formations, identities, and allies.[28] We have to be careful with this analogy. Conflict can be aesthetically satisfying in a story while being frustrating in a political movement. Nevertheless, the analogy offers a worthwhile thought experiment for considering how conflict can be a generative force that keeps a coalition developing. Much as the turns of a plot are generated by its conflicts, the dynamism of a movement comes from dissent. As *I Hotel* shows, moments of conflict and divergence, narrative climaxes like the schism between the Japantown Collective and the Committee Against Nihonmachi Eviction, are not endings but inflection points that open possibilities for the movement to take new forms and new directions.

In *I Hotel* the tensions troubling Asian American coalition are a source of propulsion. Giving form to Kandice Chuh's idea of "collaborative antagonisms,"[29] *I Hotel* rethinks Asian American coalition as a conflict-driven narrative. In the face of a theoretical impasse that sees the concept of Asian American as incoherent, the novel's narrative practices rejuvenate the concept by re-imagining its internal conflicts not as disabling problems but as generative forces driving the unfinished story of Asian American struggle.

More specifically, *I Hotel* offers a transfictional narrative model, which argues that internal conflicts can transform the political ambitions of panethnicity. As Jinqi Ling notes, the events described in each novella in *I Hotel* are "entangled" in relations that extend beyond the boundaries of the novella.[30] What Ling hints at is the novel's transfictional form. In this form, the conflicts within a story are not contained by the borders of its concerns. Unresolved conflicts are embedded in indirect yet consequential relations that extend beyond one story's spatial and temporal boundaries to implicate other stories and settings. With this form, *I Hotel* portrays the Asian American movement as a story whose internal conflicts are not simply internal. They are connected to broader social contradictions. The novel proposes that internal conflicts can orient Asian American politics toward expansive horizons of justice. Asian American politics can and should be able to think beyond the boundaries of Asian American concerns.

A passage in the last novella that meditates on the conflicted racial identity of the movement offers a rich example of how Asian American politics is part of larger struggles:

Now if we were going to have to work with the rules of a color wheel, well then
maybe we should get to define what our color is. But creating that definition
turned out to be a complicated and impossible task no matter how we circled
around it or tried to confine it, and we argued long and hard about this until
perhaps we've never really resolved it. Maybe there's no resolution; the problem
of the color wheel in America has a long and deep history. (593)

The necessary yet impossible task of defining Asian American generates an ongoing argument that unifies the "we" in this passage. Here the argument within
the Asian American community is inseparable from the longer history of U.S.
racism and its full "color wheel" of racializations. No matter how they try to
draw a circle around the problem of Asian American racialization, they find that
they cannot "confine" it. It is always part of larger struggles. This vision implies
that conflicts within Asian America are productive because they point to the
contradictions extending beyond Asian America that generate them. The struggle
of defining Asian American cannot be resolved internally; its resolution would
require transforming the entire "color wheel," the racial order of the United States
as an interrelated system. This political vision argues for the inextricable relation
of Asian American conflicts to broader horizons of justice.

This expansive vision requires an interpretive practice, a way of reading the
ramifications of particular struggles in the larger world. The Asian American
movement tried to develop such perception. The activists Yamashita depicts
strive for a sense of "the general picture" by placing different oppressions in
relation rather than seeing them in isolation (211). As Jinqi Ling observes, *I Hotel*
defies the image of the Asian American movement as a narrow ethnic nationalist concern to show its transnational ambitions and the multiracial context in
which it formed.[31] The movement saw itself as part of global struggles against
imperialism and multiracial struggles against racism. These broader alignments
helped bring together the Asian American coalition.[32] Transfictional works can
help train this vision by asking readers to situate individual stories within a
world much broader than the scope of any one story. Much as *The Book of Unknown Americans* invites readers to perceive latent solidarities across the struggles
of particular ethnic groups, *I Hotel* also spurs readers to engage in a form of
coalitional vision. This experience is especially clear in the final novella, "1977,"
which narrates in separate chapters clashing groups within the Asian American

community: the group of young activists trying to save the International Hotel, an older generation of Chinese, Japanese, and Filipina/o Americans who grew up in the ethnic enclaves of the Bay Area, and the communities that arrived in the post-1965 waves of immigration. The novella switches among these different panethnic collectives, each chapter rendering a distinct context that overlaps with but doesn't coincide with the contexts of the other groups. The distinctions and relations that emerge in reading these stories together invite us to reframe the conflicts between these groups within a broader vision.

The first two chapters focus on the young activists, their anticapitalist critique of urban redevelopment, and their outrage at the displacement of the Chinese and Filipino laborers who live in the International Hotel. The activists call out an American standard that sees suburban single-family houses as "proper" homes, a standard that delegitimizes the lives of the tenants living in the shared spaces of the International Hotel (590). In a mass protest circling the building, they defend the tenants against the eviction. At the heart of their rallying cries is a call to consider the "refuge" that older generations deserve after working for a lifetime (592).

The next chapter shifts to an older generation of Asian Americans but not the one the activists lionize. Instead it's a group that left behind ethnic enclaves to settle in the kind of suburban single-family homes their children critique. Some of them look on the radical politics of the activists with disdain. And to the young activists, their politics seem reactionary. "Our kids thought we'd betrayed them," they reflect. In turn, the older generation complains that the young activists were "giving up the opportunities of college educations to go back to the towns we had worked so hard to get them out of." The sentiment could come across as simply upward mobility and assimilation politics were it not for the history of struggle implied in the last clause, a history that Yamashita carefully unpacks by giving this group its own narrative space. Like the young activists, the older generation recognizes the disruptive impact of urban redevelopment on minority communities. "It's not as if we didn't know it was happening," they insist. But their perspective on the redevelopment of ethnic enclaves is very different, shaped by a history of having struggled for citizenship rights, social mobility, and freedom from ethnic ghettoization. The struggle against racial segregation bound this panethnic "we." They had little choice but to be confined to ethnic enclaves whose borders outsiders and tourists could easily cross. But they recall with pride, "we were the first merchants, the town patriarchs, the educated sons and daughters, the rising professionals, the veterans of war, whose hard work and sacrifice proved that, given opportunities, we could be worthy citizens" (594–595). Confronting the challenges of their day, this generation too waged a racial political struggle via their own methods.

The story of the young activists describes a situation of racialized displacement while this story describes a seemingly incompatible situation of racial enclosure. The novella's transfictional form helps us think through this conundrum. Confronting readers with distinct yet related stories, this form fosters an interpretive practice attuned to political situations where different and even opposite struggles are nevertheless connected. To link the stories of the young activists and older generation, readers must see their political differences not as internecine conflicts but as symptoms of their different positions within larger systems of injustice. Their political conflict stems from linked but distinct forms of racialized spatial violence—the residential segregation of racialized communities and the displacement of racialized communities by urban redevelopment. These instances give rise to opposing struggles: for the freedom not to have to live in an ethnic enclave and for the freedom to continue living in an ethnic enclave. *I Hotel* asks us to think more broadly, to situate political differences in their underlying conditions, and to envision the Asian American politics that could address those conditions. Sensing the larger stakes of its internal differences, a pliant Asian American politics would be able to encompass conflicting social struggles, for this is the uneven and connected landscape of racial injustices that striate Asian American social realities.

The conflicts introduced by another panethnic "we" stretch the foci of Asian American politics to take on a transnational scope. The fourth chapter in the novella introduces the post-1965 waves of Asian immigration, linked by the "cycle upon cycle of global conflict" driving migration (602). The struggles of this group fall outside the purview of the movement defending the International Hotel. As discussed in the last chapter, established panethnic organizations do not necessarily address the needs of new arrivals. The new immigrants acknowledge how more established Asian Americans must see them: "their old wave did not really want the trouble of our new wave, did not want our neediness, . . . the cynicism and dishonesty of our survival strategies, or the fervor of our grasping capitalism" (602–3). The new arrivals keep their distance from the Asian American movement. While one panethnic group pursues a radical struggle against capitalist exploitation, another remains uninvolved and even embraces the capitalism the movement is fighting. The activists may see the politics of the new arrivals as apathetic or suspect, but the distinct slice of the storyworld opened by this chapter reveals the political effects of the conditions the new arrivals confront. Explaining why they turned away from the struggle at the International Hotel, the new immigrants confess, "we hurried away, fearing any chance of arrest or assault. We had come too far and sacrificed too much to risk such involvement" (603). Yamashita shows how this political schism arises from the broader conditions of legal and economic precarity that new immigrants face and the global inequalities and conflicts that make migration such a sacrifice. These realities constrain the immigrants' political possibilities. From their tenuous positions in the nation, they cannot afford to stick out and stick up for others. With this view, the radicalism of the Asian American activists appears as a kind of power afforded by native-born citizenship in a nation whose power imbalances with Asian nations conditioned the migration of the new arrivals. Through this contrasting story, their relatively privileged position vis-à-vis the new migrants comes into focus. The novella juxtaposes conflicting parts of the Asian American community and asks us to think transfictionally across and beyond their distinct stories to construct a view of the broader world. *I Hotel*'s form insists on seeing the conflicts within Asian America as nexus points of larger social forces and deeper contradictions, pressure points that when probed reveal the interconnected struggles in which Asian America is embedded. The tensions of a panethnic coalition do not call Asian Americans simply to turn inward and set their affairs in order; the tensions are imperatives to open their political vision out onto the world.

I Hotel trains a broad political vision that perceives the conflicts in Asian America as local eruptions of vaster social contradictions. Advancing the argument for embracing dissensus, the novel shows how internal tensions can orient panethnic politics toward transformative projects of justice. Asian American coalitions, then, should welcome their conflicts. These conflicts can hamper organizing and complicate efforts but they are also reminders of the larger stakes of which these efforts are a part. Rather than covering them over or setting them aside, organizing around these conflicts is a way to reimagine the breadth of panethnic politics.

THE UTOPIAN IMAGINATION AND THE
POWERS OF CLOSURE

In response to the crisis of the categories of Asian American and Latinx, many scholars have narrowed the scope of panethnic politics, calling for situational and specific instances of cross-ethnic solidarity rather than overarching unity. *I Hotel* offers a radically different response. It pursues the proliferating and even promiscuous range of the Asian American concept to rethink panethnic politics as a broad program of social struggle. The contrast brings out some limitations of the turn toward situational panethnicity. Situational coalitions are responsive to particular issues and they bring to the foreground the active work of coalition building. But what are the costs of letting go of a grand unified vision of panethnic alliance? How does focusing on specific issues affect the ambitions of Asian American and Latinx politics? *I Hotel* wagers that it's possible to address the conflicts within panethnicity without losing the passionate ambitions that gave rise to the Asian American idea in the first place. Its argument is even stronger: that only through an expansive sense of Asian American politics can the conflicts within panethnicity be understood. In its view, Asian American politics cannot extricate itself from struggles that lie beyond the purview of what seems properly Asian American. Far from a flaw as some suggest, the incoherence of the panethnic concept may be its power. If we welcomed the way the concept cannot resolve its own conflicts and overflows its own boundaries, we might discover the stakes of Asian American politics in the broader world.

The cross-racial and transnational breadth of causes the novel addresses under the banner of the Asian American movement may appear incoherent, but this overreach is important. Its imagined shape for the Asian American movement rejects isolated, issue-focused models of organizing to orient Asian American coalition toward large-scale transformation. This shape strives to grasp systemic orders of oppression and insists that we cannot transform these orders piecemeal. The struggle for the International Hotel at the heart of the novel seems like a local struggle. Its setting is San Francisco's Manilatown and its primary antagonists are the city government and its redevelopment policies. But as the activists investigate the issue, they discover it extends far beyond the local. Tracing the hotel's tangled networks of ownership, they find transnational capital. The domestic owners of the hotel sold it to the Enchanted Seas Corporation, an investment company based in Hong Kong. Already the scope is daunting: "What you gonna do? Catch a plane, go picket Hong Kong?" (424). Tracing the links further, they find that Enchanted Seas is a front for a Thai businessman, Samut Songkram, who runs a whiskey monopoly and controls the police and military in Thailand. Songkram, they find out, bought the hotel as part of investments in California designed to get his assets out of Thailand where mass student protests have broken out and been met with military suppression. The putatively local struggle is entangled in a vast web of economic, political, and military interests. Such thick embeddedness is an argument for the Asian American movement to take on a broader scope. The antagonists cannot be simply isolated and located. Quoting Marx and Engels at one point, the novel acknowledges that the capitalist system and world market "establish connexions everywhere" (317). The demands this understanding places on resistance movements help explain the urgency driving the novel's range and proliferating connections. The counterforce to vast systems of injustice must strive to be similarly ambitious in its vision.

I Hotel conceives the site of political struggle as having no fixed boundaries. Yamashita models this openness with the narrative relations that cross in and out of each novella, which, we might recall, she thinks of as a kind of hotel. As Xiaojing Zhou observes, the novellas are "open spaces of multiple vectors of histories and events that intersect, converge in, or emerge with the multifaceted Asian American movement."[33] But if we see the site of Asian American political struggle as unbound, do we risk losing the specific identity of this struggle? Yamashita's choice to organize the narratives of the movement around a place helps alleviate this concern, because the identity of a place is compatible with unfixed boundaries and multiple relations. I Hotel's understanding of the site of Asian American struggle resonates with Doreen Massey's theory of place. Against theories that see places as bounded, fixed, and coherent in identity, she argues for understanding a place as a specific nexus of social relations that extend beyond the place itself. The particular identity of a place is not determined by the boundaries separating it from everything "which lies beyond." Its identity lies in "the specificity of the mix of links and interconnections to that 'beyond.'"[34] In I Hotel, the specific identity of Asian America as a site of struggle does not come from a clear demarcation between what is part of Asian American politics and what is not. Instead, Asian America marks a particular nexus of social relations and vectors of power that extend far beyond Asian

American contexts. By treating a central metaphor of the Asian American movement as a place in this sense, *I Hotel* implies that Asian American politics is both particular and more than particular. It is a unique vantage point on systemic struggles that extend across ethnic and racial groups and across the globe. *The Book of Unknown Americans* proposed that a panethnic coalition does not dissolve when it is part of broader formations. *I Hotel* runs with this idea, arguing that the specificity of panethnic politics can have expansive scope.

Theodor W. Adorno argues that if concepts cannot achieve identity with the objects they purport to represent, it is because these concepts are not isolated from the antagonisms of the world. "No single thing is at peace in the unpacified whole," he insists. Conceptual aporias are signs of unresolved objective problems, which in plainer words are "the sufferings of humankind."[35] Building on Adorno, Marcial González argues that concepts of racial identity are inseparable from the unequal world in which we live; resolving their contradictions would require no less than the abolition of unequal social relations.[36] Panethnic identity is full of contradictions because it is part of an unjust world. As *I Hotel* reveals, the schisms within Asian American communities are signs of Asian Americans being on the front lines of entangled struggles. The struggle then to define Asian American, to make it do justice to the complexities of the Asian American community, necessarily involves the struggle for justice in the broader world. Difficult to close off, the panethnic concept calls Asian Americans to the broad importance that their politics can and indeed must have. In this view, the Asian American idea can only become resolved to itself by embracing what is beyond itself, following its entangled implications to become a movement for justice on multiple fronts.

A utopian impulse drives this expansive vision of the Asian American movement. Utopian political visions hold that the elements of injustice in the world are bound up with each other so change must be systemic rather than piecemeal and reformist.[37] Several theorists of Asian American and Latinx panethnicity have hinted at the utopian potential of these political concepts. Min Hyoung Song recuperates the term *Asian American* by emphasizing its future-oriented possibilities. Song highlights Asian American literature as particularly powerful for opening futurities. Acting as "a literature of the not-yet," it can posit an Asian American being that is deferred for now but which "promises euphoria and utopia."[38] Positioning Asian American identity in the future is a promising idea that I'll return to shortly. In Latinx studies, Juan Flores proposes a "Latino imaginary" in which Latinxs create community from convergent histories, shared desires, and "intertwining utopias."[39] Latinxs can come together over a shared sense of the futures they want to build rather than an already existing communal identity.

The utopian horizon of the transformed future is a theme that many voices in *I Hotel* invoke. The sense that a different world can be made is crucial to the energy of those in the movement. The novel honors this passionate belief. The narrator of "1972" seeks "to pay tribute to the lives of young revolutionaries" whom she describes as "young men and women who sacrifice their youth for a new idea of the future" (296). As Song and Flores insist, imaginative work is central to the activists' ideas of the future. In "1975," Estelle Hama and her son Sen frequently argue over the political merits of fiction, but Sen gets his mother to realize the fictional work that she is already doing. Estelle believes that her disabled son Harry walks just "like everyone else." "Now, Mrs. Hama," Sen replies, "you've got to admit that that's fiction. It's like, what do you call it, the 'dream work of revolutionary ideas.'" "I didn't think of that," Estelle admits (520). The exchange emphasizes the power of fiction in developing revolutionary ideas.

But there is also a subtler current of utopian thought in *I Hotel*, in the structure of the novel. Utopian desire, I argue, is inherent to the conflicts and transfictional tensions that drive the novel. For example, the juxtaposed but divergent stories of young activists and new migrants that we saw in the last novella cannot converge into a unified narrative of Asian American community until the global inequalities and precarity that isolate new migrants are addressed. By making aesthetically perceptible the systemic social contradictions that Asian American politics must address, these tensions outline a different world. This outline is not a direct representation of that world in the vein of classic utopian texts. The future world instead emerges through negative implication in much the same way that Adorno's theory of negative dialectics contains glimpses of "utopian possibility." Dialectics for Adorno is the necessity "to think in contradictions" in a world full of contradictions. "Dialectics," he argues, "is the ontology of the wrong state of things. The right state of things would be free of it."[40] By thinking in conflicts and exposing social tensions so thoroughly, *I Hotel* suggests their obverse, the possible world that would be freed from these tensions and the scale of transformations it would take to get there.

This chapter concludes with the idea of utopia, because the utopian horizons of *I Hotel* are its most important contributions to the debates on panethnic politics. By committing to utopian horizons, *I Hotel* goes against an emerging consensus that argues for panethnic coalition to remain "permanently open." This consensus is a culmination of the values advocated in current proposals on panethnicity: fluidity, multiplicity, resistance to totalization, and embrace of infinite differences. These values are recognizable as a legacy of poststructuralist theory. Poststructuralist-informed proposals argue for rethinking panethnic categories as "permanently contested, permanently contingent" sites of "ongoing resignifiability."[41] This argument embraces the unresolved qualities that have plagued the Asian American and Latinx categories.[42] As Cristina Beltrán contends, "*Latinidad*'s indeterminacy is not its failure but its promise."[43] Advocates of open-ended panethnicity reject closure to avoid the pitfalls of identity politics and the exclusions that marred earlier movements. Kandice Chuh critiques identity politics as "teleological narrative" that "posits a common origin and looks toward a common destiny."[44] And Beltrán asserts that "Latinidad must always remain a question." Because she rejects teleology, Beltrán is drawn to the rhizome theories of Gilles Deleuze and Félix Guattari. Viewing panethnic identity as a rhizome "helps to highlight Latino pan-ethnicity as a practice of becoming that understands itself in terms of circulation rather than arrival or completion."[45] The value of the never-ending prescribes a political skepticism of closure and telos.

This open-ended position conflicts with the utopian imagination, which is committed to the idea of eventual closure, an ending of political struggle. As Fredric Jameson observes, closure is "the very form of Utopia itself." Jameson notes that skepticism of closure has been a major theme in anti-utopian thought.[46] Though most of the scholars advocating a permanently open panethnic politics do not explicitly address the idea of utopia, their resistance to closure implies a resistance to utopian politics. The utopian impulse in *I Hotel*'s portrait of panethnic politics offers an opportunity to reconsider closure. The open-ended approach is compelling. It keeps the panethnic category from hardening into an enforced consensus that excludes marginal groups. And it recognizes that political categories will have to shift as circumstances change.

Yet, in the effort to analyze the costs of closure, this discussion shortchanges its powers. In what ways is a sense of ending, however potential, crucial to political movements? Conversely, these proposals have yet to reckon with the potential costs of justice movements thinking of themselves as "permanently open." Yamashita's work is no stranger to poststructuralist thought and aesthetics, but at the same time, *I Hotel*'s utopian imagination allows us to question whether the values of open-endedness are effective stopping points for political thought.

The troubling possibility is that open-ended panethnicity may curtail a sense of hope, drive, and direction. *I Hotel* shows that envisioning the end of political struggles is essential for generating the feelings of possibility that sustain the long work of a movement. But if panethnicity "must always remain a question,"[47] does this accept that there will never be a resolution to the social contradictions that complicate panethnic unity? How does the open-ended model imagine panethnic movements achieving their goals? To put it strongly, I worry that permanent openness comes too close to suggesting that justice is permanently deferred. Some scholars come close to this. Kandice Chuh invokes the "(im)possibility of justice."[48] Granted, she makes an important point. Because of changing conditions justice is difficult to define let alone achieve; open-endedness calls coalitions to be vigilant about forms of injustice they haven't yet recognized and to navigate shifting possibilities of justice. But if committing to open-endedness as a permanent value means that movements lose the sense that they can arrive at an ending of achieved justice, that is a debilitating loss.[49] Risking ideas of closure and utopia may be necessary to the hope for an alternate world. For this purpose, Fredric Jameson concludes, "there is no alternative to Utopia." For all its possible flaws, utopian thought is the mode through which we conceive the possibilities of other social systems: "one cannot imagine any fundamental change in our social existence which has not first thrown off Utopian visions like so many sparks from a comet."[50]

I argued before that *I Hotel* helps us rethink panethnic movements by introducing the powers of narrative. For the question of closure, narrative again proves illuminating. For Jameson, arguments against utopia are in essence arguments against narrative closure.[51] Indeed, the argument for open panethnicity envisions panethnic movements as unending stories. Cristina Beltrán calls for permanent contestation in the concept of Latinidad because these conflicts will generate continually "new narratives of political structure and change."[52]

Such unrest is inherent to narrative movement. D. A. Miller calls this open-ended element the "narratable," "the instances of disequilibrium, suspense, and general insufficiency" that give rise to stories.[53] Miller's concept resonates with the terms of poststructuralist panethnicity theory. The narratable is open ended and it suspends signification.[54] But Miller's key insight is that both open-ended narratability *and* closure are necessary for the movements of narrative. The desire for a "'utopic' state" of full meaning and settlement is what drives the narratable.[55] The narratable needs its other. The utopian horizon of closure matters even if it's not achieved.

This narrative perspective on movements lets us consider how central closure is to political drive. It helps recuperate closure as a political value. Rather than a suppression of dynamism and difference, closure can be a generative horizon that draws movements to enact broad transformations. Closure, then, is not necessarily an oppressive or conservative force. Closure can be radical. Jameson notes that the closure of utopian form is what makes it possible to imagine a future that breaks from the current situation. "It is the very principle of the radical break as such," he argues, "which insists that its radical difference is possible and that a break is necessary. The Utopian form itself is the answer to the universal ideological conviction that no alternative is possible."[56]

Utopian closure is not simple. And neither is utopian hope, a value skeptics often conflate with naïve idealism. *I Hotel* shows how by orienting Asian American politics toward ambitious transformations while harboring no illusions about easy endings. Instead, it argues for a long view of political movements that understands the extended efforts necessary for radical change. In one scene, a group of Japanese American activists recall the victories they have achieved, such as the repeal of title II of the McCarran Act, which allowed the executive branch in national emergencies to detain anyone suspected of being a threat to national security. These victories did not occur overnight, and as they look on to their next battle, they remind themselves, "Sometimes it takes twenty-five years. . . . Sometimes it takes thirty" (506). This is a model of political struggle that accepts multiple stages, even generations. The novel ends with the dramatic eviction at the International Hotel in August 1977 but implies that the work continues. The language of conditionality—"we may"—and futurity—"in time"—pervade the final page (605). It's an apt ending, as it took another twenty-eight years for the struggle to bear fruit. In 2005, because of the anti-eviction movement and continued pressure from community groups, a new International Hotel was built on the site of the one that was torn down. The new hotel includes low-income housing for elderly residents and a community center dedicated to preserving the history and extending the mission of this icon of the Asian American movement.

I Hotel combines conflicting impulses, fluid openness—no easy endings, no fixed ethnic categories, unexpected plot paths and convergences—and utopian desire for closure. The conflict is an opportunity to think through how panethnic politics might embrace the political drive of closure without losing the nonexclusionary openness that poststructuralist arguments have made possible. The novel offers several guiding images to think through this duality. The chapter "Cormorant" opens with a metaphor of dancing toward the future: "the world turns in strange serendipity, and destiny, if there is such a thing at all, is not a simple destination, a straight predictable line to some inevitable end. Maybe you do get to turn, turn again, and turn back, dance a two-step, waltz in three-four, or chant a wakening that opens up a space of possibility, the great yawning mouth of your future" (393). The passage detaches the idea of destiny from straightforward teleology. The path toward destiny instead is full of unpredictable turns, serendipity and contingency, steps backward and forward. While this meditation embraces "a space of possibility," it doesn't abandon the idea of destination. The image of a shifting dance toward a future horizon combines openness and closure. The future ending is a driving force for this movement, but its content is not necessarily fixed or "inevitable." The end of the novella of which "Cormorant" is a part emphasizes this point: "there are prophecies and they do come to pass, but . . . prophecies are like any other story—they can be changed" (420). The statement affirms hope, that anticipated futures do come true, and holds that the future that we are writing can change in the process of writing. The passage celebrates narrative's mutability and anticipatory desire. What's powerful about narrative for political movements is this open directedness. Narrative moves toward a utopian horizon even as it maintains its open form.

I Hotel draws on dance, prophecy, and story to offer metaphors for an open path toward the future. This variety of art forms recalls the most stunning study of utopia, Ernst Bloch's *The Principle of Hope*, which ranges from daydreams to medicine to the novel. Bloch offers a theory of utopian teleology that describes the open paths in *I Hotel*. Bloch's teleology is more nuanced than the targets of poststructuralist critique. He defends the politics of hope, insisting that the end is achievable, but, like Yamashita, argues that the path to this end must remain open; "hasty hypotheses" and "fixed definitions of essence" merely "block the way."[57] Together, Yamashita and Bloch offer a way to incorporate critiques of essentialism, as elaborated by poststructuralist critics, into a politics that retains the powers of closure. The key is not to dismiss closure outright but to stave off premature closure while retaining it as an inspiring destination at the ends of political efforts. Bloch does not reject teleology altogether; he critiques "pre-ordered" teleological thinking that authorizes itself to know ahead of time the precise contours of the utopian future.[58] José Esteban Muñoz observes that Blochian utopia is not about "prescriptive ends" but laying out a future "horizon."[59] As a horizon, it provides a direction for political struggle without fixing what lies over its threshold. Instead of a fixed image of the future, Bloch argues that we build the vision of a utopian world in the course of pursuing it, much like the prophecy that changes in the act of its writing. "The *truth* of teleology," he contends, "never consists of purposes already existing in finished form, but rather of those which are only just forming in active process."[60] The still forming vision of what is over the utopian horizon does not prevent that horizon from exerting an essential pull on political efforts: "The goal as a whole is and remains still concealed, . . . and yet the nunc stans of the driving moment, of the striving filled with its content, stands ahead, utopian and clear."[61] *I Hotel* operates with this Blochian sense of teleology. It suggests that movements should be wary of the pitfalls of premature closure while retaining the powers of closure as a horizon inspiring the struggle for a future world.

THE FUTURE HORIZON OF UNITY

I Hotel helps recuperate closure and teleology, two ideas that current debates on panethnicity largely reject. By doing so, it also reopens the cases of panethnic unity and identity, which have likewise been targeted by those advocating a politics of difference. The novel's utopian imagination allows a different view that holds onto the fraught idea of panethnic identity. *I Hotel* takes to heart many of the concerns scholars have raised. It details the political purges and exclusions that result from enforcing unity, the folly of rigid definitions of Asian American identity, and the way that movement unity can become an end in itself, eclipsing the goals of justice that were the movement's raison d'être. *I Hotel* shares the skepticism of scholars such as Cristina Beltrán that unity must be the starting point for political action. But unlike Beltrán, the novel does not reject unity altogether. It explores instead how movements might refigure the temporality of unity. In one revealing moment, the activists wrestle with the ideas of Lenin and Mao and debate when and how to evoke unity in their struggle:

> we may have followed their principles of democratic-centralism, meaning in theory that we should all participate in our arguments but finally follow in the fierce unity of our majority decision. And we also believed that our arguments were necessary to our collective struggle, that each group was pursuing a line of thinking that would eventually be proven or disproven in practice, that at the end of our struggle, we would finally unite in common unity. (600)

The passage contains an ambiguity: What does the term "struggle" refer to? Following the democratic-centralism model, struggle may refer to a period of debate within a movement after which its members unite behind the "majority decision" to carry out their plan. Unity in this reading is a prerequisite to effective political action. The idea of whittling away tactical lines through practice supports the reading of struggle as internal debates. But the hermeneutics in which this novel trains readers—of seeing internal movement conflicts as part of systemic social contradictions—offers a way to read struggle differently, as the broad struggle for justice the movement is pursuing. The two possible readings offer different temporalities for panethnic unity. It may be "at the end of our struggle" over internal questions of tactics that the movement will "finally unite in common unity." But the more startling reading is that it is at the end of the struggle for justice that Asian Americans will finally unite. This idea combines two major themes in *I Hotel*: that Asian American identity is unsettled and full of tensions and that there is a utopian horizon for Asian American politics, a possible ending at which tensions will be resolved. The provocation is that Asian American unity is not the prerequisite to Asian American political struggle but a part of the future world that this struggle seeks to build.

Transforming the place of unity and identity in political struggle, *I Hotel* offers a different path forward than the rejection of unity and identity as political values. Rejecting identity was never going to be easy anyway. Identity,

Christopher Lee points out, cannot "simply be left behind."[62] By placing identity as a future horizon, *I Hotel* envisions a way that panethnic politics might hold onto identity's "liberatory possibilities."[63] *I Hotel* aligns with José Esteban Muñoz's moving reworking of minority identity. Building on Ernst Bloch's theory of utopia, Muñoz argues that a minority identity like queerness is less powerful as a collective identity that is already available than as an "ideality," a future "horizon imbued with potentiality."[64] This collective "we" can move beyond "a merely identitarian logic" to act as a critical form of "futurity." This we "is not content to describe who the collective is but more nearly describes what the collective and the larger social order could be, what it should be."[65] Instead of focusing on an already existing and ostensibly unified identity politics, our politics can orient toward the unified identity we could build and the changed society in which it could live. With a transfictional form that implies connections across disparate settings, groups, and stories and that situates the tensions internal to a story as part of broader contradictions, *I Hotel* helps us see how future identity and a transformed world are intertwined. Its form argues that achieving unity is entangled with a utopian horizon of change across interconnected fields of struggle. Unity and identity, then, can help us imagine a just future, if we consider the future that would allow unity free of contradiction to be possible. A utopian panethnic politics contends that part of achieving a just world would be resolving the inequalities that generate the conflicts within the panethnic community. It would not mean an erasure of differences; it would be an easing of the economic, social, and political inequities that currently make differences among Asian Americans so materially consequential, that make the life chances and political possibilities of different Asian American groups so uneven, and that position Asian Americans so divergently in the hierarchies of the panethnic coalition. Rather than a starting point or something to be set aside in a politics of difference, Asian American unity can be an orienting horizon toward which Asian American politics aims. Placing panethnic identity as part of the horizon of justice is a way to hold onto the idea of a grand political project that gave rise to the Asian American idea in the first place.

For Asian American and Latinx coalitions in the present, this orientation of unity means that panethnic identity is powerful not as a premise but as a promise. Drawing on Min Song's idea of a literature of the not-yet and Muñoz's concept of ideality,[66] I argue that *I Hotel* helps us rethink panethnic identity as not yet available. Identity instead is something to struggle for. It is the lack of full unity, in other words the conflicts within panethnicity, that can draw the narrative of a panethnic movement forward. With unity as a horizon, Asian American and Latinx politics would not try to presume unity in the present by suppressing conflicts. Such unity is premature, enforced when the deeper conditions for it have not yet been achieved. Rather it would use those conflicts in their ramifying connections as generative forces for change. In this vision, Asian Americans do not come together because they are already a unified community. They are not. Likewise, Latinxs do not come together because they are already a unified community. They also are not. Neither group should be satisfied with a panethnic community still rent with inequalities. Instead, Asian Americans and Latinxs come together for the hope of the just community they might make possible and the transformed world that would be its condition of possibility.

In the face of a conceptual impasse that sees the panethnic categories organizing Asian American and Latinx politics as incoherent, the panethnic literary fictions of the Asian and Latinx United States are vibrant. As *I Hotel* and *The Book of Unknown Americans* show, the transfictional imagination, by exploring the many possibilities for how different stories of struggle can diverge, converge, and interrelate, by thriving on the sustained conflicts among the parts of a movement, offers rejuvenating form to the ideas of Asian American and Latinx.

It is common now to call out Asian American and Latinx communities as fictions, constructions that cannot meet the realities of the vastly different politics, histories, and lives that they attempt to encompass. In such discussions, fictionality comes across as a weakness, a sign that these political identities are only abstracted ideas, not lived truths that bring people together and draw out their fiercest energies. But for many of us writing, reading, and sharing Asian American and Latinx fiction, this bleak view of fictionality is strange. Fictions are not secondhand substitutes for reality; they are vital spaces of imaginative possibility where we work out not only how we should see our communities and world but how our communities and world could be. As Muñoz reminds us, imaginative artworks allow us "to see different worlds and realities" and to realize that the present world "is simply not enough."[67] Instead of seeing the fictionality of Asian American and Latinx panethnicities as a liability, we can see it as one of their greatest strengths. To borrow from Yamashita, panethnic fictions are "like any other story—they can be changed." That panethnic coalitions are not fixed and given but stories that we are actively writing, fictions that can change and shift, is what suggests that it would be silly to think that we have already exhausted their creative possibilities. Asian American and Latinx panethnic literary fictions are energized and brimming with possibility. It's hard for me in the face of such energy to feel bleak about Asian American and Latinx possibilities. If we're willing to listen to them and draw on their aesthetic and conceptual energy, they offer hope that those other panethnic fictions, the ideas of Asian American and Latinx themselves, still have many more stories in them.

CONCLUSION

A POLITICS OF BEYOND

AS THIS BOOK nears its end, it's probably apparent that it has not been simply about transfictional aesthetics. Its thinking has been inspired by this aesthetics as well. The seepage of transfictional form into this book's methods comes from my commitment to the idea that the fictions of the Asian and Latinx United States are not just works to be interpreted but works that themselves interpret the challenging worlds that Asian Americans and Latinxs navigate. This idea takes inspiration from the participatory reading experiences offered by transfictional works and from scholars who argue for the theorizing powers of minority literatures.[1] But the idea as practiced here has been most wonderfully expressed by art historian Yve-Alain Bois, who developed a methodology that credits the artwork (in his case painting) as a "theoretical operator, a producer of models." Bois insists that artworks generate models by themselves "for anyone who takes the trouble to notice." Crucially, this approach does not mean handling the work as a piece of propositional content. "Can one designate the place of the theoretical in painting," Bois asks, "without doing violence to it, without, that is, disregarding painting's specificity?" Artworks, he argues, offer modes of theorizing rather than being simply illustrations of or objects for applied theories, and their mode of thinking is specific to their nature. This medium specificity is where form comes in. In taking the artwork as model, the critic approaches form as a way of ordering, modeling, and making sense, an aesthetic structure scaffolding thought. Offering such form, the artwork becomes "a key to the interpretation of the world."[2] The particular formal powers of fiction to theorize the world comes from the fact that each fictional work itself lays out a world, what David Herman calls a "storyworld" and Eric Hayot describes as a "literary world."[3] For Hayot, a literary world is "the diegetic totality" of the elements of a literary text as they are formed into "a structure or system." Literary worlds, he argues, are "always relations to and theories of the lived world," whether as reflections, reworkings, or critiques to prevailing models of the world in their time.[4] Fictional works, by forming worlds, help us construct our ideas of the world. Resonating with Bois's idea of a theorizing operator, Hayot suggests that by attending to how literary works construct their worlds, we can situate literature as a key medium for theorizing the world alongside models in other disciplines.[5] Running with Bois's and Hayot's proposals, I have tried to credit transfictional works as medium-specific thought partners and inspirations for our methods.

This book has followed the stakes of transfictional form for collective politics, global displacements, neoliberal stratification, and panethnic and cross-racial coalitions. I hope that readers have come away with the sense that many of the historical formations and central struggles of Asian American and Latinx communities are intertwined and that literary comparison is a powerful way to perceive their intertwining and the solidarity that can emerge from them. Following transfictional aesthetics across distinct communities and contexts has been pivotal to this comparative work. But a decidedly transfictional-like operation has also been crucial. Transfictional works are inherently comparative. They imply relationships between stories without collapsing their differences and distinctions; they register the boundaries separating stories while attending to their crossings. Likewise, perceiving an Asian and Latinx America as a potential solidarity requires such transfictional operations. We must recognize the specificities of distinct groups and stories of struggle while drawing out the possible alliances, shared challenges, and historical connections between them. The preceding chapters grappled with this challenge. They looked across separate categories and histories of migration to draw out the linked positions of Asian

American and Latinx diasporas in a U.S. Cold War machine. They examined opposed positions in the neoliberal immigration system to reveal the historical entanglements of Latinx and Asian American immigrants. Sustaining a transfictional tension of separation and relation, they revealed some of the contours of an Asian and Latinx America.

But the Asian American and Latinx ideas, as political projects and fields of thought, have followed largely separate paths. They have each faced a crisis of definition and institutional pressures to sharpen the particular boundaries of their concerns. These tendencies work against comparative scholarship and convergent solidarities. Transfictional aesthetics, however, offers a countervailing vision. With its *trans* prefix, transfictional marks an aesthetics of beyond. Each story in a transfictional work opens up a specific slice of the larger storyworld in which all the stories take place. Each story draws its own borders, making a distinction between the circle of events, people, and settings concerned in the story and those that are not. Much as the *trans* in *transnational* marks relations that unsettle and interrupt the nation as a bounded, coherent whole,[6] the *trans* in *transfictional* describes relations that trouble the narrative borders a story draws and unsettle the sense that it is complete in itself.[7] Transfictional form continually opens connections to parts of the world beyond the borders of a story, intimating the implication of any one story within broader conflicts and networks of consequence involving many others beyond its immediate horizons. In *The House on Mango Street* we saw this aesthetic insist on communal responsibilities and collective conditions extending beyond the outcome of an individual story of mobility. With *The Woman Warrior* we realized how this form can push the individual voice to encompass a collective story of ethnic and feminist struggle. *Drown* showed us the detainment of an immigration story by stories set elsewhere, revealing the inability of American immigrant myths to close themselves off from the full scope of peoples entangled in America's imperial histories. In *We Should Never Meet* we followed ethical responsibilities closed by the ending of a story set in one location only to be jolted back open by relations to other places and people in the global networks of effect generated by warfare. And in *The Book of Unknown Americans* and *I Hotel* we encountered transfictional links and transethnic slips that revealed the affinities among the stories of distinct ethnic and racial groups. In these works, transfictional aesthetics draws our thought beyond individual scales of action and justice, beyond national boundaries on our responsibilities and histories, and beyond the limits of ethnic community.

The transfictional imagination flourishing in Asian American and Latinx literatures can provide crucial inspiration, spurring panethnic communities to look beyond their own borders and see their struggles as interconnected with others. We saw *The Book of Unknown Americans* and *I Hotel* using transfictional form to propose new shapes for Latinx and Asian American coalitions. It's crucial to emphasize that these new shapes of panethnic politics do not rethink Latinx and Asian American coalitions as isolated affairs; they clarify that each of these panethnic formations extends beyond its own ostensible boundaries. *The Book of Unknown Americans* suggested that Latinx coalition can involve people who don't identify as Latinx and can form within broader solidarities with other minorities. The aesthetics of *I Hotel* proposed that we cannot address the conflicts within a panethnic coalition without becoming involved in broader social struggles. The internal conflicts plaguing these coalitions are never simply internal. They are part of an interconnected world of injustice. Panethnic politics, then, is inescapably interminority and cross-racial politics. (When we consider that the category Latinx already brings together groups with different racial experiences as does the category Asian American, it's clear that cross-racial politics is constitutive of panethnic politics. These cross-racial affiliations do not end at the established boundaries of Latinidad and Asian Americanness.)

The limitations of Asian American coalitions and Latinx coalitions may stem from their attempts to draw boundaries around the histories and political horizons of each group, attempts that founder on the relational nature of racialization and on the embeddedness of Asian American and Latinx struggles within broader landscapes of inequality. Take the class divides troubling each of these coalitions. As *Karma* and *The People of Paper* helped us map so intricately, these class divisions are not separable from the stratified immigration system that has differentially selected for, restricted, and compelled people from many different economic and social circumstances into the United States and different sectors of the economy. To truly grapple with their class cleavages, these communities must address the immigration and labor system in its complete scope including all the groups caught in it. For Asian Americans and Latinxs to address the full range of their struggles will mean confronting their interrelations with each other and with other groups. Thinking beyond group boundaries is not about erasing the specificity of each group's struggles. It's about insisting that the concerns of each group are not parochial but widely connected and far-reaching in consequence, indeed central to the future of the United States and the world.

As we consider this future and the transfictional imagination that helps us envision it, it's stirring to recall José Esteban Muñoz's account of art's futurity. While the work of Yve-Alain Bois and Eric Hayot help us see the powers of artworks to theorize the world, Muñoz's thinking holds that these powers are not limited to modeling the present world. The aesthetic, he insists, can offer anticipatory "blueprints and schemata"; it can map the "future social relations" of a transformed world. This imaginative power to think beyond the current world is necessary to resist the sense of the present social order as a self-enclosed given, a world unto itself. It helps us reject the "notion of nothing existing outside the sphere of the current moment," a status quo that resigns us to current arrangements. "We must strive," Muñoz argues, "in the face of the here and now's totalizing rendering of reality, to think and feel a *then and there*."[8] A key insight emerges when we place Muñoz's call to think beyond the current world alongside the form of transfictional works, which embeds the struggles in one story as part of a broader world of struggles. An important part of thinking and acting toward a then and there beyond the present social order may be to think beyond its given divisions. The racial order encourages minority groups to see their struggles as separate, each group's history with its own track, each group's politics with its proper boundaries. So long as minority groups accept this "rendering of reality," the transformation of this interconnected order will remain elusive.

It can be tempting in the face of the incoherence and conflict troubling Asian American and Latinx coalitions to hunker down and narrow the scope of politics. Panethnic politics is already messy, enough of a stretch as it is. But to narrow in this way is to remain within the here and now, to limit the possibilities of each community's politics to its established scope. From the perspective of the transfictional aesthetics of beyond, this messiness, the difficulty panethnic collectives have bounding themselves off cleanly, is not a limitation but a strength. As Lisa Lowe argues about Asian Americans, a racialized formation's unclear boundaries "opens political lines of affiliation with other groups in the challenge to specific forms of domination."[9] Likewise, Juan Flores insists that because of the shared coloniality of racialized difference in the United States and beyond "the 'Latino' concept needs to be seen as conjoined and partially overlapping with, rather than categorically distinct from" other racial groups.[10] Transfictional aesthetics articulates relations that extend beyond the boundaries of one story of struggle, connecting it to other distinct struggles. It offers conceptual form to the political possibilities that follow from embracing the porous edges of racial groups. The porosity of Latinx and Asian American political narratives can draw these groups into broader stories of struggle. Each of these political narratives is a potent fiction, a story that is mutable rather than fixed. Embracing their porosity and mutability, we can envision a transfictional solidarity that extends across these political fictions and beyond their traditional boundaries. A transfictional politics of beyond welcomes the porousness of political horizons and offers a different view of Asian American and Latinx politics. It opens two striking propositions:

1.   To engage in Latinx struggles is an essential act of Asian American politics.
2.   To engage in Asian American struggles is an essential act of Latinx politics.

A coalition built on these ideas would have broad potential and stakes. It could, for instance, combine forces to reconfigure U.S. foreign policy from the perspective of the Asian and Latinx displaced, redrawing the boundaries of U.S. citizenship and political community to respond to the claims of all those impacted by U.S. actions abroad. This effort would fight to claim justice for Latinxs and Asians driven from the proxy zones of the Cold War while aligning with the claims of the next waves of the displaced the nation must recognize, the millions fleeing the ill-defined battlegrounds of the "War on Terror."[11]

Instead of working in isolation, these communities can recognize the potential power of an Asian and Latinx America, a possible formation that must be given form through comparative scholarship, activism, and culture. This formation has the potential to reshape the United States, its racial landscape, its relations to the world, and the global networks of labor and capital in which it is embedded. But this solidarity is not inevitable. Like the utopian identity that is not yet available but whose power takes shape in the course of working toward the horizons of justice, an Asian and Latinx America only coalesces in the active pursuit of the conditions of equality that will enable its unity to be realized. Forging unity between groups occupying opposed positions will require, for example, dismantling the relational immigration system that both links and separates them. Overhauling this system is a project that depends on Asian American and Latinx solidarity. But at the same time, overhauling the regime seems a precondition for that solidarity. Does that leave us in a troubling bind? Within this convoluted timeline of struggle there is a possibility for a positively reinforcing cycle of political momentum. If the hope of future unity can inspire cooperative work today that can establish some of the conditions of equality for that unity to emerge as a nascent reality, that emerging reality would strengthen the allied work toward shared projects of justice. As the solidarity coalesces, these projects would appear more approachable and feed back into the strength of the solidarity.

But how can we give shape to such a strange temporality of justice? Many of the writers of the Asian and Latinx United States are already doing so. For this is the temporality of their transfictional works. Their fictions preclude readers from dissolving boundaries and positing the unity of distinct pieces in their current form. But they also imply within their tensions of unity and multiplicity, borders and crossings the possibility of a transformed world where these tensions would be addressed and a story of unity could unfold without contradiction or fantasy. Think of the refugee life stories that *We Should Never Meet* invites us to reconstruct but never quite allows us to complete, the harmony of individual and ethnic community that *The House on Mango Street* yearns for but cannot portray, the unified panethnic movement that *I Hotel* evinces utopian desire for while its form captures the social contradictions dividing this collective. These works testify to a world that remains ruptured by warfare, communities marred by uneven opportunities, and political movements split by conflicts internal and external. These narratives desire a formal unity that they cannot yet deliver because they are too perceptive to offer easy resolutions. They hold that we cannot take unified narrative for granted. The world that makes it credible must be built. So there is ambitious desire and potential encoded within these sustained tensions. Transfictional works suggest that in and through the tensions of the present lies the possible unity of the future.

To set in motion the cycle of political momentum and tap the power of an Asian and Latinx America requires a leap into what is not yet available. It demands a vision that sees in the differences and divisions of the U.S. racial order today not implacable obstacles but potential solidarities that extend beyond the scope of what Asian Americans and Latinxs see as the edges of their concerns. The ties of shared fate and claims of justice pulling on these edges are important occasions to contest the given divisions of the racial order, to engage in projects that cut across those divisions, to understand that the perceived givenness of the racial order is one of the most powerful ways it resists change, and to see the latent possibilities within the racial landscape, a first step toward the alignments that could transform it. Making the leap means drawing on a possible future and our desires for it to propel the stories of struggle we are writing in the present. That this leap is unavoidably an act of imagination explains why the fiction of the Asian and Latinx United States is so vital.

NOTES

INTRODUCTION

1. De Genova, "Migrant 'Illegality.'"

2. Colby and Ortman, "Projections," 9.

3. I am very grateful to Daniel Y. Kim who, in a stimulating conversation, suggested that I use these two stories of 1965 as an opening.

4. I am taking up Jesse Hoffnung-Garskof's call for a migration history of the Cold War by showing how the aesthetics of communities shaped by the Cold War can be a revealing axis of comparison. See *A Tale of Two Cities*, xiv.

5. U.S. military advisors to the Army of the Republic of Vietnam (ARVN) had been deployed in Vietnam before 1965, but this date marked the official entry of U.S. combat troops into the Vietnam War, as authorized by the Gulf of Tonkin Resolution in August 1964. From about 23,000 military advisors in Vietnam at the end of 1964, the American presence escalated drastically in 1965 to over 180,000 combat troops by the year's end.

6. While the Dominican displacement was on a smaller scale than that of the Southeast Asian displacement, it produced the fifth largest Latinx ethnic group in the United States. It is an important story because it is not an exceptional story but rather one representative episode in the recurrent drama of U.S. Cold War interventions across Latin America that each generated displacements.

7. Quoted in Kumar, *US Interventionism*, 142.

8. The Cold War was a crucial context for the 1965 immigration reforms. Along with civil rights legislation, these reforms were seen by Cold War liberals as a way to project an image

of U.S. racial democracy as the battle for the hearts and minds of Third World nations was at its most intense. See Ngai, *Impossible Subjects*, 228–29, and Dudziak, *Cold War Civil Rights*.

9. The indefinite article here is important since the Asian and Latinx America that has formed in the United States is one of many Asian and Latinx Americas across the Americas. To that end, I also use the term *Asian and Latinx United States* when the specification seems necessary. While this book focuses on Asian Americans and Latinxs in the United States, it registers their intertwined histories in the American hemisphere and more globally as well. See especially Chapters 2 and 3 on how the Cold War and neoliberal labor migrations linked Asian Americans and Latinxs on these broader scales.

10. This is not to say that alliances do not exist. For an important case study of Asian American–Latinx political alliance that formed around shared causes of immigration, bilingual education, discrimination, employment, and legislative redistricting, see Saito, *Race and Politics*.

11. Anemona Hartocollis and Stephanie Saul, "Affirmative Action Battle Has a New Focus: Asian-Americans," *New York Times*, August 2, 2017.

12. Southern Poverty Law Center, "Ten Days After."

13. Ibid.; Chetanya Robinson, "Forever the Foreigner—'Disturbing' Rise in Hate Crimes Targeting Asian Americans," *International Examiner*, August 8, 2017.

14. "Full Text: Donald Trump Announces a Presidential Bid," *Washington Post*, June 16, 2015.

15. Thananopavarn, *LatinAsian Cartographies*, 20.

16. De Genova, "Latino and Asian Racial Formations," 11.

17. Claire Jean Kim, *Bitter Fruit*, 10–12.

18. De Genova, *Racial Transformations*; Ngai, *Impossible Subjects*; O'Brien, *Racial Middle*.

19. Parikh, *Ethics of Betrayal*.

20. Sae-Saue, *Southwest Asia*.

21. Lim, *Bilingual Brokers*.

22. Thananopavarn, *LatinAsian Cartographies*.

23. I draw on Michael Omi and Howard Winant's concept of racial projects. See Omi and Winant, *Racial Formation in the United States*.

24. The political commitments of ethnic studies coupled with its organization as an interdisciplinary effort place distinct pressures on the balance of form and content in approaches to ethnic literatures. See Ling, *Narrating Nationalisms*, on the mobilization of culture, literature, and scholarship to serve political functions in the foundations of ethnic studies. On tendencies to overlook aesthetic concerns and reduce ethnic literatures to social content, see Gates, *Figures in Black*; Rocío G. Davis and Lee, *Literary Gestures*; and Zhou and Najmi, *Form and Transformation*. For other studies that seek to balance form and politics in ethnic literary studies, see Rocío G. Davis, *Transcultural Reinventions*, and Marcial González, *Chicano Novels*.

25. See Ryan, "Transmedial Storytelling," and Thon, "Converging Worlds," for transmedia studies accounts of transfictional storytelling. I clarify my relation to this scholarship in more detail later in the introduction.

26. I draw on David Herman's definition of storyworld: the world "evoked" by a narrative, the "global mental representations" of the events, characters, settings, processes,

relationships, situations, and physical environments mentioned or implied by a narrative work (*Basic Elements of Narrative*, 106).

27. I take causal disconnection from other stories as a central determinant of the relative autonomy of a story because causal connection has been fundamental to definitions of what makes a story a story. As David Herman and other narrative theorists observe, "causal-chronological connections" are an essential part of what makes a group of events a story and not just a group of events (*Basic Elements of Narrative*, 11; see also Bal, *Narratology*). Richard J. Gerrig has shown that many of the processes of comprehending narratives revolve around "the search for causal relations." Such relations are crucial for giving a story a sense of "global coherence" and unity (*Experiencing Narrative Worlds*, 46). Thus, the question of whether many stories ultimately form one unified story or whether they remain relatively autonomous turns in large part on the factor of causal relation.

28. These relations are crucial for giving the sense that these stories occur in the same world. As Roberta Pearson explains, the traces and overlaps of storyworld elements between stories are what allow readers to identify the connection to an established storyworld ("Additionality and Cohesion," 114).

29. Not all causal relations in transfictional works are so ambiguous or indirect. Such works often include some stories that are linked with clear causal connections. But transfictional works include several or more stories that stand apart from each other causally.

30. The following story, "Song for a Barbarian Reed Pipe," opens with a brief reference to Moon Orchid but quickly drops the subject.

31. Elaine H. Kim, *Asian American Literature*, 207.

32. Another recent novel that illustrates the boundary between the transfictional novel and the multiplot novel is Nicole Krauss's *Great House* (2010). A lonely writer in New York, a father and son confronting each other in Jerusalem, a husband in London trying to uncover his wife's past, and a man searching for his father's desk—these are the four disparate stories Krauss presents. The reading experience mimics the storyworld construction of transfictional works as it's not clear until very late in the book how or if the four plots relate to each other. But in the end it emerges that each story has one or more life-changing connections to the other stories. The novel sustains a quasi-transfictional tension of separation and interconnection for much of its duration, but in the end resolves it.

33. On borders and crossings in Latinx studies, see Concannon, Lomelí, and Priewe, *Imagined Transnationalism*. In Asian American studies, see Palumbo-Liu, *Asian/American*.

34. On the asymmetric histories of economic interdependencies and political relations that link the United States and Latin America, see Suárez-Orozco and Páez, "The Research Agenda." On economic, military, and imperial relations with Asia affecting Asian immigration to the United States, see Lowe, *Immigrant Acts*, and Jodi Kim, *Ends of Empire*. For a comparative view of U.S. imperialism and its impacts on Asian Americans and Latinxs, see De Genova, "Latino and Asian Racial Formations."

35. On the conflicts of local and diasporic commitments in Asian American studies, see Dirlik, "Asians on the Rim." For a useful overview of the debate between the transnational and national orientations of Asian American studies and politics, see Zhou, "Critical Theories and Methodologies," 4–13. See also Sau-Ling C. Wong, "Denationalization Reconsidered,"

and Koshy, "Fiction." On the conflicts of national and transnational orientations and scales of analysis in Latinx studies, see, for example, Saldívar, "Social Aesthetics"; Mariscal, *Brown-Eyed Children*, 91; and Torres-Saillant, "Problematic Paradigms."

36. Ong, *Flexible Citizenship*; Ty, *Unfastened*; Gimenez, "Latino/'Hispanic'"; Caminero-Santangelo, *On Latinidad*.

37. On the crisis of panethnic Latinidad, see Beltrán, *Trouble with Unity*, and Caminero-Santangelo, *On Latinidad*. On the impasses of Asian American panethnicity, see Koshy, "Fiction," and Chuh, *Imagine Otherwise*. I discuss this issue at length in Chapters 4 and 5.

38. Readers may notice that I seem to conflate the challenges of Asian American and Latinx immigrants with the struggles of Asian Americans and Latinxs more broadly here. This conflation is intentional because the immigration and racial regimes have routinely conflated Asians and Asian Americans, U.S. Latinxs and Latin Americans. This conflation is central to the foreignness that continues to shape the racialization of Asian Americans and Latinxs, whether they are native-born or immigrants.

39. Molina, *How Race Is Made*, 4.

40. Ibid., 6.

41. Ngai, *Impossible Subjects*, 64.

42. Chinese immigrants were the first to be excluded, beginning in 1882. This was followed by the Gentlemen's Agreement of 1907 with Japan, which barred Japanese immigration, and the implementation of an "Asiatic barred zone" in 1917, which excluded all of Asia. See Hing, *Making and Remaking*.

43. Ngai, *Impossible Subjects*, 64.

44. Douglas S. Massey, "Past and Future," 252–53.

45. Molina, *How Race Is Made*, 60.

46. Douglas S. Massey, "Past and Future," 253.

47. Ngai, *Impossible Subjects*, 58.

48. Molina, *How Race Is Made*, 38–40, 53.

49. Ibid., 40.

50. Erika Lee, *Making of Asian America*, 380. For an in-depth discussion of the model minority transformation and its roots in immigration policy, see Madeline Y. Hsu, *Good Immigrants*, 198–250.

51. Ngai, *Impossible Subjects*, 261.

52. Molina, *How Race Is Made*, 143.

53. Ibid., 35.

54. Ibid., 46.

55. This is not to deny that some Asian American activists have joined the immigrant rights movement. See Erika Lee, *Making of Asian America*, 398–402. My point is that this has not been a movement anywhere near the scale of mobilization by Latinx activists.

56. Lim, *Bilingual Brokers*, 18.

57. López and Radford, "Facts on U.S. Immigrants."

58. Signs of nativist hostility to Asian Americans are already clear. Coverage of the anti-immigrant fervor whipped up by the Trump administration has focused on anti-Latinx and anti–Arab American sentiment, but Asian Americans are also targets, as the 2017 elections

in Edison, New Jersey, illustrated. In the run-up to the local school board election, Edison households received anonymous flyers calling on voters to "deport" two Asian American candidates in order to "Make Edison Great Again." "The Chinese and Indians," it warned, "are taking over our town!" (Amy B. Wang, "'DEPORT': Racist Campaign Mailers Target Asian School Board Candidates," *Washington Post*, November 2, 2017).

59. Daniel Y. Kim, *Writing Manhood*; Julia H. Lee, *Interracial Encounters*; Ho and Mullen, *Afro Asia*.

60. Lutenski, *West of Harlem*; Milian, *Latining America*; Román, *Race and Upward Mobility*.

61. See, for example, Budick, *Blacks and Jews*; Goffman, *Imagining Each Other*; Sundquist, *Strangers in the Land*.

62. On literary connections between Asian Americans and Jewish Americans, see Schlund-Vials, *Modeling Citizenship*. On the intersections of Chicanx and Native American literatures, see Hebebrand, *Native American and Chicana/o Literature*.

63. For examples of shared themes as a comparative axis, see Milian, *Latining America*; Schlund-Vials, *Modeling Citizenship*; Parikh, *Ethics of Betrayal*; Daniel Y. Kim, *Writing Manhood*; and Lim, *Bilingual Brokers*. For examples of histories and representations of direct encounter and interaction as comparative axis, see Lutenski, *West of Harlem*; Hebebrand, *Native American and Chicana/o Literature*; and Prashad, *Everybody Was Kung Fu Fighting*. For examples of cross-influences as comparative axis, see Mullen, "Persisting Solidarities"; Oliver Wang, "These Are the Breaks"; and Sundquist, *Strangers in the Land*. Reciprocal representations power the comparison in works such as Sae-Saue, *Southwest Asia*; Julia H. Lee, *Interracial Encounters*; and Goffman, *Imagining Each Other*.

64. There have been important historical contacts between Asians and Latinxs in the Americas due to labor migrations and recruitment. Additionally, these groups have intersected in multiracial cities that are oriented to Asia and Latin America, such as Los Angeles. On these points, see Hu-DeHart, "Latin America in Asia-Pacific Perspective," and Thananopavarn, *LatinAsian Cartographies*. Such encounters are important, but I want to emphasize as well the range of relationships beyond direct contact that have shaped both groups.

65. This point of methods linking across different positions builds on Shu-mei Shih's idea of "relational comparison," whose goal is not to keep objects of study separate while considering their similarities and differences but rather "excavating and activating" the historical relations between distinct literary works and social contexts. Relational comparison can reveal "unpredictable entanglements" between "terms that have traditionally been pushed apart . . . due to certain interests" ("Comparison as Relation," 79–84). A related inspiration has been Lisa Lowe's work, which activates "relation across differences" to map the "distinct yet connected racial logics" of settler colonialism, slavery, and indentured labor by which empire governed and exploited various racialized groups (*Intimacies of Four Continents*, 20, 161). I see my method of relational comparison through historicized form as a way to grasp the less visible links between groups that are positioned in different yet related ways for the benefit of the racial order and capitalist labor systems.

66. Raymond Williams, *Marxism and Literature*, 160.

67. Ibid., 186.

68. Ibid., 133–34, 210, 212.

69. Other fascinating examples of transfictional form in contemporary Asian American and Latinx literatures include Jessica Hagedorn's *Dogeaters* (1990), Helena María Viramontes's *Their Dogs Came with Them* (2007), and Daniyal Mueenuddin's *In Other Rooms, Other Wonders* (2009). But there are also important earlier examples, such as Edith Eaton's *Mrs. Spring Fragrance* (1912), Jovita González's *Dew on the Thorn* (written in 1935 but not published until 1997), Toshio Mori's *Yokohama, California* (1949), and Rolando Hinojosa's *Estampas del valle / The Valley* (1973/1983).

70. For an insightful comparative reading of *Tropic of Orange* and *The Lady Matador's Hotel*, see Thananopavarn, *LatinAsian Cartographies*. Interactions of Asian American and Latinx characters can be found in the margins of many works, but Yamashita's and García's novels stand out as among the few works where these relationships are central.

71. Ryan, "Transmedial Storytelling"; Thon, "Converging Worlds." Richard Saint-Gelais first introduced the term. See Saint-Gelais, "Transfictionality."

72. Ryan, "Transfictionality Across Media," 386.

73. Ryan, "Transmedial Storytelling," 366.

74. Ibid., 366.

75. Ong, *Flexible Citizenship*, 15.

76. Chare and Willis, "Trans-: Across/Beyond," 284.

77. By *narrative borders* I mean the distinctions between the delimited diegetic scope concerned in a story and the broader fictional world that its world making opens up. As a narrative renders a world, it inevitably makes some distinction within that world, between the events, people, times, and places concerned in the story and those that are not. "Every discourse," D. A. Miller observes, "is uttered against a background of all those things that it chooses, for one reason or another, not to say" (*Narrative and Its Discontents*, 4). I call these distinctions a narrative border. Seymour Chatman observes that the story layer of a narrative is theoretically infinite; it could include "the total set of all conceivable details." In practice though we normally think of the story layer as "only that continuum and that set actually inferred by a reader" (*Story and Discourse*, 28). Only a limited portion of this indefinitely expansive world is part of a story. A narrative border then is a way to conceptualize fundamental narrative principles of inclusion and exclusion, focus and extent. The broader fictional world implied by a narrative is a potentially unbound and comprehensive world whereas the part of the storyworld concerned in the story, is a bounded piece "cut out from the universe" (Bunia, "Diegesis and Representation," 686).

78. Phan, interview by the author, March 29, 2018, San Francisco, CA.

79. Prosser, *Second Skins*, 200. Sandy Stone argues for attention to states in between gender categories and calls for rethinking this "position which is nowhere" as its own space of possibility ("*Empire* Strikes Back," 230).

80. Consider Paul Haggis's film *Crash* (2004), which appears to be transfictional yet resolves in a problematic manner. The film's gambit of multiple narratives to examine racial conflicts in Los Angeles is weakened by its plot resolutions, which improbably bring the stories of different individuals back together so that their conflicts can be diffused. In one case, a white police officer who sexually assaulted a black woman during a traffic stop has a

chance to make amends when, by improbable coincidence, he saves the same woman from a car explosion later in the film. The decision to converge separate stories and resolve their tensions produces a facile idea of racial conflict as an interpersonal issue rather than the systemic result of structures of power.

81. Sue-Im Lee, "Aesthetic"; Lye, "Racial Form"; Marcial González, *Chicano Novels*; Harford Vargas, *Forms of Dictatorship*; Ralph E. Rodriguez, *Brown Gumshoes*. For other significant studies of form and race in recent Asian American criticism, see Dorothy J. Wang, *Thinking Its Presence*; Zhou and Najmi, *Form and Transformation*; Tang, *Repetition and Race*; and Tsou, *Unquiet Tropes*. The attention to form and genre in Chicanx and Latinx literary studies is not new. For some foundational studies of genre and form in the field, see Saldívar, *Chicano Narrative*; Limón, *Mexican Ballads, Chicano Poems*; and Calderón, *Narratives of Greater Mexico*. The case in Asian American literary studies is different as the attention to literary form has been a more recent phenomenon. For an important earlier exception, see Ling, *Narrating Nationalisms*.

82. Hamilton, *Of Space and Mind*; Chuh, *Imagine Otherwise*; Song, *Children of 1965*. See also Goellnicht, "Blurring Boundaries."

83. Caminero-Santangelo, *On Latinidad*; Koshy, "Fiction." Many other scholars have debated the constructed and artificial nature of these concepts. See Christopher Lee, *Semblance of Identity*; Espiritu, *Asian American Panethnicity*; Beltrán, *Trouble with Unity*; and Flores, *From Bomba to Hip-Hop*.

84. Dudziak, *Cold War Civil Rights*; Cindy I-Fen Cheng, *Citizens of Asian America*.

85. Examples include Sarah Orne Jewett's *The Country of the Pointed Firs* (1896), Edith Eaton's *Mrs. Spring Fragrance* (1912), and Ernest Hemingway's *In Our Time* (1925).

86. We can think of Louise Erdrich's *Love Medicine* (1984), Anna Deavere Smith's *Twilight: Los Angeles* (1993), or Colum McCann's *Let the Great World Spin* (2009). One notable example in Native American literature that uses transfictional form to encompass an expansive range of places and peoples in disadvantaged movements and alignments is Leslie Marmon Silko's *Almanac of the Dead* (1991).

87. In this formulation, I take inspiration from Min Hyoung Song's suggestion that contemporary American literature is wrestling with many of the same questions that Asian American literature had already been wrestling with. Thus, examining Asian American literature has import beyond Asian America: "One does not read and study Asian American literature to understand only Asian Americans. One also does so to understand American literature in its expansive plasticity and its potential for constant renewal" (*Children of 1965*, 8).

CHAPTER I

1. The story of Nilda's long-suffering mother, for example, serves as a warning to Nilda to build a life where something belongs to her alone and not to her children and family.

2. Chávez's story cycle actually develops some of *Mango Street*'s formal tendencies further. For instance, it extends Cisneros's experiments with narrator positions beyond the singular "I" of the protagonist to have other characters around the protagonist narrate.

3. In *Fifth Chinese Daughter*, the protagonist's desire for independence from her family and her culture's constraints on women coexists with a craving for recognition from that

family and culture. This ambivalent negotiation is central to Kingston's work as well. With respect to *Nisei Daughter*, Kingston reproduces almost wholesale a key scene in which the protagonist feels unable to speak in school and realizes this silence was racially specific to the Japanese students.

4. Naylor, *Women of Brewster Place*, 84. Subsequent references will be noted parenthetically in the text.

5. O'Brien, *Racial Middle*.

6. Ngai, *Impossible Subjects*, 268. Many scholars have scrutinized the model minority discourse framing Asian Americans. See, for example, Palumbo-Liu, *Asian/American*, 395–416; Viet Thanh Nguyen, *Race and Resistance*, 143–49; and Takaki, *Strangers*, 474–84. Less frequently acknowledged is how Latinxs may figure as emergent model minorities. Aggregate economic data and popular images of undocumented immigration have obscured the growing Latinx middle class (Agius Vallejo, *Barrios to Burbs*, 183). There is emerging evidence of white, non-Hispanic Americans viewing Mexican Americans as hard-working minorities, in contrast to African Americans. Some views explicitly link Mexican and Asian immigrants as successful minorities (Wortham, Mortimer, and Allard, "Mexicans as Model Minorities," 390–92, 397). This convergence shows the need for comparative scholarship on model minority discourses. For Asian American studies, this is a call to expand the work already done. See Schlund-Vials, *Modeling Citizenship*, for a compelling study of Jewish and Asian American writing that does comparative work on model minority discourses. Such work can push Latinx studies to examine how upwardly mobile strata complicate models of Latinx critique. For one study addressing the questions middle-class and upper-class status creates within Chicanx culture see Román, *Race and Upward Mobility*.

7. Baym, "Melodramas of Beset Manhood"; Fraiman, *Unbecoming Women*; TuSmith, *All My Relatives*.

8. On the female bildungsroman's revisions of individualism see Fraiman, *Unbecoming Women*, and Abel, Hirsch, and Langland, *The Voyage In*.

9. JanMohamed and Lloyd, *Nature and Context of Minority Discourse*, 10.

10. On minority revisions of the bildungsroman using a story cycle form, see Bolaki, "Weaving Stories," and Kelley, "A Minor Revolution."

11. Moretti, *Way of the World*.

12. Humboldt, "Theory of Bildung," 58.

13. Woloch, *One vs. the Many*, 29.

14. Humboldt, *Limits of State Action*, 17.

15. Ibid., 64.

16. Fraiman, *Unbecoming Women*, 131, 139–40, 125.

17. Moretti, *Way of the World*.

18. Slaughter, *Human Rights, Inc.*, 27.

19. These reforms and the repeal of laws that had denied them citizenship and landownership changed the landscape for Asian Americans (Takaki, *Strangers*, 473–74). These reforms also helped some Mexican Americans enter the middle class (Agius Vallejo, *Barrios to Burbs*, 42). Bolstered by these openings and post–World War II shifts in the gender composition of U.S. labor, Chicanas increasingly joined the labor force and attained higher levels of education (Karen

Anderson, *Changing Woman*, 123). As discussed in the introduction, the effect of immigration reforms on Latinxs was more vexed than for Asian Americans as the laws placed numerical restrictions on immigration from the Americas. These restrictions intensified undocumented immigration, which has been a primary factor in the continuing aggregate poverty of Mexican Americans up to the present (Agius Vallejo, *Barrios to Burbs*, 6). But even as low-wage Mexican immigration remained dominant, contemporary immigration from Latin America varies dramatically in socioeconomic status (Portes, "The New Latin Nation").

20. The proportion of Mexican Americans entering the middle-class remained small (Agius Vallejo, *Barrios to Burbs*, 16). For many Asian Americans, economic struggles persisted even as aggregate measures of the population showed increasing affluence. The image of Asian American success covers over the many groups, including refugees, undocumented and/or working-class immigrants, who face economic hardships.

21. Omi and Winant, *Racial Formation*, 105.

22. Román, "'Jesus, When Did You Become So Bourgeois, Huh?'" 14.

23. Liu, Geron, and Lai, *Snake Dance*, 39–45.

24. Klinkner and Smith, *Unsteady March*, 5.

25. For a useful overview of these conditions, see Mills, "Racial Liberalism."

26. Omi and Winant, *Racial Formation*, 117

27. Steinberg, *Turning Back*, 101–2.

28. Klinkner and Smith, *Unsteady March*, 292.

29. Omi and Winant, *Racial Formation*, 136

30. Klinkner and Smith, *Unsteady March*, 304.

31. Ibid., 290–91.

32. Omi and Winant, *Racial Formation*, 88, 117.

33. Vaïsse, *Neoconservatism*, 205.

34. "Affirmative Action Conversion," 32.

35. Glazer, *Affirmative Discrimination*, 220.

36. Humboldt, *Limits of State Action*, 52.

37. Vaïsse, *Neoconservatism*, 7, 53.

38. Glazer, *Affirmative Discrimination*, 168.

39. Glazer, *Limits of Social Policy*, 189.

40. Slaughter, *Human Rights, Inc.*, 112.

41. I am not arguing that the bildungsroman has a direct causal relationship to neoconservatism. I'm noting that the bildungsroman has been massively influential for cultural narratives of social mobility that converge with neoconservative policy. We can trace an indirect linkage in the influence of ideas of *bildung* on liberalism. Consider a central text of liberalism, John Stuart Mill's *On Liberty*. In his autobiography, Mill acknowledges the influence of Goethe and Humboldt. The value of self-development and a delimited role for government in fostering the conditions for such development characterize this intersection of *bildung* and liberalism (Valls, "Self-Development").

42. Glazer, *Affirmative Discrimination*, 220, 7.

43. Vaïsse, *Neoconservatism*, 46–47.

44. Moretti, *Way of the World*.

45. Slaughter, *Human Rights, Inc.*, 116.
46. On the shift to individual blame in post–civil rights scholarship, see Steinberg, *Turning Back.*
47. Lukács, *Theory of the Novel*, 135.
48. Vaïsse, *Neoconservatism*, 43, 89–91.
49. Stories of individual mobility have long been problematic for U.S. minority literatures, but not until the legal equality of civil rights legislation had been achieved could these stories be coupled with an ideology of "equality" free of conspicuous qualifications like the Jim Crow regime's "separate but equal" logic. Formal legal equality presents a powerful basis for concluding that the United States has arrived at a colorblind meritocracy where individual mobility is possible for all.
50. Steinberg, *Turning Back*, 125.
51. Parikh, *Ethics of Betrayal*, 68.
52. Lukács, *Theory of the Novel*, 135.
53. For a critique of the novel's individualism, see Juan Rodriguez, review of *The House on Mango Street*. See Mayock, "Bicultural Construction of Self," and Valdés, "In Search of Identity," for celebrations of the novel's individualism. On the novel's collective values, see McCracken, "Sandra Cisneros' *The House on Mango Street*," and Kelley, "Minor Revolution." Finally, for accounts that take compromise positions on this debate, see Bolaki, "Weaving Stories"; Gutiérrez-Jones, "Different Voices"; and Yarbro-Bejarano, "Chicana Literature."
54. Moya, "Resisting the Interpretive Schema," 123–24.
55. McCracken, "Sandra Cisneros' *The House on Mango Street*," 63–64.
56. Ibid., 66.
57. Moretti, *Way of the World*, 21.
58. McCracken, "Sandra Cisneros' *The House on Mango Street*," 68.
59. For other examples of functionalizing the other characters, see Karafilis, "Crossing the Borders of Genre," and Yarbro-Bejarano, "Chicana Literature."
60. Kelley, "Minor Revolution," 74.
61. For other exceptionalist readings of Esperanza, see Gonzáles-Berry and Rebolledo, "Growing Up Chicano"; Valdés, "In Search of Identity"; and Bolaki, "Weaving Stories."
62. Mayock, "Bicultural Construction of Self," 225.
63. Moya, "Resisting the Interpretive Schema," 125–26.
64. Cisneros, "Returning to One's House," 166.
65. Elaine H. Kim, *Asian American Literature*, 207.
66. Cisneros, *House on Mango Street*, 24. Subsequent references will be cited parenthetically in the text.
67. Cisneros, "Do You Know Me?" 78.
68. Humboldt, "Theory of Bildung," 60.
69. One could argue that the stories where Esperanza chronicles others are occasions for her development as a writer. But Esperanza's artistic agency is downplayed in many of these stories and she narrates frequently through subject positions other than the individual "I." This strategy subordinates the development of her voice to the stories of other people in themselves.
70. Brady, "Contrapuntal Geographies."

71. Cisneros, "Notes," 75.

72. Few critics emphasize these differences in circumstances. Inés Salazar's "Can You Go Home Again?" is an exception.

73. Mayock, "Bicultural Construction of Self"; Salazar, "Can You Go Home Again?"

74. Gutiérrez-Jones, "Different Voices," 299.

75. Robbins, *Upward Mobility*, 193.

76. Fraiman, *Unbecoming Women*, 10.

77. See Gutiérrez-Jones, "Different Voices," for an example of this conflation.

78. Cisneros, "Notes," 75–76.

79. Cisneros, "Returning to One's House," 176, 178.

80. Sanborn, "Keeping Her Distance," 1343.

81. Cisneros, "Notes," 75.

82. Collins, *Black Feminist Thought*, 309.

83. There may seem to be a generic problem in this comparison, as *Mango Street* is a work of fiction and *The Woman Warrior* is a memoir. But as many critics note, *The Woman Warrior* blurs the lines between memoir and fiction. One of the novelistic traditions it dialogues with is the bildungsroman. See Chu, "Invisible World," for an extensive situation of *Woman Warrior* within this genre.

84. The influence of Kingston's work on Cisneros also suggests the productivity of this comparison. Cisneros employs an epigraph from *The Woman Warrior* in her poetry collection *My Wicked, Wicked Ways* (Cutler, *Ends of Assimilation*, 144). It's not clear when Cisneros read *The Woman Warrior* (1976). *My Wicked, Wicked Ways* was first written as part of her MFA thesis (submitted in 1978), but it wasn't until the published version (1987) that the epigraph appeared. It's possible that she read Kingston by the time of the writing of the poems and *Mango Street* (which was written between 1977 and 1982), but it's also possible she recognized the resonances in their concerns later on.

85. Anne Anlin Cheng, *Melancholy of Race*, 66, 81.

86. Kingston, *Woman Warrior*, 171. Subsequent references will be cited parenthetically in the text.

87. Sau-Ling C. Wong, *Reading Asian American Literature*, 78; Sidonie Smith, "Filiality," 77; Cheung, *Articulate Silences*, 88; Li, "Naming," 509; Elaine H. Kim, *Asian American Literature*, 205.

88. Moretti, *Way of the World*, 4.

89. Sau-Ling C. Wong, *Reading Asian American Literature*, 109.

90. Cheung, *Articulate Silences*, 77.

91. Chu, "Invisible World," 109; Li, "Naming," 499.

92. Li, "Naming," 500.

93. Kingston originally conceived of the two books as one. She considers *China Men* a "companion volume" to *The Woman Warrior* (Kingston, "Susan Brownmiller Talks with Maxine Hong Kingston," 178).

94. Cheung, *Articulate Silences*, 99–100.

95. Sidonie Smith, "Filiality," 75.

96. Sau-Ling C. Wong, *Reading Asian American Literature*, 89–90.

CHAPTER 2

  1. Benedict Anderson, *Imagined Communities*.

  2. I am inspired by work in British and postcolonial literary studies on form and the transnational. Stephen Clingman's *The Grammar of Identity* examines the syntax of postcolonial novels and Rebecca L. Walkowitz's *Cosmopolitan Style* explores how modernist techniques develop cosmopolitan thought. I break from these scholars by considering how narrating the transnational may require forms beyond the dominant form of the novel. Peter Hitchcock's *The Long Space* offers an interesting possibility by examining novelistic series. I complement this focus on narrative extensiveness by exploring the productivity of narrative gaps.

  3. Jodi Kim, *Ends of Empire*; Ortiz, "Cold War in the Americas"; Thananopavarn, *LatinAsian Cartographies*.

  4. For a perspective on how Asian American and Latinx literatures bear witness to suppressed histories of the Cold War, see Thananopavarn, *LatinAsian Cartographies*. For a very helpful survey of the post–Cold War generation of Latinx writers, see Ortiz, "Cold War in the Americas."

  5. Espiritu, *Body Counts*, 48.

  6. Briggs, *Somebody's Children*, 130, 152; David L. Eng, *Feeling of Kinship*, 102.

  7. On the limitations of linear models of immigration for Latinx formations see Poblete, "Introduction."

  8. Concannon, Lomelí, and Priewe, *Imagined Transnationalism*, 3.

  9. Kandiyoti, *Migrant Sites*, 24, 5–6, 43.

  10. Phan, interview by the author, March 29, 2018, San Francisco, CA.

  11. Pease, "Re-Mapping the Transnational Turn," 5.

  12. Briggs, McCormick, and Way, "Transnationalism."

  13. Tsing, *Friction*, 270.

  14. Schiller, "U.S. Immigrants," 408.

  15. Sarah J. Mahler, *American Dreaming*, 31.

  16. Sarah J. Mahler, *American Dreaming*; Schiller, Basch, and Blanc, "Transnationalism."

  17. Irizarry, "This Is How You Lose It," 148.

  18. Chu, *Assimilating Asians*, 143, 186.

  19. For the theory of the chronotope, see Bakhtin, "Forms of Time." David Cowart describes this binary between America and the rest of the world as a pitting of "old world fatalism" against "the new world paradigm of self-fashioning" (*Trailing Clouds*, 161).

  20. John Riofrio acknowledges the book's fragmentation but does not examine it ("Situating Latin American Masculinity"). Aitor Ibarrola-Armendáriz views the sequence as "a random and rather incomplete choice of snapshots" ("Puerto Rican and Dominican Self-Portraits," 189). Although Christopher González thinks of *Drown* as a story cycle with a coherent effect, he argues for analyzing the stories out of order in thematic clusters (*Reading Junot Díaz*, 13).

  21. This male-first migration pattern is widespread among Dominican migrants and others from Latin America. Men travel first to make money and establish a home. The difficulty of crossing borders and the price of travel prevent families from migrating together. See Sarah J. Mahler, *American Dreaming*, 80. John Riofrio notes that Rafa and Yunior are part

of "an entire generation of Dominican boys forced to grow up without fathers" ("Situating Latin American Masculinity," 26).

22. Díaz, *Drown*, 199. Subsequent references will be cited parenthetically in the text.

23. Christopher González, *Reading Junot Díaz*, 24.

24. In contrast, Julia Alvarez's novels, as nonlinear and multiplot as they are, offer largely reconstructed family histories. For instance, the forward-flowing mother's story and backward-flowing daughter's story in *In the Name of Salomé* eventually converge into a narrative whole. Díaz's work pushes Dominican American fiction towards transfictional gaps that Alvarez's novels hint at but do not sustain. Such gaps are powerful aesthetic features with which to register the ruptures in Dominican American history.

25. Irizarry, "This Is How You Lose It," 150.

26. Díaz, *The Brief Wondrous Life of Oscar Wao*, 3. See Atkins and Wilson, *The Dominican Republic*, for a history of U.S. imperialism in the Dominican Republic.

27. For a detailed history of the civil war and U.S. intervention, see Chester, *Rag-Tags*.

28. Tammy Lee, *Operation Babylift*.

29. Sachs, *Life We Were Given*, 102–5.

30. Ibid., 58–63.

31. Ibid., 190.

32. Ibid., 212–13.

33. The stories also focus on Mai and Vinh, who came to the United States as boat refugees.

34. Van, "Aimee Phan."

35. Phan, "Interview with Aimee Phan."

36. Jungha Kim, "Affects and Ethics," 61.

37. Marguerite Nguyen and Fung, "Refugee Cultures," 2.

38. Espiritu, *Body Counts*, 48, 100, 104.

39. Ibid., 10, 18.

40. Briggs, *Somebody's Children*, 156.

41. Jodi Kim observes that American popular culture obsessively remembers American warfare in Vietnam but privileges stories of what American men endured in Vietnam while silencing the stories of Vietnamese people (*Ends of Empire*, 196). On masculinity in representations of the Vietnam War, see Jeffords, *Remasculinization of America*.

42. Wills, "Claiming America."

43. Briggs, *Somebody's Children*, 152.

44. Ibid., 130.

45. Deann Borshay Liem's documentary *First Person Plural* about her experience as a Korean adoptee makes this point powerfully. On how contemporary adoption practices have shifted away from abandoning the child's past, see Volkman, "New Geographies of Kinship," 4–14.

46. Both Michele Janette and Isabelle Thuy Pelaud survey examples of the Vietnamese American family saga. And they stress the dominance of personal memoir (Janette, *Mỹ Việt*, xix; Pelaud, *This Is All*, 27). Janette observes that works that go farther afield in genre, style, and subject matter have become more prominent since the 1990s (xxii). I situate Phan's work as part of these movements beyond memoir.

47. The American story cycle emerged in regionalist texts like Sarah Orne Jewett's *The Country of the Pointed Firs* (1896) and Sherwood Anderson's *Winesburg, Ohio* (1919).

48. Foote, *Regional Fictions*; Hsuan L. Hsu, *Geography*; Lutz, *Cosmopolitan Vistas*; Joseph, *American Literary Regionalism*; Arthur, *Violet America*.

49. Kennedy, *Modern American Short Story Sequences*; Harde, *Narratives of Community*; Rocío G. Davis, *Transcultural Reinventions*.

50. Ingram, *Representative Short Story Cycles*, 44.

51. Koshy, "Minority Cosmopolitanism."

52. Phan, *We Should Never Meet*, 20. Subsequent references will be cited parenthetically in the text.

53. Phan's stories give form to Viet Thanh Nguyen's argument that the "violence that had supposedly ended erupted once more in the refugee community, caused by those traumatized by the war or by those who had no other opportunities because of the war" ("Just Memory," 146).

54. Joseph, *American Literary Regionalism*, 157.

55. David L. Eng, *Feeling of Kinship*, 103.

56. Espiritu, *Body Counts*, 5; Malkki, "National Geographic," 443.

57. David L. Eng, *Feeling of Kinship*, 137.

58. Hsuan L. Hsu, *Geography*, 13.

59. Melissa S. Williams, "Citizenship as Agency," 41, 43, 41.

60. Neil Smith, "Contours of a Spatialized Politics," 60.

61. Koshy, "Minority Cosmopolitanism," 595.

62. Foote, *Regional Fictions*, 13.

63. Kandiyoti, *Migrant Sites*, 39.

64. Foote, *Regional Fictions*, 3–14.

65. Sohn, "These Desert Places," 166.

66. August, "Re-Placing the Accent," 68.

67. Lowe, *Immigrant Acts*, 16.

68. On the gaps of American historical memory about the Vietnam War, see Truong, "Emergence of Voices," and Lieu, *American Dream in Vietnamese*.

69. Melissa S. Williams, "Citizenship as Agency," 42.

70. Ibid., 43.

71. As the story is focalized through Lien, the word *it* functions as a translation of the Vietnamese word *nó*, the gender-neutral pronoun that would be used to refer to an infant. I thank erin Khuê Ninh for this point. The choice has an additional effect of removing identity information to make the linkages between this infant and other characters more difficult to ascertain.

72. Melissa S. Williams, "Citizenship as Agency," 52.

73. Hoffnung-Garskof, *Tale of Two Cities*, xiv.

74. Kumar, *US Interventionism*, 120.

75. Chester, *Rag-Tags*, 2–3.

76. Hoffnung-Garskof, *Tale of Two Cities*, 94–95.

77. Ibid., 74.

78. For more on how Cold War foreign policy shaped refugee recognition, see Loescher and Scanlan, *Calculated Kindness*.

79. Quoted in Hoffnung-Garskof, *Tale of Two Cities*, 94.

80. Lieu, *American Dream in Vietnamese*, xxi.

81. For an important exception that deeply explores Asian–Latin American connections, though not the Vietnam War, see Rothwell, *Transpacific Revolutionaries*. Studies that make only passing mention of Vietnam–Latin American connections during the Cold War include Marchesi, *Latin America's Radical Left*; Grandin, *Last Colonial Massacre*; and Brands, *Latin America's Cold War. In from the Cold*, edited by G. M. Joseph and Daniela Spenser, dwells on U.S. Chicano responses to the Vietnam War but has little to say about its impact on Latin American nations.

82. Prashad, *Darker Nations*; Christopher J. Lee, "Between a Moment and an Era"; Westad, *Global Cold War*.

83. Young, "Postcolonialism," 17.

84. The one Latin American–Asian solidarity that is often noted is between Cuba and Vietnam. See Westad, *Global Cold War*.

85. Young, "Postcolonialism," 19.

86. Anne Garland Mahler, "Global South," 108.

87. Young, "Postcolonialism," 18–19.

88. Anne Garland Mahler, "Global South," 107.

89. The other key work will be revealing the connections between Latin American and African struggles. We can think, for example, of Che Guevara's task force that fought alongside rebels in eastern Congo against U.S., Congolese, and Belgian troops.

CHAPTER 3

1. Reddi, *Karma*, 31. Subsequent references will be cited parenthetically in the text.

2. Plascencia, *People of Paper*, 114. Subsequent references will be cited parenthetically in the text.

3. Chan et al., *Aiiieeeee!*, xxi.

4. Paredes, *"With His Pistol,"* 15–23.

5. It would be reductive to assume that all Asian American and Latinx writers seek to represent their ethnic or racial groups. David Leiwei Li, however, has argued that whether the author intends it or not, ethnic minority texts are caught in a state of "compulsory representation" in which the author and/or text are taken to stand in for the ethnic community by many audiences (*Imagining the Nation*, 181). King-Kok Cheung also notes "the peculiar burden" placed on ethnic writers. Because the histories of many minority communities have been so invisible to the U.S. mainstream, readers look to "biological insiders" for "authentic" representations (*Articulate Silences*, 12).

6. On spreading ideas of American racial equality as a motive for immigration reforms see Ngai, *Impossible Subjects*, 243–45. See Madeline Y. Hsu, *Good Immigrants*, on the desire for an economic edge informing immigration reforms.

7. Ong, *Buddha Is Hiding*, 9, 266.

8. Madeline Y. Hsu, *Good Immigrants*, 201.

9. Lim, *Bilingual Brokers*, 16.

10. Brown, *Undoing the Demos*, 110.

11. Madeline Y. Hsu, *Good Immigrants*, 247. See also Ong, *Buddha Is Hiding*, 261.

12. Madeline Y. Hsu, *Good Immigrants*, 239, 245.

13. Ong, *Flexible Citizenship*, 130.

14. Madeline Y. Hsu, *Good Immigrants*, 237.

15. Ong, *Buddha Is Hiding*, 12.

16. Madeline Y. Hsu, *Good Immigrants*, 243.

17. Zahir Janmohamed, "Illegal Indian Immigrants in US: Many Overstayed Their Tourist or Student Visas or Are from Broken Marriages," *Economic Times*, October 8, 2017.

18. Portes and Hoffman, "Latin American Class Structures," 71.

19. Delgado-Wise, "Critical Dimensions of Mexico-US Migration," 595.

20. Ong, *Buddha Is Hiding*, 282.

21. Reddi, "The Indian Community I Knew," 7.

22. Srikanth, *World Next Door*, 12.

23. Bal, *Narratology*, 152. See Forster, *Aspects of the Novel*, 100–125, on flat and round characters.

24. "Nuclei" and "catalysers" are Roland Barthes's terms ("Introduction," 93). "Kernels" and "satellites" are Seymour Chatman's (*Story and Discourse*, 53–54).

25. Genette, *Narrative Discourse*, 94–112.

26. Of course many story cycles include reversals of major and minor character positions. What's distinctively transfictional about the transposition is the opening of a separate story that is not merged into a larger causally interconnected story whose overarching positioning of characters tends to subsume the local character distributions in each story. We can think of Sherwood Anderson's *Winesburg, Ohio*, in which the stories interconnect into a larger story centered on George Willard. The other characters may change positions from minor to major in different stories, but in the overall structure of the work they are subordinated to the overarching hierarchy of characters around George. In transfictional story cycles, the different arrangements of characters in different stories have equal weight in the overall work since each story remains relatively autonomous and there is no broader overarching narrative that connects them all. It is this equally weighted co-presence of many conflicting distributions that sustains the tensions of major and minor, center and periphery.

27. Balgamwalla, "Bride and Prejudice," 26.

28. Brown, *Undoing the Demos*, 106–7.

29. Woloch, *One vs. the Many*, 41.

30. Ibid., 22.

31. I am not arguing that the narrative attention allocated to minor characters in novels cannot fluctuate. It often does. Minor characters may receive expanded attention as a novel progresses. Still, the transfictional technique of opening another *independent* narrative for a minor character is distinct. Rather than reconfiguring the economy of narrative attention within the same story, the transposition opens a separate economy, loosely connected to but also relatively autonomous of the other.

32. James, "Preface to 'Daisy Miller,'" 278.

33. Appiah, "Identity, Authenticity, Survival," 161–63.

34. See Li, *Imagining the Nation*, for a balanced assessment of cultural nationalism. He recognizes how its essentialist tendencies were both problematic and generative. He notes that the model was powerful in asserting an Asian American presence and contesting the hegemonic monologue of U.S. public discourse on Asians (37).

35. Efforts to wrest control over Mexican and Mexican American representations became widespread with the rise of Chicano cultural nationalism. See, however, Limón, "Stereotyping and Chicano Resistance" for an account of early twentieth-century efforts by Mexican Americans to resist such stereotypes.

36. Alarcón, "Chicana Feminism," 250.

37. Rosaldo, *Culture and Truth*, 149.

38. Chen, *Double Agency*, 61.

39. Alonzo, *Badmen*, 11, 15–17; Chen, *Double Agency*, 60–85; Christian, *Show and Tell*, 17, 22–23.

40. Pickering, *Stereotyping*, 70–71.

41. Said, *Orientalism*, 72.

42. Bhabha, "Other Question," 107.

43. The classic theorization of type characters in E. M. Forster's *Aspects of the Novel* is very suggestive for the formal features of stereotyping. But Forster's focus on the craft of the novel means that he doesn't address the relationship of type characters to social types. David Galef's study of type characters is formalist and largely eschews questions of social types and stereotypes. See Galef, *Supporting Cast*. Peter Demetz's discussion of how type characters arise in Balzacian realism's attempts to capture the complex social totalities of the urbanized world does not address the issue of stereotypes explicitly but it dovetails neatly with Michael Pickering's argument that the urgency of stereotyping has intensified in modernization's proliferation of difference. See Demetz, "Balzac and the Zoologists."

44. Woloch, *One vs. the Many*, 69.

45. Ibid., 83–85.

46. Fanon, *Black Skin, White Masks*, 109, 116, 117.

47. See, for example, Colleen Lye's account of naturalism's use of the Asiatic figure (*America's Asia*, 47–95).

48. Woloch, *One vs. the Many*, 70, 71.

49. It doesn't make sense to categorically vilify a formal structure that is part of the craft of fiction. As E. M. Forster contends, novels that are complex often require flat as well as round characters (*Aspects of the Novel*, 108).

50. Chuh, *Imagine Otherwise*, 7.

51. Here I draw from David Palumbo-Liu's point about the representation of Asian American diaspora, that we need to interrogate how "any *discrete* notion of diasporic experience comes to stand in for an *essential* experience" (*Asian/American*, 356).

52. Plascencia, "An Interview with Salvador Plascencia," by Angela Stubbs.

53. Plascencia, "Interview by Max Benavidez," 27.

54. Ibid., 27.

55. Plascencia frequently notes his interest in book design. The material construction of the novel, he reflects, "has a profound effect on the way we construct narrative. If we understand the novel as a single column of prose spread over five hundred pages . . . the stories and paragraphs we write are in a very real sense just conforming to this arbitrary guide" (Plascencia, "An Interview with Salvador Plascencia," by Matthew Baker).

56. Harford Vargas, *Forms of Dictatorship*, 63–64.

57. Melamed, *Represent and Destroy*, 2, 34. For an important discussion of the fraught choice between recognition and redistribution politics, see Fraser, "From Redistribution to Recognition?" See Taylor, "Politics of Recognition," for an influential defense of the centrality of recognition and social images in racial politics.

58. Ibid., 34.

59. Delgado-Wise, "Critical Overview of Migration," 646, 652; Robinson, *Latin America and Global Capitalism*, 104, 107, 121.

60. Robinson, *Latin America and Global Capitalism*, 207.

61. Harvey, *Brief History of Neoliberalism*, 29–30.

62. Delgado-Wise, "Critical Overview of Migration," 651.

63. Robinson, *Latin America and Global Capitalism*, 203.

64. Foster, McChesney, and Jonna, "Global Reserve Army."

65. Robinson, *Latin America and Global Capitalism*, 204–5.

66. Vargas, *Forms of Dictatorship*, 79.

67. "Paul and Daisy Soros Fellowship for New Americans," Paul and Daisy Soros Foundation, 2018, https://www.pdsoros.org/fellowship.

68. This alignment is most apparent in the kinds of young immigrants supported by the foundation. For example, 80 percent of the 2018 fellowship cohort were young immigrants working in science, technology, engineering, and mathematics (STEM) fields, law, or business.

69. Melamed, *Represent and Destroy*, 37, 42.

70. Plascencia, "Interview by Max Benavidez," 27.

71. Saldívar, "Historical Fantasy," 576. Kevin Cooney draws out another way that the novel critiques stereotypes that emerge through Chicano representation, by exposing the established discourse of committed Chicano men and betraying Chicana women in the subplot of Sal's vitriolic accusations of his ex-girlfriend Liz ("Metafictional Geographies," 213).

72. Saldívar, "Historical Fantasy," 581.

73. In the first edition of *The People of Paper*, published by McSweeney's, these black blocks were cut out of the page, a different kind of absence, but equally obscuring. See Hayles, "Future of Literature," for a reading of surface and subtext effects in this novel.

74. Alonzo, *Badmen*, 7.

75. For a sense of the pervasiveness of these impulses, consider how many anthologies and critical studies in ethnic studies take up some version of these phrases in their titles. In Asian American studies, these include *Breaking Silence: An Anthology of Contemporary Asian American Poets; Breaking the Silence: Redress and Japanese American Ethnicity; Nisei Soldiers Break Their Silence; Asian American Voices: A Coffee House Press Sampler; Voices of the Asian American and Pacific Islander Experience*, and many others. In Chicanx studies, they include

Decolonial Voices: Chicana and Chicano Cultural Studies in the 21st Century; Speaking Chicana: Voice, Power, and Identity; Voices of Resistance: Interdisciplinary Approaches to Chicana Children's Literature; Chicana Voices: Intersections of Class, Race, and Gender, and so forth.

76. Melamed, *Represent and Destroy*, 36.

77. Bhabha, "Other Question," 101.

CHAPTER 4

1. See Lopez and Espiritu, "Panethnicity," for their originary formulation.

2. Certainly, we can think of exceptions to this tendency. In Latinx literature, Judith Ortiz Cofer's poem "The Latin Deli" comes to mind, as well as the multiethnic Latinx neighborhood in Cisneros's *Mango Street* or the Nueva York depicted in Junot Díaz's *Drown*, where Cubans, Puerto Ricans, and Dominicans commingle. Francisco Goldman's *The Ordinary Seaman* is another intriguing example that shows a multiethnic Central American boat crew and multiple Latinx groups in Brooklyn. See Caminero-Santangelo, *On Latinidad*, for further discussion of the single ethnic focus of the literatures we organize under the rubric Latinx. In Asian American literature, literature from multiethnic Hawaii stands out, as does the tradition of Vietnam War stories where Asian American soldiers who aren't Vietnamese find themselves racialized as Vietnamese. We might also think of Frank Chin's *Chickencoop Chinaman*, with its Japanese American and Chinese American protagonists, or Younghill Kang's depiction of Korean exiles in New York's Chinatown in *East Goes West*. Beyond the few exceptions we might cite, however, it's apparent that the texts whose subject matter is panethnically Asian American or Latinx are far outnumbered by texts whose subject matter is a single ethnic group.

3. We might see the emergence of self-consciously Asian American and Latinx texts as made possible by years of institutionalization of these categories in public discourse, academic programs, and the world of letters. The lag between the invention of these categories and the flourishing of panethnic literatures speaks to the gap between the categories and the communities they attempt to encompass, communities for whom panethnicity may be an abstraction distant from their lived realities.

4. The socioeconomic divide between the Asian American and Latinx communities is perhaps the most overt contrast. In 2014, Asian American households had a median income of $74,297 while Hispanic households had a median income of $42,491 (DeNavas-Walt and Proctor, "Income and Poverty," 6). This points to different kinds of coalitions: a working-class Latinx panethnicity versus a professional-class Asian American panethnicity. Aggregate measures like median income, however, do not capture the growing socioeconomic stratifications that characterize both populations. While their overall socioeconomic indicators diverge, both of these coalitions are struggling with forging coalition across widening class divides. Many of the differences between these groups become more nuanced if we break down the aggregate blocs to analyze the transformations and diversities within each. At this level of granularity, some of the distinctions between these communities give way to overlaps and parallels. Shared language as a basis for solidarity, for example, seems to favor panethnicity among Latinxs more than among Asian Americans, who trace ties back to many different ethnic groups speaking myriad languages. But the image of a unifying Spanish language covers over the linguistic diversity among Latinxs and the differences between national and regional

variations of Spanish (Caminero-Santangelo, *On Latinidad*, 14–15). Neither Asian American nor Latinx coalitions can rely on uniform language as a solid grounding for unity. One could argue that Asian American and Latinx panethnic coalitions are different because the former is premised on shared racialization while the latter must bring together multiple races. (For this argument, see Lopez and Espiritu, "Panethnicity," 204. See De Genova and Ramos-Zaya, *Latino Crossings*, for an opposing view that many Latinxs have come to understand and deploy Latino as a racial category positioned in relation to whiteness and blackness.) Racial identification is indeed complex within Latinx communities, but Asian American racialization is not uniform either. Filipina/os and South Asians are among the groups whose experiences of racialization do not square with the dominant racial image of Asian Americans, which centers on phenotypes associated with East Asia. (On Filipina/o racialization, see Ocampo, *Latinos of Asia*. On the racial experiences of South Asian Americans, see Shankar and Srikanth, *A Part, yet Apart*.) Common racialization, then, is not as straightforward for Asian Americans as it might seem. Asian American panethnic cooperation has also been facilitated by the concentration of Asian ethnic groups in the same regions of the United States (the West and Hawaii, for example). Meanwhile, Latinx groups had relatively little interaction as they lived in separate regions for much of their histories in the United States (Lopez and Espiritu, "Panethnicity," 207). Today this difference between Asian American and Latinx panethnicity is closing, as Latinx settlement increasingly moves beyond established ethnic enclaves and those enclaves themselves are becoming more multiethnic (Mora, *Making Hispanics*, 4, 165–67).

5. Latinxs participated in the radical racial politics of the period, not as Latinxs but in ethnic-specific Chicano and Puerto Rican movements. See Oboler, *Ethnic Labels, Latino Lives*, 50–70.

6. Padilla, *Latino Ethnic Consciousness*, 81; Espiritu, *Asian American Panethnicity*, 17.

7. Though we might point to the political tradition of pan–Latin American solidarity, as expressed in the writings of José Martí or Simón Bolívar, as an important symbolic resource in the absence of a Latinx movement history in the United States.

8. For the most influential account of the formation of Asian American panethnicity, see Espiritu, *Asian American Panethnicity*. For a more recent history, see Maeda, *Chains of Babylon*. See Mora, *Making Hispanics*, for an illuminating history of the construction of the panethnic term *Hispanic* through the combined efforts of federal agencies, activist organizations, and media companies. While the terms *Hispanic* or *Latinx* are quite recent as highly visible political bodies, several scholars note that there were earlier histories of smaller-scale panethnic identification among Latinxs in the United States. See Dávila, *Latinos, Inc.*, 15; Laó-Montes, "Niuyol," 124–25; Flores, *From Bomba to Hip-Hop*, 148.

9. Caminero-Santangelo, *On Latinidad*, 1–2; Espiritu, *Asian American Panethnicity*, 14.

10. Espiritu, *Asian American Panethnicity*, 14.

11. Flores and Rosaldo, *Companion to Latina/o Studies*, xxiii–xxiv.

12. Lopez and Espiritu, "Panethnicity," 205–6.

13. Yén Lê Espiritu gives the example of refugee populations from Southeast Asia that arrived with few resources to start new lives in the United States; such groups may have urgent needs but can be the least represented within existing Asian American political organizations (Espiritu, *Asian American Panethnicity*, 98).

14. Ibid., 60.

15. For examples of the argument of panethnic incoherence, see Koshy, "Fiction," 323; Chuh, *Imagine Otherwise*, 21; and Song, *Children of 1965*, 11.

16. Beltrán, *Trouble with Unity*, 6.

17. Suárez-Orozco and Páez, "Research Agenda," 3.

18. Gimenez, "Latino/'Hispanic,'" 559.

19. Torres-Saillant, "Problematic Paradigms."

20. As Suzanne Oboler rightly observes, even the term "entered" is complicated by Latinx differences, as Puerto Ricans and many Mexican Americans did not "enter" the United States at all; rather the United States entered their lands and brought these populations into the nation through conquest and colonization (Oboler, *Ethnic Labels, Latino Lives*, xii).

21. Ibid., 10.

22. Gimenez, "Latino/'Hispanic,'" 558.

23. Cuban Americans, who, as an aggregate, tend to be more affluent than other Latinx groups have been frequent examples for this argument (Caminero-Santangelo, *On Latinidad*, 165). Several South American national origin groups, whose migrations are characterized by professionals, have also been examples (Gimenez, "Latino/'Hispanic,'" 567).

24. While some scholars argue that there is no such thing as a single Hispanic race (Caminero-Santangelo, *On Latinidad*, 14), others counter that we should recognize how government practices and popular discourse position Hispanic as a racial category determining social policy and the distribution of resources (De Genova and Ramos-Zayas, *Latino Crossings*, 16; Mora, *Making Hispanics*, 118).

25. Caminero-Santangelo, *On Latinidad*, 14–15.

26. Gimenez, "Latino/'Hispanic,'" 560.

27. Caminero-Santangelo, *On Latinidad*, 163.

28. Beltrán, *Trouble with Unity*, 9.

29. Ty, *Unfastened*, xxvii.

30. Chinese Americans were favored allies during World War II while the United States fought Japan and forced thousands of Japanese Americans into internment camps; but they found themselves the targets of anticommunist raids and deportations after the Chinese revolution in 1949 (Koshy, "Fiction," 319–20). For a detailed history of the anticommunist campaigns waged on Chinese American communities, see Ngai, *Impossible Subjects*.

31. Ong, *Flexible Citizenship*.

32. Though both panethnic formations exhibit class diversity, each faces particular challenges in acknowledging this diversity. For Asian Americans, currently racialized as an affluent "model minority," the distinct economic and political struggles of disadvantaged Asian American groups such as Filipina/o Americans or Southeast Asian refugees conflict with the economic and political priorities of more affluent groups (Espiritu, *Asian American Panethnicity*, 107–8).

33. Lye, "Racial Form," 95.

34. On the fissures between the Asian American movement and Asian American communities, see Maeda, *Chains of Babylon*, and Espiritu, *Asian American Panethnicity*.

35. Viet Thanh Nguyen, *Race and Resistance*.

36. Espiritu, *Asian American Panethnicity*, 50.

37. Oboler, *Ethnic Labels, Latino Lives*, 172.

38. Lye, "Racial Form," 94.

39. On the consolidation of the concept Hispanic in the federal government, nonprofit organizations, and the media, see Mora, *Making Hispanics*. For an account of how Latino has become a powerful commercial and market category, see Dávila, *Latinos, Inc.*, which also includes a useful discussion of Asian Americans emerging as a distinct market. See Kwon, "Politics and Institutionalization" for an analysis of how Asian American politics has become entrenched in state and nonprofit organizations.

40. Mora, *Making Hispanics*, 157.

41. The phrase is from Kwon, "Politics and Institutionalization," 145. See Beltrán, *Trouble with Unity*, 99, on the professionalization of Latinx politics.

42. Mora, *Making Hispanics*, 159.

43. Chuh, *Imagine Otherwise*, 149.

44. See Kwon, "Politics and Institutionalization," and Mora, *Making Hispanics*, especially 14–15, 34–36, and 55.

45. See Song, *Children of 1965*, and Caminero-Santangelo, *On Latinidad*, for nuanced assessments of this question. See also Christopher Lee, *Semblance of Identity*, which shows how difficult it can be to move beyond identity categories.

46. De Genova and Ramos-Zayas, *Latino Crossings*, 21. See also Lye, "Racial Form," 94.

47. Beltrán, *Trouble with Unity*, 158.

48. Koshy, "Fiction," 316.

49. Espiritu, *Asian American Panethnicity*, 134–60.

50. The irony of these Latinx characters lamenting the strike on American soil is that many Latinxs were displaced to the United States by American strikes on their soil. Indeed among the most convincing potential unifying principles for Latinxs is a widely shared historical experience of the disruptive relations of the United States with Latin America. See Suárez-Orozco and Páez, "Research Agenda."

51. Melissa S. Williams, "Citizenship as Agency," 41.

52. This idea builds on Cristina Beltrán's suggestion that Latinidad may be less about identity and being than about mobilization and doing. See Beltrán, *Trouble with Unity*, 19.

53. Beltrán, *Trouble with Unity*, 119.

54. Chuh, *Imagine Otherwise*, 10; Beltrán, *Trouble with Unity*, 128; Caminero-Santangelo, *On Latinidad*, 21. This proposal is not entirely new, as Yén Lê Espiritu, in her foundational work on Asian American panethnicity, noted that panethnic coalitions tend to emerge and organize around specific issues and conditions that bring together multiple ethnic groups (*Asian American Panethnicity*, 82).

55. David Rodriguez, *Latino National Political Coalitions*, 88–89.

56. Caminero-Santangelo, *On Latinidad*, 215.

57. Agustín Laó-Montes's study of Latinx social movements in New York finds movements engaged "in a plurality of struggles addressing a diversity of axes of injustice" ("Niuyol," 141). On the national level, there is no single encompassing Latinx political organization; instead there are multiple panethnic organizations addressing different issues. While the Mexican American Legal Defense and Education Fund (MALDEF) brings legal expertise to

advocate for Latinxs, and the League of United Latin American Citizens (LULAC) addresses civil rights, the National Council of La Raza (NCLR) coordinates local groups serving Latinx communities. For more on national Latinx organizations, see David Rodriguez, *Latino National Political Coalitions*.

58. Chuh, *Imagine Otherwise*, 114.

59. It's important to note that many multiplot forms do comparative work but by eschewing direct plot and causal connections transfictional form places distinctive emphasis on drawing out the latent and less direct parallels that may thread across distinct stories.

60. Christopher Lee, *Semblance of Identity*, 121.

61. Torres-Saillant, "Problematic Paradigms," 449–50.

62. Caminero-Santangelo, *On Latinidad*, 17.

63. Flores, *From Bomba to Hip-Hop*, 8.

CHAPTER 5

1. Ragain, "Revolutionary Romance," 138.

2. Yamashita, *I Hotel*, 124. Further citations will be noted parenthetically in the text.

3. Nathan Ragain offers one of the most intriguing formal treatments of *I Hotel*. I build on his work, in particular his observation that the novel sustains a "double movement of fragmentation and relation," a tension that we can recognize as transfictional. His work though focuses on a single novella and argues that "it would be impossible to deal adequately with the variety of story-lines and formal experiments in this long novel's 'complex architecture.'" Though my approach does not claim comprehensiveness, I hope to show that *I Hotel*'s full powers for theorizing Asian American panethnicity can only be appreciated by attempting a view of the whole. See Ragain, "Revolutionary Romance," 138, 141. For other important studies of the novel, see Zhou, *Cities of Others* and Ling, *Across Meridians*.

4. Padilla, *Latino Ethnic Consciousness*, 68.

5. Ibid., 138.

6. Caminero-Santangelo, *On Latinidad*, 214.

7. In describing this continual play of convergence and divergence, I'm building on Yén Lê Espiritu's formulation that panethnicity is a "process of fusion as well as of fission" (Espiritu, *Asian American Panethnicity*, 14).

8. Okamoto, "Theory of Panethnicity," 835.

9. Espiritu, *Asian American Panethnicity*, 2.

10. Gimenez, "Latino/'Hispanic,'" 569.

11. Ibid., 562.

12. Chuh, *Imagine Otherwise*, 9, 147.

13. Beltrán, *Trouble with Unity*, 170.

14. Caminero-Santangelo, *On Latinidad*, 204, 217.

15. Palumbo-Liu, "Embedded Lives," 17.

16. See, for example, Flores, *Bomba to Hip-Hop*, 165.

17. Beltrán, *Trouble with Unity*, 9.

18. Ibid., 5, 10.

19. Ibid., 58, 56.

20. See Moraga, *Loving in the War Years* and Bow, *Betrayal*.

21. Lowe, *Immigrant Acts*, 72.

22. Beltrán, *Trouble with Unity*, 65.

23. Ibid., 16.

24. Ibid., 160.

25. Chuh, *Imagine Otherwise*, 147.

26. Ibid., 28.

27. Ragain, "Revolutionary Romance," 151.

28. Yamashita's portrayal of narratives constructing movements squares with emerging research in the sociology of social movements. This research has taken a narrative turn, arguing for the role narrative plays in how movements come together, shift directions, draw in their members, persuade the public, and make sense of their pasts and futures. See Joseph E. Davis, *Stories of Change*, 4, 20–27. These scholars conclude that narratives are constitutive to the identities of movements and the formation of new collective political agents (Polletta, "Plotting Protest," 47). Motivating this narrative turn is the insight that imaginative and emotional appeals, not just rational arguments and interests, fuel movements. Sociologists have focused so far on nonliterary narratives constructed by movements, but this turn toward the imaginative and affective creates an opening to consider the work that literary fictions can do for the creative work of coalition.

29. Chuh, *Imagine Otherwise*, 28.

30. Ling, *Across Meridians*, 173.

31. Ibid., 174, 187.

32. Maeda, *Chains of Babylon*.

33. Zhou, *Cities of Others*, 297.

34. Doreen Massey, *Space, Place, and Gender*, 5.

35. Adorno, *Negative Dialectics*, 153.

36. Marcial González, *Chicano Novels*, 198.

37. Jameson, *Archaeologies of the Future*, 39.

38. Song, *Children of 1965*, 232.

39. Flores, *From Bomba to Hip-Hop*, 198.

40. Adorno, *Negative Dialectics*, 11, 145, 11.

41. Beltrán, Trouble with Unity, 9.

42. Ibid., 161

43. Ibid., 74. For a similar argument in Asian American studies, see Song, *Children of 1965*, 51.

44. Chuh, *Imagine Otherwise*, 33.

45. Beltrán, *Trouble with Unity*, 162, 167.

46. Jameson, *Archaeologies of the Future*, 210–11.

47. Beltrán, *Trouble with Unity*, 162.

48. Chuh, *Imagine Otherwise*, 8.

49. I draw here on Fredric Jameson who acknowledges that attacks on teleology have been useful to rid Marxism of the bourgeois notion of progress. He insists however that we should be nervous about whether the attack on teleology also abandons a "vision of the future altogether." See Jameson, "Marxism and Historicism," 47.

50. Jameson, *Archaeologies of the Future*, xii.

51. Ibid., 210.

52. Beltrán, *Trouble with Unity*, 160.

53. Miller, *Narrative and Its Discontents*, ix.

54. Ibid., 265–67.

55. Ibid., x.

56. Jameson, *Archaeologies of the Future*, 231–32.

57. Bloch, *Principle of Hope*, 1373.

58. Ibid., 1373.

59. Muñoz, *Cruising Utopia*, 91.

60. Bloch, *Principle of Hope*, 1374.

61. Ibid., 1375.

62. Christopher Lee, *Semblance of Identity*, 151. Lee demonstrates the enduring hold of identity by revealing the vestiges of identitarian thinking that endure even in anti-identitarian thought.

63. Ibid., 152.

64. Muñoz, *Cruising Utopia*, 1. The relation of Muñoz's theory of queer identity to Yamashita's rethinking of Asian American identity is not just a case of aligned logics. Chris A. Eng observes that *I Hotel*'s opening novella is centrally focused on relations of "queer (be)longing" that have been central to the radical possibilities of Asian American coalition but have been obscured by metaphors of generational transmission in our histories. Eng argues that *I Hotel* envisions a utopian horizon "of interdependent and coalitional intimacies" of the kind Muñoz theorizes. See Eng, "Queer Genealogies of (Be)Longing," 347, 364.

65. Ibid., 20.

66. Song, *Children of 1965*, 232; Muñoz, *Cruising Utopia*, 1.

67. Muñoz, *Cruising Utopia*, 171.

CONCLUSION

1. Chuh, *Imagine Otherwise*, 16–20; Hamilton, *Of Space and Mind*, 3, 16.

2. Bois, "Painting as Model," 257, 246, 245, 253.

3. Herman, *Basic Elements of Narrative*; Hayot, "On Literary Worlds."

4. Hayot, "On Literary Worlds," 137. Hayot's invocation of fictional totality and system resonates with recent discussions of realism that see realism's totalizing ambitions as critically useful for attempts to make sense of the world system. See Esty and Lye, "Peripheral Realisms Now," 284–85. This resonance is intriguing, but Hayot shows that we can analyze the features of fictional world construction and the ways they engage the world across realist and nonrealist works. Focusing analysis in this way can move our thinking beyond familiar literary categories ("On Literary Worlds," 160). This is especially helpful for transfictional form, which, as we've seen, can structure realist works like *We Should Never Meet* but can also structure metafictional fantasies like *The People of Paper*, multigeneric works like *I Hotel*, and mixtures of legend and myth like *The Woman Warrior*. Focusing on fictional world construction can also help de-emphasize entrenched ways of debating the politics of literature, which for too long have been structured by an opposition between realist literature

and modernist/nonrealist literature, with modernism usually appearing as the subversive genre. (This opposition was most influentially consolidated in the conversations involving Theodor Adorno, Walter Benjamin, Ernst Bloch, Bertolt Brecht, and Georg Lukács, which are collected in Adorno, Benjamin, Bloch, Brecht, and Lukács, *Aesthetics and Politics*.) I agree with the many scholars of realism who call for moving beyond this entrenched opposition (see Esty and Lye, "Peripheral Realisms Now," and Goodlad, "Introduction: Worlding Realisms Now"). Transfictional form, from its early instances around the turn of the twentieth century to the contemporary examples we've examined, cuts across these divides, showing up in realist, regionalist, modernist, and postmodernist works. Its powers for theorizing the world and giving aesthetic shape to social contradictions comes from its narrative structure and the way it constructs fictional worlds across distinct stories; these features aren't best described within the terms of the realism-modernism debates, so they push us to articulate the political stakes of aesthetics in other ways.

5. Hayot, "On Literary Worlds," 142.

6. Briggs, McCormick, and Way, "Transnationalism," 627.

7. Transfictional works emphasize a tension between seeing each story as a self-enclosed world or as part of a much broader world beyond any one story's scope. Their form highlights a central ambivalence in the concept of world that Eric Hayot notes: the sense of world as "a generic totality of any size and world as the most total totality" ("On Literary Worlds," 132).

8. Muñoz, *Cruising Utopia*, 1, 12, 1.

9. Lowe, *Immigrant Acts*, 70.

10. Flores, *From Bomba to Hip-Hop*, 11.

11. For a compelling and urgent argument linking the fates of Asian Americans and Arab Americans in the post-9/11 period, see Maira and Shihade, "Meeting Asian / Arab American Studies." The case for solidarity between Latinxs and those targeted in the war on terror is evident from at least two developments: the increased militarization of the U.S.-Mexico border post-9/11 for the purported purpose of securing U.S. borders against terrorists and the alibi of antiterrorism efforts for the increased policing of U.S. Latinxs and Latin American immigrants. See Romero, *Hyperborder*.

BIBLIOGRAPHY

Abel, Elizabeth, Marianne Hirsch, and Elizabeth Langland, eds. *The Voyage In: Fictions of Female Development*. Hanover, NH: University Press of New England, 1983.

Adorno, Theodor, Walter Benjamin, Ernst Bloch, Bertolt Brecht, and Georg Lukács. *Aesthetics and Politics*. London: Verso, 2007.

Adorno, Theodor W. *Negative Dialectics*. Translated by E. B. Ashton. London: Routledge, 1973.

"The Affirmative Action Conversion of Nathan Glazer." *Journal of Blacks in Higher Education* 20 (Summer 1998): 32.

Agius Vallejo, Jody. *Barrios to Burbs: The Making of the Mexican American Middle Class*. Stanford, CA: Stanford University Press, 2012.

Alarcón, Norma. "Chicana Feminism: In the Tracks of 'the' Native Woman." *Cultural Studies* 4, no. 3 (October 1990): 248–56.

Alonzo, Juan J. *Badmen, Bandits, and Folk Heroes: The Ambivalence of Mexican American Identity in Literature and Film*. Tucson: University of Arizona Press, 2009.

Alvarez, Julia. *How the García Girls Lost Their Accents*. New York: Penguin, 1991.

———. *In the Name of Salomé*. New York: Penguin, 2000.

Anderson, Benedict. *Imagined Communities: Reflections on the Origin and Spread of Nationalism*. Rev. ed. London: Verso, 2006.

Anderson, Karen. *Changing Woman: A History of Racial Ethnic Women in Modern America*. New York: Oxford University Press, 1996.

Anderson, Sherwood. *Winesburg, Ohio*. 1919. Edited by Glen A. Love. Oxford: Oxford University Press, 1997.

Appiah, Kwame Anthony. "Identity, Authenticity, Survival: Multicultural Societies and Social Reproduction." In *Multiculturalism: Examining the Politics of Recognition*, edited by Amy Gutmann, 149–63. Princeton, NJ: Princeton University Press, 1994.

Arthur, Jason. *Violet America: Regional Cosmopolitanism in U.S. Fiction Since the Great Depression*. Iowa City: University of Iowa Press, 2013.

Atkins, G. Pope, and Larman C. Wilson. *The Dominican Republic and the United States: From Imperialism to Transnationalism*. Athens: University of Georgia Press, 1998.

August, Timothy K. "Re-placing the Accent: From the Exile to Refugee Position." *MELUS* 41, no. 3 (2016): 68–88.

Bakhtin, M. M. "Forms of Time and of the Chronotope in the Novel: Notes Toward a Historical Poetics." In *The Dialogic Imagination: Four Essays*, edited by Michael Holquist, translated by Caryl Emerson and Michael Holquist, 84–258. Austin: University of Texas Press, 1981.

Bal, Mieke. *Narratology: Introduction to the Theory of Narrative*. 3rd ed. Toronto: University of Toronto Press, 2009.

Balgamwalla, Sabrina. "Bride and Prejudice: How U.S. Immigration Law Discriminates Against Spousal Visa Holders." *Berkeley Journal of Gender, Law and Justice* 29, no. 1 (January 2014): 25–71.

Barthes, Roland. "Introduction to the Structural Analysis of Narratives." In *Image, Music, Text*, edited and translated by Stephen Heath, 79–124. New York: Hill and Wang, 1977.

Baym, Nina. "Melodramas of Beset Manhood: How Theories of American Fiction Exclude Women Authors." *American Quarterly* 33, no. 2 (Summer 1981): 123–39.

Beltrán, Cristina. *The Trouble with Unity: Latino Politics and the Creation of Identity*. Oxford: Oxford University Press, 2010.

Bhabha, Homi K. "The Other Question: Stereotype, Discrimination and the Discourse of Colonialism." In *The Location of Culture*, 94–120. London: Routledge, 1994.

Bloch, Ernst. *The Principle of Hope*. Translated by Neville Plaice, Stephen Plaice, and Paul Knight. Vol. 3. Cambridge, MA: MIT Press, 1986.

Bois, Yve-Alain. "Painting as Model." In *Painting as Model*, 245–57. Cambridge, MA: MIT Press, 1990.

Bolaki, Stella. "Weaving Stories of Self and Community Through Vignettes in Sandra Cisneros's *The House on Mango Street*." In Harde, *Narratives of Community: Women's Short Story Sequences*, 14–36.

Bow, Leslie. *Betrayal and Other Acts of Subversion: Feminism, Sexual Politics, Asian American Women's Literature*. Princeton, NJ: Princeton University Press, 2001.

Brady, Mary Pat. "The Contrapuntal Geographies of *Woman Hollering Creek and Other Stories*." *American Literature* 71, no. 1 (1999): 117–50.

Brands, Hal. *Latin America's Cold War*. Cambridge, MA: Harvard University Press, 2012.

Briggs, Laura. *Somebody's Children: The Politics of Transracial and Transnational Adoption*. Durham, NC: Duke University Press, 2012.

Briggs, Laura, Gladys McCormick, and J. T. Way. "Transnationalism: A Category of Analysis." *American Quarterly* 60, no. 3 (September 2008): 625–48.

Brown, Wendy. *Undoing the Demos: Neoliberalism's Stealth Revolution*. Brooklyn: Zone Books, 2015.

Budick, E. Miller. *Blacks and Jews in Literary Conversation*. Cambridge: Cambridge University Press, 1998.

Bunia, Remigius. "Diegesis and Representation: Beyond the Fictional World, on the Margins of Story and Narrative." *Poetics Today* 31, no. 4 (2010): 679–720.

Calderón, Héctor. *Narratives of Greater Mexico: Essays on Chicano Literary History, Genre, and Borders*. Austin: University of Texas Press, 2004.

Caminero-Santangelo, Marta. *On Latinidad: U.S. Latino Literature and the Construction of Ethnicity*. Gainesville: University Press of Florida, 2007.

Chan, Jeffery Paul, Lawson Fusao Inada, Shawn Wong, and Frank Chin, eds. *Aiiieeeee! An Anthology of Asian-American Writers*. Washington, DC: Howard University Press, 1974.

Chare, Nicholas, and Ika Willis. "Introduction: Trans-: Across/Beyond." *Parallax* 22, no. 3 (2016): 267–89.

Chatman, Seymour. *Story and Discourse: Narrative Structure in Fiction and Film*. Ithaca, NY: Cornell University Press, 1978.

Chávez, Denise. *The Last of the Menu Girls*. Houston: Arte Público Press, 1986.

Chen, Tina. *Double Agency: Acts of Impersonation in Asian American Literature and Culture*. Stanford, CA: Stanford University Press, 2005.

Cheng, Anne Anlin. *The Melancholy of Race: Psychoanalysis, Assimilation, and Hidden Grief*. Oxford: Oxford University Press, 2001.

Cheng, Cindy I-Fen. *Citizens of Asian America: Democracy and Race During the Cold War*. New York: New York University Press, 2013.

Chester, Eric Thomas. *Rag-tags, Scum, Riff-raff, and Commies: The U.S. Intervention in the Dominican Republic, 1965–1966*. New York: Monthly Review Press, 2001.

Cheung, King-Kok. *Articulate Silences: Hisaye Yamamoto, Maxine Hong Kingston, Joy Kogawa*. Ithaca, NY: Cornell University Press, 1993.

Christian, Karen. *Show and Tell: Identity as Performance in U.S. Latina/o Fiction*. Albuquerque: University of New Mexico Press, 1997.

Chu, Patricia. *Assimilating Asians: Gendered Strategies of Authorship in Asian America*. Durham, NC: Duke University Press, 2000.

———. "'The Invisible World the Emigrants Built': Cultural Self-Inscription and the Antiromantic Plots of *The Woman Warrior*." *Diaspora: A Journal of Transnational Studies* 2, no. 1 (Spring 1992): 95–115.

Chuh, Kandice. *Imagine Otherwise: On Asian Americanist Critique*. Durham, NC: Duke University Press, 2003.

Cisneros, Sandra. "Do You Know Me?: I Wrote *The House on Mango Street*." *Americas Review* 15, no. 1 (1987): 77–79.

———. *The House on Mango Street*. 1984. New York: Vintage, 1991.

———. "Notes to a Young(er) Writer." *Americas Review* 15, no. 1 (1987): 74–76.

———. "Returning to One's House: An Interview with Sandra Cisneros." Interviewed by Martha Satz. *Southwest Review* 82, no. 2 (1997): 166–85.

Clingman, Stephen. *The Grammar of Identity: Transnational Fiction and the Nature of the Boundary*. New York: Oxford University Press, 2009.

Colby, Sandra L., and Jennifer M. Ortman. "Projections of the Size and Composition of the U.S. Population: 2014 to 2060." Washington, DC: U.S. Census Bureau, 2015.

Collins, Patricia Hill. *Black Feminist Thought: Knowledge, Consciousness, and the Politics of Empowerment*. 2nd ed. New York: Routledge, 2009.

Concannon, Kevin, Francisco A. Lomelí, and Marc Priewe, eds. *Imagined Transnationalism: U.S. Latino/a Literature, Culture, and Identity*. New York: Palgrave Macmillan, 2009.

Cooney, Kevin. "Metafictional Geographies: Los Angeles in Karen Tei Yamashita's *Tropic of Orange* and Salvador Plascencia's *People of Paper*." In *On and Off the Page: Mapping Place in Text and Culture*, edited by M. B. Hackler and Ari J. Adipurwawidjana, 189–218. Newcastle upon Tyne, UK: Cambridge Scholars, 2009.

Cowart, David. *Trailing Clouds: Immigrant Fiction in Contemporary America*. Ithaca, NY: Cornell University Press, 2006.

Cutler, John Alba. *Ends of Assimilation: The Formation of Chicano Literature*. New York: Oxford University Press, 2015.

Dávila, Arlene M. *Latinos, Inc.: The Marketing and Making of a People*. Berkeley: University of California Press, 2001.

Davis, Joseph E., ed. *Stories of Change: Narrative and Social Movements*. Albany: State University of New York Press, 2002.

Davis, Rocío G. *Transcultural Reinventions: Asian American and Asian Canadian Short-story Cycles*. Toronto: TSAR Publications, 2001.

Davis, Rocío G., and Sue-Im Lee, eds. *Literary Gestures: The Aesthetic in Asian American Writing*. Philadelphia: Temple University Press, 2005.

De Genova, Nicholas. "Latino and Asian Racial Formations at the Frontiers of U.S. Nationalism." In De Genova, *Racial Transformations*, 1–20.

———. "Migrant 'Illegality' and Deportability in Everyday Life." *Annual Review of Anthropology* 31 (2002): 419–47.

———, ed. *Racial Transformations: Latinos and Asians Remaking the United States*. Durham, NC: Duke University Press, 2006.

De Genova, Nicholas, and Ana Y. Ramos-Zayas. *Latino Crossings: Mexicans, Puerto Ricans, and the Politics of Race and Citizenship*. New York: Routledge, 2003.

Delgado-Wise, Raúl. "Critical Dimensions of Mexico—US Migration Under the Aegis of Neoliberalism and NAFTA." *Canadian Journal of Development Studies/Revue canadienne d'études du développement* 25, no. 4 (January 2004): 591–605.

———. "A Critical Overview of Migration and Development: The Latin American Challenge." *Annual Review of Sociology* 40, no. 1 (July 2014): 643–63.

Demetz, Peter. "Balzac and the Zoologists: A Concept of the Type." In *The Disciplines of Criticism: Essays in Literary Theory, Interpretation, and History*, edited by Peter Demetz, Thomas Greene, and Lowry Nelson, 397–418. New Haven, CT: Yale University Press, 1968.

DeNavas-Walt, Carmen, and Bernadette D. Proctor. "Income and Poverty in the United States: 2014." Washington, DC: U.S. Census Bureau, 2015.

Díaz, Junot. *The Brief Wondrous Life of Oscar Wao*. New York: Riverhead, 2007.

————. *Drown*. New York: Riverhead, 1996.

Dirlik, Arif. "Asians on the Rim: Transnational Capital and Local Community in the Making of Contemporary Asian America." In *Across the Pacific: Asian Americans and Globalization*, edited by Evelyn Hu-DeHart, 29–60. New York: Asia Society and Temple University Press, 1999.

Dudziak, Mary L. *Cold War Civil Rights: Race and the Image of American Democracy*. Princeton, NJ: Princeton University Press, 2000.

Egan, Jennifer. *A Visit from the Goon Squad*. New York: Anchor, 2010.

Eng, Chris A. "Queer Genealogies of (Be)Longing: On the Thens and Theres of Asian America in Karen Tei Yamashita's *I Hotel*." *Journal of Asian American Studies* 20, no. 3 (2017): 345–72.

Eng, David L. *The Feeling of Kinship: Queer Liberalism and the Racialization of Intimacy*. Durham, NC: Duke University Press, 2010.

Espiritu, Yến Lê. *Asian American Panethnicity: Bridging Institutions and Identities*. Philadelphia: Temple University Press, 1992.

————. *Body Counts: The Vietnam War and Militarized Refuge(es)*. Oakland: University of California Press, 2014.

Esty, Jed, and Colleen Lye. "Peripheral Realisms Now." *Modern Language Quarterly* 73, no. 3 (2012): 269–88.

Fanon, Frantz. *Black Skin, White Masks*. Translated by Charles Lam Markmann. New York: Grove, 1982.

Flores, Juan. *From Bomba to Hip-hop: Puerto Rican Culture and Latino Identity*. New York: Columbia University Press, 2000.

Flores, Juan, and Renato Rosaldo, eds. *A Companion to Latina/o Studies*. Malden, MA: Blackwell, 2007.

Foote, Stephanie. *Regional Fictions: Culture and Identity in Nineteenth-Century American Literature*. Madison: University of Wisconsin Press, 2001.

Forster, E. M. *Aspects of the Novel*. New York: Harcourt, 1927.

Foster, John Bellamy, Robert W. McChesney, and R. Jamil Jonna. "The Global Reserve Army of Labor and the New Imperialism." *Monthly Review*, November 1, 2011.

Fraiman, Susan. *Unbecoming Women: British Women Writers and the Novel of Development*. New York: Columbia University Press, 1993.

Fraser, Nancy. "From Redistribution to Recognition? Dilemmas of Justice in a 'Postsocialist' Age." In *Justice Interruptus: Critical Reflections on the "Postsocialist" Condition*, 11–39. New York: Routledge, 1997.

Galef, David. *The Supporting Cast: A Study of Flat and Minor Characters*. University Park: Pennsylvania State University Press, 1993.

Gates, Henry Louis, Jr. *Figures in Black: Words, Signs, and the "Racial" Self*. New York: Oxford University Press, 1987.

Genette, Gérard. *Narrative Discourse: An Essay in Method*. Translated by Jane E. Lewin. Ithaca, NY: Cornell University Press, 1980.

Gerrig, Richard J. *Experiencing Narrative Worlds: On the Psychological Activities of Reading*. New Haven, CT: Yale University Press, 1993.

Gimenez, Martha E. "Latino/'Hispanic'—Who Needs a Name?: The Case Against a Standardized Terminology." *International Journal of Health Services* 19, no. 3 (1989): 557–71.

Glazer, Nathan. *Affirmative Discrimination: Ethnic Inequality and Public Policy*. New York: Basic Books, 1975.

———. *The Limits of Social Policy*. Cambridge, MA: Harvard University Press, 1988.

Goellnicht, Donald. "Blurring Boundaries: Asian American Literature as Theory." In *An Interethnic Companion to Asian American Literature*, edited by King-Kok Cheung, 338–65. Cambridge: Cambridge University Press, 1997.

Goethe, Johann Wolfgang von. *Wilhelm Meister's Apprenticeship*. 1795–96. Edited by Eric A. Blackall. Translated by Eric A. Blackall and Victor Lange. Vol. 9 of *Goethe's Collected Works*. New York: Suhrkamp, 1989.

Goffman, Ethan. *Imagining Each Other: Blacks and Jews in Contemporary American Literature*. Albany: State University of New York Press, 2000.

Gonzáles-Berry, Erlinda, and Tey Diana Rebolledo. "Growing Up Chicano: Tomás Rivera and Sandra Cisneros." *Revista Chicano-Riqueña* 13, no. 3–4 (1985): 109–19.

González, Christopher. *Reading Junot Díaz*. Pittsburgh: University of Pittsburgh Press, 2015.

González, Marcial. *Chicano Novels and the Politics of Form: Race, Class, and Reification*. Ann Arbor: University of Michigan Press, 2009.

Goodlad, Lauren M. E. "Introduction: Worlding Realisms Now." *Novel: A Forum on Fiction* 49, no. 2 (2016): 183–201.

Grandin, Greg. *The Last Colonial Massacre: Latin America in the Cold War*. Chicago: University of Chicago Press, 2004.

Gutiérrez-Jones, Leslie S. "Different Voices: The Re-Bildung of the Barrio in Sandra Cisneros' *The House on Mango Street*." In *Anxious Power: Reading, Writing, and Ambivalence in Narrative by Women*, edited by Carol J. Singley and Susan Elizabeth Sweeney, 295–312. Albany: State University of New York Press, 1993.

Haggis, Paul, dir. *Crash*. 2004. Santa Monica, CA: Lion's Gate Entertainment, 2005. DVD.

Hamilton, Patrick Lawrence. *Of Space and Mind: Cognitive Mappings of Contemporary Chicano/a Fiction*. Austin: University of Texas Press, 2011.

Harde, Roxanne, ed. *Narratives of Community: Women's Short Story Sequences*. Newcastle upon Tyne, UK: Cambridge Scholars, 2007.

Harford Vargas, Jennifer. *Forms of Dictatorship: Power, Narrative, and Authoritarianism in the Latinx Novel*. New York: Oxford University Press, 2018.

Harvey, David. *A Brief History of Neoliberalism*. Oxford: Oxford University Press, 2005.

Hayles, N. Katherine. "The Future of Literature: Complex Surfaces of Electronic Texts and Print Books." In *A Time for the Humanities: Futurity and the Limits of Autonomy*, edited by James J. Bono, Tim Dean, and Ewa Plonowska Ziarek, 180–209. New York: Fordham University Press, 2008.

Hayot, Eric. "On Literary Worlds." *Modern Language Quarterly* 72, no. 2 (2011): 129–61.

Hebebrand, Christina M. *Native American and Chicano/a Literature of the American Southwest: Intersections of Indigenous Literature*. New York: Routledge, 2004.

Henríquez, Cristina. *The Book of Unknown Americans*. New York: Vintage, 2014.

Herman, David. *Basic Elements of Narrative*. Malden, MA: Wiley-Blackwell, 2009.

Hing, Bill Ong. *Making and Remaking Asian America Through Immigration Policy, 1850–1990*. Stanford, CA: Stanford University Press, 1993.

Hinojosa, Rolando. *The Valley/Estampas del valle*. 1973. Houston: Arte Público Press, 2014.

Hitchcock, Peter. *The Long Space: Transnationalism and Postcolonial Form*. Stanford, CA: Stanford University Press, 2010.

Ho, Fred, and Bill V. Mullen, eds. *Afro Asia: Revolutionary Political and Cultural Connections Between African Americans and Asian Americans*. Durham, NC: Duke University Press, 2008.

Hoffnung-Garskof, Jesse. *A Tale of Two Cities: Santo Domingo and New York After 1950*. Princeton, NJ: Princeton University Press, 2008.

Hsu, Hsuan L. *Geography and the Production of Space in Nineteenth-Century American Literature*. Cambridge: Cambridge University Press, 2010.

Hsu, Madeline Y. *The Good Immigrants: How the Yellow Peril Became the Model Minority*. Princeton, NJ: Princeton University Press, 2015.

Hu-DeHart, Evelyn. "Latin America in Asia-Pacific Perspective." In *What Is in a Rim? Critical Perspectives on the Pacific Region Idea*. 2nd ed. Edited by Arif Dirlik, 251–282. Lanham, MD: Rowman and Littlefield, 1998.

Humboldt, Wilhelm von. *The Limits of State Action*. Edited and translated by J. W. Burrow. London: Cambridge University Press, 1969.

———. "Theory of Bildung." In *Teaching as a Reflective Practice: The German Didaktik Tradition*, edited by Ian Westbury, Stefan Hopmann, and Kurt Riquarts, translated by Gillian Horton-Krüger, 57–61. Mahwah, NJ: Lawrence Erlbaum, 2000.

Ibarrola-Armendáriz, Aitor. "Puerto Rican and Dominican Self-Portraits and Their Frames: The 'Autobiographical' Fiction of Esmeralda Santiago, Junot Díaz, and Julia Álvarez." In *Selves in Dialogue: A Transethnic Approach to American Life Writing*, edited by Simal Begoña, 181–205. New York: Rodopi, 2011.

Ingram, Forrest L. *Representative Short Story Cycles of the Twentieth Century: Studies in a Literary Genre*. The Hague: Mouton, 1971.

Irizarry, Ylce. "This Is How You Lose It: Navigating Dominicanidad in Junot Díaz's *Drown*." In *Junot Díaz and the Decolonial Imagination*, edited by Monica Hanna, Jennifer Harford Vargas, and José David Saldívar, 147–71. Durham, NC: Duke University Press, 2016.

James, Henry. "Preface to 'Daisy Miller.'" In *The Art of the Novel: Critical Prefaces*, 267–87. Chicago: The University of Chicago Press, 2011.

Jameson, Fredric. *Archaeologies of the Future: The Desire Called Utopia and Other Science Fictions*. London: Verso, 2007.

———. "Marxism and Historicism." *New Literary History* 11, no. 1 (Autumn 1979): 41–73.

Janette, Michele, ed. *Mỹ Việt: Vietnamese American Literature in English, 1962–present*. Honolulu: University of Hawai'i Press, 2011.

JanMohamed, Abdul R., and David Lloyd, eds. *The Nature and Context of Minority Discourse*. New York: Oxford University Press, 1990.

Jeffords, Susan. *The Remasculinization of America: Gender and the Vietnam War*. Bloomington: Indiana University Press, 1989.

Joseph, G. M., and Daniela Spenser, eds. *In from the Cold: Latin America's New Encounter with the Cold War*. Durham, NC: Duke University Press, 2008.

Joseph, Philip. *American Literary Regionalism in a Global Age*. Baton Rouge: Louisiana State University Press, 2007.

Kandiyoti, Dalia. *Migrant Sites: America, Place, and Diaspora Literatures*. Hanover, NH: Dartmouth College Press, 2009.

Karafilis, Maria. "Crossing the Borders of Genre: Revisions of the Bildungsroman in Sandra Cisneros's *The House on Mango Street* and Jamaica Kincaid's *Annie John*." *Journal of the Midwest Modern Language Association* 31, no. 2 (1998): 63–78.

Kelley, Margot. "A Minor Revolution: Chicano/a Composite Novels and the Limits of Genre." In *Ethnicity and the American Short Story*, edited by Julie Brown, 63–84. New York: Garland, 1997.

Kennedy, J. Gerald, ed. *Modern American Short Story Sequences: Composite Fictions and Fictive Communities*. Cambridge: Cambridge University Press, 1995.

Kim, Claire Jean. *Bitter Fruit: The Politics of Black-Korean Conflict in New York City*. New Haven, CT: Yale University Press, 2000.

Kim, Daniel Y. *Writing Manhood in Black and Yellow: Ralph Ellison, Frank Chin, and the Literary Politics of Identity*. Stanford, CA: Stanford University Press, 2005.

Kim, Elaine H. *Asian American Literature: An Introduction to the Writings and Their Social Context*. Philadelphia: Temple University Press, 1982.

Kim, Jodi. *Ends of Empire: Asian American Critique and the Cold War*. Minneapolis: University of Minnesota Press, 2010.

Kim, Jungha. "The Affects and Ethics of the Gift in Aimee Phan's *We Should Never Meet*." *Contemporary Literature* 57, no. 1 (2016): 56–78.

Kingston, Maxine Hong. *China Men*. New York: Knopf, 1980.

———. "Susan Brownmiller Talks with Maxine Hong Kingston, Author of *The Woman Warrior*." Interview by Susan Brownmiller. In *Maxine Hong Kingston's* The Woman Warrior: *A Casebook*, edited by Sau-ling Cynthia Wong, 173–80. New York: Oxford University Press, 1999.

———. *The Woman Warrior: Memoirs of a Girlhood Among Ghosts*. New York: Vintage, 1976.

Klinkner, Philip A., and Rogers M. Smith. *The Unsteady March: The Rise and Decline of Racial Equality in America*. Chicago: University of Chicago Press, 1999.

Koshy, Susan. "The Fiction of Asian American Literature." *Yale Journal of Criticism* 9, no. 2 (1996): 315–46.

———. "Minority Cosmopolitanism." *PMLA* 126, no. 3 (May 2011): 592–609.

Krauss, Nicole. *Great House*. New York: Norton, 2010.

Kumar, V. Shiv. *US Interventionism in Latin America: Dominican Crisis and the OAS*. New York: Advent Books, 1987.

Kwon, Soo Ah. "The Politics and Institutionalization of Panethnic Identity." *Journal of Asian American Studies* 16, no. 2 (June 2013): 137–57.

Laó-Montes, Agustín. "Niuyol: Urban Regime, Latino Social Movements, Ideologies of Latinidad." In *Mambo Montage: The Latinization of New York*, edited by Agustín Laó-Montes and Arlene M. Dávila, 119–57. New York: Columbia University Press, 2001.

Lee, Christopher. *The Semblance of Identity: Aesthetic Mediation in Asian American Literature.* Stanford, CA: Stanford University Press, 2012.

Lee, Christopher J. "Between a Moment and an Era: The Origins and Afterlives of Bandung." In *Making a World After Empire: The Bandung Moment and Its Political Afterlives*, edited by Christopher J. Lee, 1–42. Athens: Ohio University Press, 2010.

Lee, Erika. *The Making of Asian America: A History.* New York: Simon and Schuster, 2015.

Lee, Julia H. *Interracial Encounters: Reciprocal Representations in African American and Asian American Literatures, 1896–1937.* New York: New York University Press, 2011.

Lee, Sue-Im. "Introduction: The Aesthetic in Asian American Literary Discourse." In Rocío G. Davis and Lee, *Literary Gestures*, 1–14.

Lee, Tammy, dir. *Operation Babylift: The Lost Children of Vietnam.* Dallas: Against the Grain, 2010. DVD.

Li, David Leiwei. *Imagining the Nation: Asian American Literature and Cultural Consent.* Stanford, CA: Stanford University Press, 1998.

———. "The Naming of a Chinese American 'I': Cross-Cultural Sign/ifications in *The Woman Warrior*." *Criticism: A Quarterly for Literature and the Arts* 30, no. 4 (1988): 497–515.

Liem, Deann Borshay. *First Person Plural.* San Francisco: Center for Asian American Media, 2000. DVD.

Lieu, Nhi T. *The American Dream in Vietnamese.* Minneapolis: University of Minnesota Press, 2011.

Lim, Jeehyun. *Bilingual Brokers: Race, Literature, and Language as Human Capital.* New York: Fordham University Press, 2017.

Limón, José E. *Mexican Ballads, Chicano Poems: History and Influence in Mexican-American Social Poetry.* Berkeley: University of California Press, 1992.

———. "Stereotyping and Chicano Resistance: An Historical Dimension." In *Chicanos and Film: Representation and Resistance*, edited by Chon A. Noriega, 3–17. Minneapolis: University of Minnesota Press, 1992.

Ling, Jinqi. *Across Meridians: History and Figuration in Karen Tei Yamashita's Transnational Novels.* Stanford, CA: Stanford University Press, 2012.

———. *Narrating Nationalisms: Ideology and Form in Asian American Literature.* New York: Oxford University Press, 1998.

Liu, Michael, Kim Geron, and Tracy Lai. *The Snake Dance of Asian American Activism: Community, Vision, and Power.* Lanham, MD: Lexington Books, 2008.

Loescher, Gil, and John A. Scanlan. *Calculated Kindness: Refugees and America's Half-Open Door Policy.* New York: Free Press, 1986.

Lopez, David, and Yén Espiritu. "Panethnicity in the United States: A Theoretical Framework." *Ethnic and Racial Studies* 13, no. 2 (1990): 198–224.

López, Gustavo, and Jynnah Radford. "Facts on U.S. Immigrants, 2015." *Pew Research Center's Hispanic Trends Project* (blog), May 3, 2017. http://www.pewhispanic.org/2017/05/03/facts-on-u-s-immigrants/.

Lowe, Lisa. *Immigrant Acts: On Asian American Cultural Politics.* Durham, NC: Duke University Press, 1996.

—————. *The Intimacies of Four Continents*. Durham, NC: Duke University Press, 2015.

Lukács, Georg. *The Theory of the Novel: A Historico-Philosophical Essay on the Forms of Great Epic Literature*. Translated by Anna Bostock. Cambridge, MA: MIT Press, 1971.

Lutenski, Emily. *West of Harlem: African American Writers and the Borderlands*. Lawrence: University Press of Kansas, 2015.

Lutz, Tom. *Cosmopolitan Vistas: American Regionalism and Literary Value*. Ithaca, NY: Cornell University Press, 2004.

Lye, Colleen. *America's Asia: Racial Form and American Literature, 1893–1945*. Princeton, NJ: Princeton University Press, 2005.

—————. "Racial Form." *Representations* 104 (2008): 92–101.

Maeda, Daryl J. *Chains of Babylon: The Rise of Asian America*. Minneapolis: University of Minnesota Press, 2009.

Mahler, Anne Garland. "The Global South in the Belly of the Beast: Viewing African American Civil Rights Through a Tricontinental Lens." *Latin American Research Review* 50, no. 1 (2015): 95–116.

Mahler, Sarah J. *American Dreaming: Immigrant Life on the Margins*. Princeton, NJ: Princeton University Press, 1995.

Maira, Sunaina, and Magid Shihade. "Meeting Asian / Arab American Studies: Thinking Race, Empire, and Zionism in the U.S." *Journal of Asian American Studies* 9, no. 2 (June 29, 2006): 117–40.

Malkki, Liisa. "National Geographic: The Rooting of Peoples and the Territorialization of National Identity Among Scholars and Refugees." In *Becoming National: A Reader*, edited by Geoff Eley and Ronald Grigor Suny, 434–53. New York: Oxford University Press, 1996.

Marchesi, Aldo. *Latin America's Radical Left: Rebellion and Cold War in the Global 1960s*. Translated by Laura Perez Carrara. New York: Cambridge University Press, 2018.

Mariscal, George. *Brown-Eyed Children of the Sun: Lessons from the Chicano Movement, 1965–1975*. Albuquerque: University of New Mexico Press, 2005.

Massey, Doreen. *Space, Place, and Gender*. Minneapolis: University of Minnesota Press, 1994.

Massey, Douglas S. "The Past and Future of Mexico-U.S. Migration." In *Beyond La Frontera: The History of Mexico-U.S. Migration*, edited by Mark Overmyer-Velázquez, 251–65. New York: Oxford University Press, 2011.

Mayock, Ellen C. "The Bicultural Construction of Self in Cisneros, Álvarez, and Santiago." *Bilingual Review / La Revista Bilingüe* 23, no. 3 (1998): 223–29.

McCracken, Ellen. "Sandra Cisneros' *The House on Mango Street*: Community-Oriented Introspection and the Demystification of Patriarchal Violence." In *Breaking Boundaries: Latina Writing and Critical Readings*, edited by Asunción Horno-Delgado, Eliana Ortega, Nina M. Scott, and Nancy Saporta Sternbach, 62–71. Amherst: University of Massachusetts Press, 1989.

Melamed, Jodi. *Represent and Destroy: Rationalizing Violence in the New Racial Capitalism*. Minneapolis: University of Minnesota Press, 2011.

Milian, Claudia. *Latining America: Black-Brown Passages and the Coloring of Latino/a Studies*. Athens: University of Georgia Press, 2013.

Mill, John Stuart. *Autobiography and Other Writings.* Edited by Jack Stillinger. Boston: Houghton Mifflin, 1969.

Miller, D. A. *Narrative and Its Discontents: Problems of Closure in the Traditional Novel.* Princeton, NJ: Princeton University Press, 1981.

Mills, Charles W. "Racial Liberalism." *PMLA* 123, no. 5 (October 2008): 1380–97.

Mohr, Nicholasa. *Nilda.* New York: Harper and Row, 1973.

Molina, Natalia. *How Race Is Made in America: Immigration, Citizenship, and the Historical Power of Racial Scripts.* Berkeley: University of California Press, 2014.

Mora, G. Cristina. *Making Hispanics: How Activists, Bureaucrats, and Media Constructed a New American.* Chicago: University of Chicago Press, 2014.

Moraga, Cherríe. *Loving in the War Years: Lo Que Nunca Pasó Por Sus Labios.* Cambridge, MA: South End Press, 1983.

Moretti, Franco. *The Way of the World: The Bildungsroman in European Culture.* Translated by Albert Sbragia. New edition. London: Verso, 2000.

Mori, Toshio. *Yokohama, California.* 1949. Seattle: University of Washington Press, 1985.

Moya, Paula M. L. "Resisting the Interpretive Schema of the Novel Form: Rereading Sandra Cisneros's *The House on Mango Street.*" In *Bridges, Borders, Breaks: History, Narrative, & Nation in Twenty-First-Century Chicana/o Literary Criticism,* edited by William Orchard and Yolanda Padilla, 121–38. Pittsburgh: University of Pittsburgh Press, 2016.

Mullen, Bill V. "Persisting Solidarities: Tracing the AfroAsian Thread in U.S. Literature and Culture." In *AfroAsian Encounters: Culture, History, Politics,* edited by Heike Raphael-Hernandez and Shannon Steen, 245–59. New York: New York University Press, 2006.

Muñoz, José Esteban. *Cruising Utopia: The Then and There of Queer Futurity.* New York: New York University Press, 2009.

Naylor, Gloria. *The Women of Brewster Place.* New York: Penguin, 1982.

Ngai, Mae M. *Impossible Subjects: Illegal Aliens and the Making of Modern America.* Princeton, NJ: Princeton University Press, 2004.

Nguyen, Marguerite, and Catherine Fung. "Refugee Cultures: Forty Years After the Vietnam War." *MELUS* 41, no. 3 (2016): 1–7.

Nguyen, Viet Thanh. "Just Memory: War and the Ethics of Remembrance." *American Literary History* 25, no. 1 (2013): 144–63.

———. *Race and Resistance: Literature and Politics in Asian America.* Oxford: Oxford University Press, 2002.

Oboler, Suzanne. *Ethnic Labels, Latino Lives: Identity and the Politics of (Re) Presentation in the United States.* Minneapolis: University of Minnesota Press, 1995.

O'Brien, Eileen. *The Racial Middle: Latinos and Asian Americans Living Beyond the Racial Divide.* New York: New York University Press, 2008.

Ocampo, Anthony Christian. *The Latinos of Asia: How Filipino Americans Break the Rules of Race.* Stanford, CA: Stanford University Press, 2016.

Okamoto, Dina. "Toward a Theory of Panethnicity: Explaining Asian American Collective Action." *American Sociological Review* 68 (2003): 811–42.

Omi, Michael, and Howard Winant. *Racial Formation in the United States: From the 1960s to the 1990s.* 2nd. ed. New York: Routledge, 1994.

Ong, Aihwa. *Buddha Is Hiding: Refugees, Citizenship, the New America*. Berkeley: University of California Press, 2003.

———. *Flexible Citizenship: The Cultural Logics of Transnationality*. Durham, NC: Duke University Press, 1999.

Ortiz, Ricardo L. "The Cold War in the Americas and Latina/o Literature." In *The Cambridge Companion to Latina/o American Literature*, edited by John Morán González, 72–90. New York: Cambridge University Press, 2016.

Padilla, Felix M. *Latino Ethnic Consciousness: The Case of Mexican Americans and Puerto Ricans in Chicago*. Notre Dame: University of Notre Dame Press, 1985.

Palumbo-Liu, David. *Asian/American: Historical Crossings of a Racial Frontier*. Stanford, CA: Stanford University Press, 1999.

———. "Embedded Lives: The House of Fiction, the House of History." *Profession*, 2011, 13–22.

Paredes, Américo. *"With His Pistol in His Hand": A Border Ballad and Its Hero*. Austin: University of Texas Press, 1958.

Parikh, Crystal. *An Ethics of Betrayal: The Politics of Otherness in Emergent U.S. Literatures and Culture*. New York: Fordham University Press, 2009.

Pearson, Roberta. "Additionality and Cohesion in Transfictional Worlds." *Velvet Light Trap* 79 (Spring 2017): 113–20.

Pease, Donald E. "Re-mapping the Transnational Turn." In *Re-framing the Transnational Turn in American Studies*, edited by Winfried Fluck, Donald E. Pease, and John Carlos Rowe, 1–46. Dartmouth, NH: Dartmouth College Press, 2011.

Pelaud, Isabelle Thuy. *This Is All I Choose to Tell: History and Hybridity in Vietnamese American Literature*. Philadelphia: Temple University Press, 2011.

Phan, Aimee. "An Interview with Aimee Phan." By Luan Gaines. *Curled Up with a Good Book*, 2005. http://www.curledup.com/intaphan.htm.

———. *We Should Never Meet*. New York: Picador, 2004.

Pickering, Michael. *Stereotyping: The Politics of Representation*. New York: Palgrave, 2001.

Plascencia, Salvador. "Interview by Max Benavidez." *BOMB* 98 (2007): 22–24, 26–28.

———. "An Interview with Salvador Plascencia." By Angela Stubbs. *Bookslut* (blog), June 2006. http://www.bookslut.com/features/2006_06_009056.php.

———. "An Interview with Salvador Plascencia." By Matthew Baker. *Nashville Review* 1, no. 1 (2010).

———. *The People of Paper*. Orlando, FL: Harcourt, 2005.

Poblete, Juan. "Introduction." In *Critical Latin American and Latino Studies*, edited by Juan Poblete, ix–xli. Minneapolis: University of Minnesota Press, 2003.

Polletta, Francesca. "Plotting Protest: Mobilizing Stories in the 1960 Student Sit-Ins." In Joseph E. Davis, *Stories of Change*, 31–51.

Portes, Alejandro. "The New Latin Nation: Immigration and the Hispanic Population of the United States." In Flores and Rosaldo, *A Companion to Latina/o Studies*, 15–24.

Portes, Alejandro, and Kelly Hoffman. "Latin American Class Structures: Their Composition and Change During the Neoliberal Era." *Latin American Research Review* 38, no. 1 (April 2003): 41–82.

Prashad, Vijay. *The Darker Nations: A People's History of the Third World*. New York: New Press, 2007.

———. *Everybody Was Kung Fu Fighting: Afro-Asian Connections and the Myth of Cultural Purity*. Boston: Beacon Press, 2001.

Prosser, Jay. *Second Skins: The Body Narratives of Transsexuality*. New York: Columbia University Press, 1998.

Ragain, Nathan. "A Revolutionary Romance: Particularity and Universality in Karen Tei Yamashita's *I Hotel*." *MELUS* 38, no. 1 (2013): 137–54.

Reddi, Rishi. "The Indian Community I Knew . . . and the Indian Community I Never Had." In *Karma and Other Stories*, 7–13.

———. *Karma and Other Stories*. New York: Harper, 2007.

Riofrio, John. "Situating Latin American Masculinity: Immigration, Empathy and Emasculation in Junot Díaz's *Drown*." *Atenea* 28, no. 1 (June 2008): 23–36.

Rivera, Tomás. *. . . y no se lo tragó la tierra / . . . and the earth did not devour him*. 1971. Translated by Evangelina Vigil-Piñon. Houston: Arte Público, 1992.

Robbins, Bruce. *Upward Mobility and the Common Good: Toward a Literary History of the Welfare State*. Princeton, NJ: Princeton University Press, 2007.

Robinson, William I. *Latin America and Global Capitalism: A Critical Globalization Perspective*. Baltimore: Johns Hopkins University Press, 2008.

Rodriguez, David. *Latino National Political Coalitions: Struggles and Challenges*. New York: Routledge, 2002.

Rodriguez, Juan. Review of *The House on Mango Street*, by Sandra Cisneros. *Austin Chronicle*, August 10, 1984, E1.

Rodriguez, Ralph E. *Brown Gumshoes: Detective Fiction and the Search for Chicana/o Identity*. Austin: University of Texas Press, 2005.

Rodriguez, Richard. *Hunger of Memory: The Education of Richard Rodriguez*. Boston: D. R. Godine, 1981.

Román, Elda María. "'Jesus, When Did You Become So Bourgeois, Huh?': Status Panic in Chicana/o Cultural Production." *Aztlán: A Journal of Chicano Studies* 38, no. 2 (Fall 2013): 11–40.

———. *Race and Upward Mobility: Seeking, Gatekeeping, and Other Class Strategies in Postwar America*. Stanford, CA: Stanford University Press, 2018.

Romero, Fernando. *Hyperborder: The Contemporary U.S.-Mexico Border and Its Future*. New York: Princeton Architectural Press, 2008.

Rosaldo, Renato. *Culture and Truth: The Remaking of Social Analysis*. Boston: Beacon Press, 1989.

Rothwell, Matthew D. *Transpacific Revolutionaries: The Chinese Revolution in Latin America*. New York: Routledge, 2013.

Ryan, Marie-Laure. "Transfictionality Across Media." In *Theorizing Narrativity*, edited by John Pier and José Angel Garcia Landa, 385–417. Berlin: Walter de Gruyter, 2008.

———. "Transmedial Storytelling and Transfictionality." *Poetics Today* 34, no. 3 (2013): 361–88.

Sachs, Dana. *The Life We Were Given: Operation Babylift, International Adoption, and the Children of War in Vietnam*. Boston: Beacon Press, 2010.

Sae-Saue, Jayson Gonzales. *Southwest Asia: The Transpacific Geographies of Chicana/o Literature*. New Brunswick, NJ: Rutgers University Press, 2016.

Said, Edward. *Orientalism*. New York: Vintage, 1979.

Saint-Gelais, Richard. "Transfictionality." In *Routledge Encyclopedia of Narrative Theory*, edited by David Herman, Manfred Jahn, and Marie-Laure Ryan. Routledge, 2010. ProQuest Literature Online.

Saito, Leland T. *Race and Politics: Asian Americans, Latinos, and Whites in a Los Angeles Suburb*. Urbana: University of Illinois Press, 1998.

Salazar, Inés. "Can You Go Home Again? Transgression and Transformation in African-American Women's and Chicana Literary Practice." In *Postcolonial Theory and the United States: Race, Ethnicity, and Literature*, edited by Amritjit Singh and Peter Schmidt, 388–411. Jackson: University Press of Mississippi, 2000.

Saldívar, Ramón. *Chicano Narrative: The Dialectics of Difference*. Madison: University of Wisconsin Press, 1990.

———. "Historical Fantasy, Speculative Realism, and Postrace Aesthetics in Contemporary American Fiction." *American Literary History* 23, no. 3 (2011): 574–99.

———. "Social Aesthetics and the Transnational Imaginary." In Flores and Rosaldo, *A Companion to Latina/o Studies*, 406–16.

Sanborn, Geoffrey. "Keeping Her Distance: Cisneros, Dickinson, and the Politics of Private Enjoyment." *PMLA* 116, no. 5 (2001): 1334–48.

Schiller, Nina Glick. "U.S. Immigrants and the Global Narrative." *American Anthropologist* 99, no. 2 (1997): 404–8.

Schiller, Nina Glick, Linda G. Basch, and Cristina Szanton Blanc. "Transnationalism: A New Analytic Framework for Understanding Migration." *Annals of the New York Academy of Sciences* 645 (1992): 1–24.

Schlund-Vials, Cathy J. *Modeling Citizenship: Jewish and Asian American Writing*. Philadelphia: Temple University Press, 2011.

Shankar, Lavina Dhingra, and Rajini Srikanth, eds. *A Part, yet Apart: South Asians in Asian America*. Philadelphia: Temple University Press, 1998.

Shih, Shu-mei. "Comparison as Relation." In *Comparison: Theories, Approaches, Uses*, edited by Rita Felski and Susan Stanford Friedman, 79–98. Baltimore: Johns Hopkins University Press, 2013.

Slaughter, Joseph R. *Human Rights, Inc.: The World Novel, Narrative Form, and International Law*. New York: Fordham University Press, 2007.

Smith, Neil. "Contours of a Spatialized Politics: Homeless Vehicles and the Production of Geographical Scale." *Social Text* 33 (1992): 54–81.

Smith, Sidonie. "Filiality and Woman's Autobiographical Storytelling." In *Maxine Hong Kingston's* The Woman Warrior: *A Casebook*, edited by Sau-ling Cynthia Wong, 57–83. Oxford: Oxford University Press, 1999.

Sohn, Stephen Hong. "These Desert Places: Tourism, the American West, and the Afterlife of Regionalism in Julie Otsuka's *When the Emperor Was Divine*." *Modern Fiction Studies* 55, no. 1 (Spring 2009): 163–88.

Sonei, Monica. *Nisei Daughter*. 1953. Reprint. Seattle: University of Washington Press, 2014.

Song, Min Hyoung. *The Children of 1965: On Writing, and Not Writing, as an Asian American*. Durham, NC: Duke University Press, 2013.

Southern Poverty Law Center. "Ten Days After: Harassment and Intimidation in the Aftermath of the Election." Southern Poverty Law Center, November 29, 2016. https://www .splcenter.org/20161129/ten-days-after-harassment-and-intimidation-aftermath-election.

Srikanth, Rajini. *The World Next Door: South Asian American Literature and the Idea of America*. Philadelphia: Temple University Press, 2004.

Steinberg, Stephen. *Turning Back: The Retreat from Racial Justice in American Thought and Policy*. Boston: Beacon Press, 1995.

Stone, Sandy. "The *Empire* Strikes Back: A Posttranssexual Manifesto." In *The Transgender Studies Reader*, edited by Susan Stryker and Stephen Whittle, 221–35. New York: Routledge, 2006.

Suárez-Orozco, Marcelo M., and Mariela M. Páez. "Introduction: The Research Agenda." In *Latinos: Remaking America*, edited by Mariela M. Páez and Marcelo M. Suárez-Orozco, 1–37. Berkeley: University of California Press, 2009.

Sundquist, Eric J. *Strangers in the Land: Blacks, Jews, Post-Holocaust America*. Cambridge, MA: Belknap Press, 2005.

Takaki, Ronald T. *Strangers from a Different Shore: A History of Asian Americans*. Updated and rev. ed. Boston: Little, Brown, 1998.

Tang, Amy Cynthia. *Repetition and Race: Asian American Literature After Multiculturalism*. New York: Oxford University Press, 2016.

Taylor, Charles. "The Politics of Recognition." In *Multiculturalism: Examining the Politics of Recognition*, edited by Amy Gutmann, 25–73. Princeton, NJ: Princeton University Press, 1994.

Thananopavarn, Susan. *LatinAsian Cartographies: History, Writing, and the National Imaginary*. New Brunswick: Rutgers University Press, 2018.

Thon, Jan-Noël. "Converging Worlds: From Transmedial Storyworlds to Transmedial Universes." *Storyworlds: A Journal of Narrative Studies* 7, no. 2 (Winter 2015): 21–53.

Torres-Saillant, Silvio. "Problematic Paradigms: Racial Diversity and Corporate Identity in the Latino Community." In *Latinos: Remaking America*, edited by Mariela M. Páez and Marcelo M. Suárez-Orozco, 435–55. Berkeley: University of California Press, 2009.

Truong, Monique Thuy-Dung. "The Emergence of Voices: Vietnamese American Literature 1975–1990." *Amerasia Journal* 19, no. 3 (1993): 27–50.

Tsing, Anna Lowenhaupt. *Friction: An Ethnography of Global Connection*. Princeton, NJ: Princeton University Press, 2005.

Tsou, Elda E. *Unquiet Tropes: Form, Race, and Asian American Literature*. Philadelphia: Temple University Press, 2015.

TuSmith, Bonnie. *All My Relatives: Community in Contemporary Ethnic American Literatures*. Ann Arbor: University of Michigan Press, 1993.

Ty, Eleanor Rose. *Unfastened: Globality and Asian North American Narratives*. Minneapolis: University of Minnesota Press, 2010.

Vaïsse, Justin. *Neoconservatism: The Biography of a Movement*. Translated by Arthur Goldhammer. Cambridge, MA: Belknap Press, 2010.

Valdés, Maria Elena de. "In Search of Identity in Cisnero's *The House on Mango Street*." *Canadian Review of American Studies/Revue canadienne d'études americaines* 23, no. 1 (Fall 1992): 55–72.

Valls, Andrew. "Self-Development and the Liberal State: The Case of John Stuart Mill and Wilhelm von Humboldt." *The Review of Politics* 61, no. 2 (1999): 251–74.

Van, Hong. "Aimee Phan on the Journey of Writing." *International Examiner*, September 26, 2005.

Volkman, Toby Alice. "New Geographies of Kinship." In *Cultures of Transnational Adoption*, edited by Toby Alice Volkman, 1–22. Durham, NC: Duke University Press, 2005.

Walkowitz, Rebecca L. *Cosmopolitan Style: Modernism Beyond the Nation*. New York: Columbia University Press, 2006.

Wang, Dorothy J. *Thinking Its Presence: Form, Race, and Subjectivity in Contemporary Asian American Poetry*. Stanford, CA: Stanford University Press, 2014.

Wang, Oliver. "These Are the Breaks: Hip-Hop and AfroAsian Cultural (Dis)Connections." In *AfroAsian Encounters: Culture, History, Politics*, edited by Heike Raphael-Hernandez and Shannon Steen, 146–65. New York: New York University Press, 2006.

Westad, Odd Arne. *The Global Cold War: Third World Interventions and the Making of Our Times*. Cambridge: Cambridge University Press, 2005.

Williams, Melissa S. "Citizenship as Agency Within Communities of Shared Fate." In *Unsettled Legitimacy: Political Community, Power, and Authority in a Global Era*, edited by William D. Coleman and Steven F. Bernstein, 33–52. Vancouver: University of British Columbia Press, 2009.

Williams, Raymond. *Marxism and Literature*. Oxford: Oxford University Press, 1977.

Wills, Jenny. "Claiming America by Claiming Others: Asian-American Adoptive Parenthood in *A Gesture Life* and *Digging to America*." *Americana: The Journal of American Popular Culture* 10, no. 1 (2011): n.p.

Wilson, William J. *The Declining Significance of Race: Blacks and Changing American Institutions*. Chicago: University of Chicago Press, 1978.

Woloch, Alex. *The One vs. the Many: Minor Characters and the Space of the Protagonist in the Novel*. Princeton, NJ: Princeton University Press, 2003.

Wong, Jade Snow. *Fifth Chinese Daughter*. 1950. Reprint. Seattle: University of Washington Press, 1989.

Wong, Sau-Ling C. "Denationalization Reconsidered: Asian American Cultural Criticism at a Theoretical Crossroads." *Amerasia Journal* 21, no. 1 (January 1995): 1–27.

———. *Reading Asian American Literature: From Necessity to Extravagance*. Princeton, NJ: Princeton University Press, 1993.

Wortham, Stanton, Katherine Mortimer, and Elaine Allard. "Mexicans as Model Minorities in the New Latino Diaspora." *Anthropology and Education Quarterly* 40, no. 4 (2009): 388–404.

Yamashita, Karen Tei. *I Hotel*. Minneapolis, MN: Coffee House Press, 2010.

Yarbro-Bejarano, Yvonne. "Chicana Literature from a Chicana Feminist Perspective." In *Chicana Creativity and Criticism: New Frontiers in American Literature*, edited by María

Herrera-Sobek and Helena María Viramontes, rev. ed., 213–19. Albuquerque: University of New Mexico Press, 1996.

Young, Robert J. C. "Postcolonialism: From Bandung to the Tricontinental." *Historein* 5 (2006): 11–21.

Zhou, Xiaojing. *Cities of Others: Reimagining Urban Spaces in Asian American Literature.* Seattle: University of Washington Press, 2014.

Zhou Xiaojing. "Introduction: Critical Theories and Methodologies in Asian American Literary Studies." In Zhou and Najmi, *Form and Transformation in Asian American Literature*, 3–29.

Zhou Xiaojing and Samina Najmi, eds. *Form and Transformation in Asian American Literature*. Seattle: University of Washington Press, 2005.

INDEX

Stanford Studies in
COMPARATIVE RACE AND ETHNICITY

Published in collaboration with the Center for Comparative Studies in Race and Ethnicity, Stanford University

SERIES EDITORS
Hazel Rose Markus
Paula M.L. Moya

Arab Routes: Pathways to Syrian California
Sarah M. A. Gualtieri
2019

South Central Is Home: Race and the Power of Community Investment in Los Angeles
Abigail Rosas
2019

The Border and the Line: Race, Literature, and Los Angeles
Dean J. Franco
2019

Black Power and Palestine: Transnational Countries of Color
Michael R. Fischbach
2018

Race and Upward Mobility: Seeking, Gatekeeping, and Other Class Strategies in Postwar America
Elda María Román
2017

*The Emotional Politics of Racism: How Feelings Trump Facts
in an Era of Colorblindness*
Paula Ioanide
2015

*Beneath the Surface of White Supremacy: Denaturalizing U.S. Racisms
Past and Present*
Moon-Kie Jung
2015

Race on the Move: Brazilian Migrants and the Global Reconstruction of Race
Tiffany D. Joseph
2015

The Ethnic Project: Transforming Racial Fiction into Racial Factions
Vilna Bashi Treitler
2013

On Making Sense: Queer Race Narratives of Intelligibility
Ernesto Javier Martínez
2012